Da
Cow

"America's Team"

Is Back!

Jeff Stevenson

Introduction

The Dallas Cowboys. Americas Team. The Cowboys are the original Americas Team, named as such in 1978 by NFL Films. The Cowboys have won the Super Bowl five times in their illustrious history (1971, 1977, 1992, 1993, 1995).

The Cowboys were one of the great NFL franchises in the decade of the 70's. There were no championships in the decade of the 80's. Then came Jerry Jones acquisition of the franchise in 1989. The 90's saw the Cowboys get back to the top of the NFL, and win the Super Bowl in three out of four seasons from 1992 – 1995.

After 1995 the franchise fell into a long period of relative mediocrity. While Jerry Jones enjoyed unprecedented success as an NFL owner, Jerry struggled as the Cowboys General Manager. Year after year of draft busts, bad trades and unproductive free agent moves left Cowboy fans to wonder if The Cowboys would ever measure up to their great history.

Now we look at Jerry's drafts of 2011 – 2014. We see the tremendous improvement in our Cowboys on the field in 2014. Now we look forward to 2015. Might this be the year that The Cowboys get back to the top of the NFL?

Read on for a re-telling of our Cowboys great history, for a look at Jerry's transformation as the Cowboys GM and for the look to the future for our Dallas Cowboys.

Table of Contents

Dallas Cowboys, Americas Team *Is Back*

This book is not endorsed by the Dallas Cowboys or the National Football League.

Texas Stadium, Home of the Dallas Cowboys 1971-2008

Dallas Cowboys, Americas Team Is Back

Chapter One

<u>The Jimmy Johnson Era</u>

The Dallas Cowboys. "America's Team". This world famous franchise was given the moniker "Americas Team" in 1978 by NFL Films in their "year in review" video. That famous 1978 video began with this narration in the memorable voice of John Acenda: *"The Cowboys are the Notre Dame of professional football. No matter where they play, their fans are there to greet them. Their faces are recognized by fans all across this country. The sum total of their stars are a galaxy. They are, The Dallas Cowboys, America's Team".*

The faces of the stars of the 1970s Cowboys were definitely recognizable, and abundant: Roger Staubach, Tony Dorsett, Drew Pearson, Rayfield Wright, Billy Joe Dupree, Butch Johnson, Bob Hayes, Robert Newhouse, Preston Pearson, Bob Lilly, Randy White, Ed "Too-Tall" Jones, Harvey Martin, Charlie Waters, Cliff Harris, Mel Renfro, Lee Roy Jordan, Thomas "Hollywood" Henderson, and of course there were the illustrious and innovative leaders, head coach Tom Landry and General Manager Tex Schramm.

The Dallas Cowboys are one of the preeminent NFL franchises. The Cowboys are renowned world-wide, and they have more followers, and likewise their "haters", than any other NFL team. Even in their down years the Cowboys are among the league leaders in authorized, authentic NFL merchandise sales. The NFL is a more entertaining league when the Dallas Cowboys are good, whether you are a fan, or a hater.

There are so many milestone Cowboy memories. Here are a few that all Cowboy fans can remember: the Thanksgiving Day 1974 game against the Washington Redskins, when Clint Longley hit Drew Pearson for a 50 yard touchdown pass with time running out, for a 24-23 Dallas win; the 1975 Division championship game at Minnesota when Roger Staubach threw the 50 yard "Hail Mary" touchdown pass to Drew Pearson with 30 seconds left to beat the Vikings 17-14; the 1977 Super Bowl, when Roger Staubach threw a 45 yard pass to Butch Johnson who made a spectacular diving catch into the end zone; in 1978 when NFL films "year-in-review" dubbed the Cowboys "America's Team", because of the fan support that the Cowboys often drew in opposing stadiums; the final game of the 1979 regular season, when Roger Staubach hit Tony Hill with the high arching pass in the back corner of the end zone in the final minute of the game to win 35-34, and eliminate the Redskins from the playoffs; the 1980 Division championship game at Atlanta when Danny White hit Drew Pearson for a 23 yard touch-down to win 30-27 in the final minute; Tony Dorsett's 1983 Monday night in Minnesota when he ran 99 yards for a touchdown; Troy Aikman's slant pass to Alvin Harper that turned into a 70 yard catch and run in the fourth quarter of the 1992 NFC Championship game, that buried the 'Niners in the "changing of the guard" game, which avenged "The Catch" from 1982; Jimmy Johnson exclaiming "how 'bout them Cowboys!" in the celebrating locker room after Dallas defeated San Francisco in that 1992 NFC Championship game; the dominance of the Cowboys in the 1992 Super Bowl win over Buffalo, 52-17; Emmitt Smith's heroic performance in the final regular season game of 1993, playing with a separated shoulder, and carrying Dallas to the NFC East Title with a 16-13 overtime win at the New York Giants on a cold December day; the week of the 1993 NFC Championship, when three days before the game against rival San Francisco, Jimmy Johnson declared on a radio talk show, "*you can put it in three-inch headlines, we will win the ball game*", and the Cowboys backed Jimmy up with a 38-21 whipping of the 49ers and a second straight trip to the Super Bowl; Emmitt Smith wearing out Buffalo (again) and winning MVP of Super Bowl XXVIII; Larry Brown's interception in the fourth quarter of Super Bowl XXX that lead to Emmitt Smith's clinching touchdown run, and the Cowboys fifth Super Bowl win.

The Cowboys performance declined in the second half of the 80's before the widely acclaimed, and critically covered arrival of their new owner in 1989. What followed soon thereafter was a remarkable return to greatness worthy of the title "Americas Team". The rebuilding was led by the shrewd and confident owner Jerry Jones, and his choice for the new head coach, Jimmy Johnson, and was fueled in the early nineties by Hall of Famers Troy Aikman, Emmitt Smith, and Michael Irvin, as well as many other great players including Darren Woodson, Erik Williams, Jay Novacek, Daryl Johnston, Leon Lett, Nate Newton, Alvin Harper, Mark Tuinei, Charles Haley, Tony Casillas and Tony Tolbert.

Our Dallas Cowboys have a history of greatness in the 70's, the early 80's, and the first half of the 90's, that is the envy of most of the NFL. If they don't envy the Cowboys historical greatness, they at least aspire to have achieved a similar level of success. The Cowboys in their history have won eight NFC Championships and five Super Bowls. Only one NFL franchise has won more Super Bowls than the Dallas Cowboys: The Pittsburgh Steelers have won six. Like the Cowboys, the Steelers have achieved championship greatness in multiple decades. Only one other NFL franchise has matched the Cowboys success of winning five Super Bowls: The San Francisco 49ers. The 49ers won their five Super Bowls in just over a decade (1981 – 1994). Green Bay and New England have won four Super Bowls. Our Dallas Cowboys have a history that is among an elite few of the entire National Football League in terms of Super Bowl wins.

There are thirteen NFL teams that have never won the Super Bowl. Five teams have been to just one Super Bowl, and lost: Arizona Cardinals, Atlanta Falcons, Carolina Panthers, San Diego Chargers and Tennessee Titans. Two teams have lost their only two Super Bowl berths: Cincinnati Bengals and Philadelphia Eagles. Two teams are four time Super Bowl losers: Minnesota Vikings and Buffalo Bills. Four teams have never made it to the Super Bowl: Cleveland Browns, Detroit Lions, Houston Texans and Jacksonville Jaguars.

Jerry Jones bought the Dallas Cowboys in February 1989. At that time the Cowboys on the field were not very good. They were in fact the worst team in the NFL, illustrated by their 3-13 record in the 1988 season. The starting quarterback was Steve Pelluer, who had won the job from an aging Danny White. The running back was Herschel Walker, who would later become the key to a trade that was the impetus for the re-building of the team ("the great train robbery"). Michael Irvin had just finished his rookie season.

Nate Newton (aka the "kitchen") was the left guard, Mark Tuinei the left tackle, and Kevin Gogan the right tackle. Jim Jeffcoat was a defensive end, and Kelvin Martin a slot receiver and kick returner. There were a few "pieces" in place, however most of that team had become old and slow, by NFL standards. Tom Landry had finished his 29th season as the team's only head coach. H.R. "Bum" Bright was the team's principal owner.

Michael Irvin #88 "The Play Maker" NFL Hall of Famer

Mr. Bright's business fortunes had suffered in the late eighties, prompting his willingness to sell the team to the eager and brash oilman Jerry Jones. Jerry's timing was very good. The franchise had fallen on "hard times", and the market value was relatively low. Jerry's acquisition was a very good deal financially, and he knew that he had nothing but "upside" in his new prize acquisition.

As the story has been told, as soon as Jerry "got the deal done" and purchased the Cowboys from Bum Bright, he and Tex Schramm went to Austin (coach Landry's off-season home) to meet with Tom Landry. In that meeting Jerry informed Coach Landry that he would no longer be the coach of the Cowboys. Jerry awkwardly told Mr. Landry, "I am here and so is Jimmy". Later Jerry justified his selection of a college football coach to lead the most storied franchise in the NFL, by stating that "*Jimmy Johnson is worth five number one draft picks*". There were a lot of people, both reporters and fans, who thought that Jerry's bravado was at least a little outrageous, coming from a cocky new NFL owner, who was speaking of a new head coach that had never coached at the professional level. What was missed was the fact that Jerry originally intended for Jimmy to be much more than just a head coach, as it appears in retrospect, and according to the terms of Jimmy's contract.

How else do you explain that outrageous statement by Jerry about Jimmy being worth "five number one draft picks"?

Jimmy Johnson, Dallas Cowboys head coach 1989-1993

Looking back, Jerry Jones was absolutely right! Jimmy Johnson was the best coach, and the absolute best talent evaluator in the National Football League in the early nineties.

So it would appear based on what we know now, that Jerry Jones bought the Dallas Cowboys knowing that he could make a great return on his investment. Jerry apparently knew that he needed help with player personnel decisions, the coaching staff, and the team management. It also appears that Jerry had his man selected to handle the day-to-day decisions, and that he was outrageously confident and outspoken about how qualified Jimmy Johnson was to handle the job that Jerry had hired him for. Jerry made the right moves and he put the right pieces in place in 1989, to rebuild the Dallas Cowboys and to make them great again.

Before I move on to how Jimmy Johnson rebuilt the Cowboys, and the complete substantiation that Jerry was right in 1989 to pick Jimmy to be the Cowboys head coach and "player personnel director", I need to take a moment to thank the Green Bay Packers for their contribution to the Cowboys success of the 1990s. You might be thinking, "thank Green Bay"? For what? Well you see, heading in to the final game of the 1988 season, the Cowboys and the Green Bay Packers were tied for the worst record in the league at 3-12. Troy Aikman was the consensus to be the number one pick in the 1989 NFL draft following the 1988 college football season, verified by Troy's performance for UCLA in the Cotton Bowl in Dallas on New Year's Day. Green Bay held a tie breaker with the Cowboys, so that if the two teams had finished the 1988 season with identical records, the Packers would have held the number one pick, and the opportunity to select Troy Aikman as their new quarterback. On Sunday December 18, 1988 the Cowboys hosted the Philadelphia Eagles in a noon game at Texas Stadium. By 3 pm central time that afternoon, the NFL world knew that the Cowboys had been beaten by the Eagles 23-7. Cowboy fans would then have to watch with anticipation for the outcome of the Green Bay at Phoenix Cardinals game, which was played starting at 3:30 pm central time. Again, if Green Bay would have lost that game, at Phoenix, they would have locked up the number one selection in the 1989 NFL draft. To my amazement, and my elation, Green Bay went to Phoenix and defeated the Cardinals 26-17, and by doing so they handed Troy Aikman to the eagerly waiting Cowboys with the first pick in the draft. Most people forget this "little" anomaly, and remember instead the colossal draft mistake that Green Bay made with the second pick in the 1989 draft, when they selected offensive tackle Tony Mandarich (Michigan State), rather than taking running back and eventual NFL hall of famer Barry Sanders (Oklahoma State).

The rebuilding began with the 1989 draft. The press was really having a lot of fun at the expense of Jerry and Jimmy in the early days after Jerry acquired the Cowboys franchise. They were making fun of Jerry's Arkansas colloquialisms. They made fun of Jimmy's infamous hair. They were calling Jerry and Jimmy a couple of Arkansas hillbillies, among other things. One Dallas writer nicknamed them the "J-birds", because both had the initials JJ. They were making fun of Jerry and Jimmy in any way that they could, and as often as they could. The bottom line is that the press had no respect for these two "outsiders". To the press, Jerry was just an Arkansas oilman: what does he know about the vaunted and venerable National Football League? Who is he to fire the great Tom Landry? (at least half of Dallas Cowboy fans wanted coach Landry to retire in 1989) Jimmy was just a "college coach" who was a bully, and who ran up the score on lesser teams at the University of Miami. Jimmy had no experience or knowledge of the pro game. The "big boys" at the pro level were going to teach these two rookies a lesson. The press felt superior to these two NFL outsiders. The press was part of the "fraternity", and they were appalled that these two knuckleheads thought that they could be a part of the NFL, and even more so that they were now the owner, and the head coach of one of the most revered of all NFL teams.

I remember thinking at the time that the whole episode of the change in ownership, and the change of the head coach did seem a bit outrageous, in the way that it was done by Jerry Jones. However, I was one of those Cowboy fans who knew that the old regime was done (with all due respect to coach Landry), and that a change was in fact needed. I had no idea that Jimmy Johnson could do what he was going to do as quickly as he did, but I sure was intrigued to see how it would go. Surely it couldn't be worse than the 3-13 of 1988, or any worse than the relative decline (which was building momentum) that the Cowboys had been on for those last three years. Jimmy was a winner at the highest levels in the NCAA. Having lived in Port Arthur, TX (Jimmy's original home town), I had a little personal "connection" with Jimmy that most people didn't have, so I was pulling for him to succeed. As a Cowboy fan I just hoped that Jimmy could do for the Cowboys what he had done at The University of Miami!

The 1989 NFL draft gave us the first opportunity to evaluate Jerry and Jimmy as the owner and the head coach. The Cowboys held the first overall pick in the first round. In my mind the first pick in the draft would define Jimmy as knowledgeable, or as an NFL idiot. Prior to the draft Jimmy was low key about the first pick, as he wrote in his book "Turning the Thing Around". As a result of Jimmy's "discretion" it was not clear that he was going to take Troy Aikman with the first pick. *But he did.* And when he did, he earned a lot of respect and credibility, because Troy Aikman was widely considered to be a sure NFL quarterback prospect. So now the Cowboys had a huge piece around which to build, and to start the return to greatness. Jimmy and his staff were very productive in their first draft.

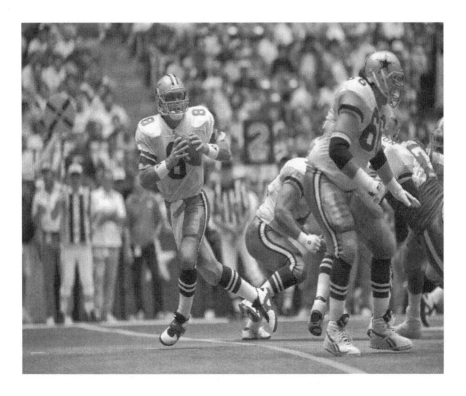

Troy Aikman, Cowboys Hall of Fame quarterback 1989-2000

After taking Troy Aikman number one overall, they selected players in the second, third, and fourth rounds who would make an immediate impact in the lineup, and who would be starters on the Super Bowl winning team four years later. In the second round they selected Daryl Johnston, a fullback from Syracuse University. He would become the lead blocker for eventual running back Emmitt Smith, and a two-time pro-bowler. In the third round the Cowboys selected Mark Stepnoski, a guard/center from the University of Pittsburgh. He would become the anchor for one of the most dominant offensive lines in NFL history, and a five-time pro-bowler. In the fourth round the Cowboys selected Tony Tolbert, a linebacker/defensive end from the University of Texas at El Paso. Tolbert would also make the pro-bowl. Jimmy would later write in his book ("Turning the Thing Around") that he was surprised at how little depth there was in the NFL draft after the fourth or fifth round. Jimmy Johnson and his new staff were "four-for-four" in the first four rounds of their first NFL draft. Not bad for a bunch of college guys working for an Arkansas oilman.

1989 draft

round	pick	position	Player name	University
1	1	QB	**Troy Aikman**	UCLA
2	29	G	Steve Wisniewski	Penn St
2	39	RB	**Daryl Johnston**	Syracuse
3	57	C	**Mark Stepnoski**	Pittsburgh
3	68	DE	Rhondy Weston	Florida
4	85	DE	**Tony Tolbert**	UTEP
5	113	TE	Keith Jennings	Clemson
5	119	LB	Willis Crocket	Ga Tech
5	125	DT	Jeff Roth	Florida
7	168	LB	Kevin Peterson	Nwestern
8	196	RB	Charvez Foger	Nev Reno
9	224	DB	Tim Jackson	Nebraska
10	252	LB	Rod Carter	Miami FL
11	280	LB	Randy Shannon	Miami FL
12	308	WR	Scott Ankrom	TCU

What none of their outspoken critics had considered about the ability of these "college coaches" to evaluate and execute on the NFL draft, was the fact that these college coaches had been spending all of their football focus on evaluating, recruiting, coaching (for and against) and game planning (for and against) the most talented college players in the country. All of the top talent that would be entering the NFL draft had been the focus of their jobs while coaching Division-I college football at The University of Miami. Jimmy Johnson and his staff probably had as much or more knowledge of the players in the 1989 draft than any other scouting staff in the entire National Football League. The results from their selections in the first four rounds are undeniable. Four players became pro bowlers during their Cowboys careers, and contributed to the Cowboys winning the Super Bowl three out of four years from 1992 to 1995. We know this now. But in May 1989 no one knew what had just begun to happen inside the Dallas Cowboys organization. It was the beginning of a remarkable turn-around that would later become the title to Jimmy Johnson's entertaining book (published in 1993).

In May 1989 the "turn-around" had begun. However, there was a long way to go, and there was a lot of work to do. Despite the draft picks that had been added to the team, the Cowboys went in to the 1989 training camp with the worst team in the league. Jimmy Johnson tells the key indicators in "Turning the Thing Around". One was that the Cowboys had no team speed.

The Cowboys had less team speed than the team that Jimmy had left behind at the University of Miami. Jimmy and his staff spent the 1989 season shuffling the bottom part of their roster looking for talent upgrades. They would bring in free-agent players who were available, nearly every week. Jimmy described this process by saying that "we would work out a player on Tuesday, sign him on Wednesday, play him on Sunday, and cut him on Monday". Can you imagine the chaos?

Jimmy Johnson knew in the 1989 pre-season that he needed to upgrade the talent on the team as quickly as possible. He also knew that the best way to do that was through astute selections in the early rounds of the draft. However, he needed to have more draft picks in those early rounds of the next draft, and/or in the near term drafts, in order to improve his team more rapidly. He knew that the only way to compile more draft picks was to make trades with other clubs for their draft picks.

Early in the 1989 season Jimmy Johnson held potential trade talks with a number of NFL teams. Jimmy had concluded in discussions with his coaching staff, that Herschel Walker was the only real tradable player that the Cowboys had that would bring them the kind of value in terms of future draft choices, that was needed to accelerate the team's rebuilding process. So Jimmy cultivated the idea of trading Herschel to the two teams that showed the most interest in doing so. In the end it was the Minnesota Vikings that were most willing to trade for Herschel, and to give up the draft choices that Jimmy so coveted.

The trade became known as "The Great Train Robbery", so named by Jimmy in his book, and also known ultimately as the most lopsided trade in NFL history. However, at the time the trade was made, the media reaction was that the Cowboys had foolishly traded away their most valuable player, and that in return they had gotten five average NFL players and "a couple of draft picks". First, the initial reactions were more of the same from that point in time. That is to say, that Jerry and Jimmy had no credibility with the press. So in their analysis of the trade, the press was very short sighted and critical in their perception of Jimmy's negotiation. They saw the Minnesota Vikings getting a great running back, and possibly the one missing piece that could propel the Vikings to the elusive Super Bowl championship that they had lost in four previous trips in franchise history (and that they still do not have). They did not understand that the Cowboys (Jimmy) were not making this trade for the players that came along immediately. The Cowboys were making this trade to create the multiple draft pick opportunities that it would generate in the next two drafts. And oh how Jimmy and the Cowboys did take advantage of those "conditional" draft picks! In summary, in return for Herschel Walker, the Cowboys ultimately drafted four starters for their 1992 and 1993 Super Bowl championship teams, including the NFL all-time rushing leader!

So, let's go through who the Cowboys got from the conditional draft picks in return for Hershel Walker. It is astounding. There were five players that Jimmy and the Cowboys added as a result of draft picks from the trade, four of whom contributed significantly to the Cowboys turn-around from NFL cellar dweller to NFL champion between 1989 and 1992. First and foremost is Emmitt Smith. Emmitt was drafted with Minnesota's twenty-first pick of the first round in 1990, after Dallas traded that number twenty-one pick and a later round selection to Pittsburgh, for the right to move up four spots to number seventeen in the first round.

All Emmitt Smith did was become one of the anchors of three Super Bowl winning teams, and one of "the triplets" (Emmitt, Michael Irvin and Troy Aikman). Emmitt Smith is an NFL Hall of Famer, and to this date (2015) he is the all-time leading rusher in NFL history. Emmitt was an elusive and durable running back, and his strength was that he rarely fumbled. If Emmitt had been the only player that Dallas had gotten from the trade, he alone would have been a complete success for Jimmy and the Cowboys.

But Emmitt is only one of five drafted players, plus four Vikings players, that the Cowboys obtained in return for Hershel Walker! In the second round of the 1990 draft the Cowboys selected Alexander Wright, a wide receiver (Auburn). He was not highly productive for the Cowboys, and he was eventually traded to Oakland in 1992 for a fourth round pick.

In the 1991 draft the Cowboys used two of the conditional draft picks from the Walker trade. Both picks were highly productive, and both were starters on the 1992 Super Bowl Championship team. With the number twelve pick in the first round the Cowboys selected Alvin Harper, a big play wide receiver from Tennessee. Harper complimented Michael Irvin and made it difficult for defenses to double cover Irvin. He was a starter on the 1992 and 1993 Super Bowl teams. Harper made a critical seventy yard catch and run late in the fourth quarter of the 1992 NFC championship game against San Francisco, to help seal the dramatic win. In the second round of the 1991 draft the Cowboys took Dixon Edwards, a linebacker from Michigan State. Edwards was a starter on all three Super Bowl winning teams (1992, 1993 and 1995).

The fifth player drafted by the Cowboys with a pick from the Hershel Walker trade, and along with Emmitt the most impactful, was Darren Woodson. Woodson was taken in the second round of the 1992 draft. He was a linebacker for Arizona State, but the Cowboys drafted him with the intention to convert him to a safety. Woodson started all three Super Bowl wins, became a five time pro bowl selection and his Cowboy career lasted from 1992 to 2004. He is the only Cowboy to have played for both Jimmy Johnson and Bill Parcells. Woodson was an outstanding safety because he had the ability to cover slot receivers as well as any cornerback. He is arguably the best safety ever to have played for the Dallas Cowboys.

In addition to the five draft picks, the Cowboys originally received five Vikings players in the Hershel Walker trade. Jesse Solomon was a linebacker, and he played for the Cowboys through the 1990 season, and then was traded to New England. David Howard was a linebacker, played through 1990 and was traded to New England in the Russell Maryland draft pick transaction. Darrin Nelson was a running back. He refused to report to Dallas, and was traded to San Diego for a draft pick. Alex Stewart was a defensive end, and he was waived by the Cowboys. Isaac Holt was the most productive of the Viking veterans for the Cowboys, from the trade. Holt was a cornerback who started for the Cowboys through the 1992 season, and in Super Bowl XXVII. Holt was eventually waived in 1993 after Kevin Smith was drafted.

Summary of the 1989 Hershel Walker trade

Conditional draft picks	Veterans from Vikings
* Emmitt Smith - drafted 1st round 1990	Jesse Sollomon - traded
Alexander Wright - drafted 2nd round 1990	David Howard - traded
Alvin Harper - drafted 1st round 1991	Darrin Nelson - traded
Dixon Edwards - drafted 2nd round 1991	Alex Stewart - waived
Darren Woodson - drafted 2nd round 1992	Issaic Holt - starter 1992

* NFL Hall of Fame & all-time NFL leading rusher

So, to recap the beginning of the rebuilding, in 1989 Jimmy and his staff had gone "four-for-four" in their first four rounds of the NFL draft (Aikman, Johnston, Stepnoski and Tolbert). In addition to the conditional draft picks from the Hershel Walker trade, the Cowboys were also successful with their own picks in the 1990, 1991 and 1992 drafts as well. In 1990 they took Emmitt Smith in the first round, and Alexander Wright in the second round. In the third round the Cowboys selected Jimmie Jones, a defensive tackle from The University of Miami. He was a very effective pass rusher from the tackle position, and added unprecedented depth to Jimmy's defensive line roster. The other notable pick in 1990 was the ninth round selection. The Cowboys took Kenneth Gant, a defensive back from Albany State. Gant was a very productive late round pick, as he became a special teams star, as well as a contributor in the Cowboys "nickel" defensive package, as an extra safety. Gant played for the 1992 and 1993 Super Bowl champions.

1990 draft

Round	Pick	Position	Player name	University
1	17	RB	Emmitt Smith	Florida
2	26	WR	Alexander Wright	Auburn
3	64	DT	Jimmie Jones	Miami (FL)
5	123	DB	Stan Smagala	Notre Dame
9	221	DB	Kenneth Gant	Albany St (Ga)
11	277	LB	Dave Harper	Humboldt ST

In the 1991 draft the Cowboys held the number eleven pick in the first round. The pre-draft consensus for the number one pick was Raghib "Rocket" Ismael (Notre Dame). The

New England Patriots held the number one pick. Before the draft Ismael signed a lucrative contract with the CFL Toronto Argonauts, so New England was willing to trade the top pick. Jimmy and the Cowboys traded three players (Ron Francis, David Howard and Eugene Lockhart) and the number eleven pick in the first round for the rights to the top pick in the draft. The Cowboys used the number one pick to select Russell Maryland, a defensive tackle from The University of Miami. Maryland was a high energy interior lineman who was very effective at stopping the running game.

As previously mentioned, in 1991 the Cowboys selected Alvin Harper in the first round with one of the Hershel Walker conditional picks, as well as Dixon Edwards in the second round with another of the Walker picks. Jimmy and the Cowboys were also productive in the third round with their own picks. At number sixty-two in the third round they selected Godfrey Myles, a linebacker from Florida. He contributed to all three Super Bowl winning teams, and started in the Super Bowl in 1995. At number seventy in the third round, the Cowboys selected Erik Williams, an offensive tackle from Central State of Ohio. This was an extraordinary pick of a player from an NAIA football program. Erik Williams became arguably one of the most dominant offensive tackles in the NFL in his era, and one of the greats in NFL history. As a rookie he dominated the great Reggie

White (the "Minister of defense") who was still in his prime. In the seventh round, Jimmy and the Cowboys selected Leon Lett, a defensive tackle from Emporia State (KS). Leon became infamous for two silly plays, one in the Super Bowl in 1992 and the other in the Thanksgiving Day game against Miami in 1993. However, he was a very productive player in the defensive tackle rotation on all three Super Bowl champions, was a two time pro bowler, and had a ten year NFL career, again as a seventh round pick! Finally, in the twelfth round of the 1991 draft the Cowboys took a corner back from TCU, Larry Brown. The twelfth rounder started at corner as a rookie, was a starter on all three Super Bowl winners and was selected as the MVP of Super Bowl XXX in 1995. Again, a twelfth round pick!

In what in retrospect appears to be a comedy of riches, the Cowboys also acquired defensive tackle Tony Casillas in a trade from the Atlanta Falcons prior to the 1991 season. The Cowboys gave up a second, and an eighth round pick to acquire the second overall pick from the 1986 draft.

1991 draft

Round	Pick	Position	Player name	University
1	1	DT	**Russell Maryland**	Miami (FL)
1	12	WR	**Alvin Harper**	Tennessee
1	20	DT	Kelvin Pritchett	Mississippi
2	37	LB	Dixon Edwards	Mich ST
3	62	LB	Godfrey Myles	Florida
3	64	G	James Richards	California
3	70	T	**Erik Williams**	Central ST (OH)
4	97	RB	Curvin Richards	Pittsburgh
4	106	QB	Bill Musgrave	Oregon
4	108	DE	Tony Hill	Tenn-Chatt.
4	110	DE	Kevin Harris	Texas Southern
5	132	LB	Darrick Brownlow	Illinois
6	153	G	Mike Sullivan	Miami (FL)
7	173	DT	**Leon Lett**	Emporia ST
9	235	WR	Damon Mays	Missouri
10	264	G	Sean Love	Penn ST
11	291	RB	Tony Boles	Michigan
12	320	DB	Larry Brown	TCU

In the 1992 draft Jimmy and the Cowboys were again very productive, although the team was becoming relatively loaded with talent, so the needs were not as great. In the first round with the seventeenth pick, the Cowboys drafted Kevin Smith, a defensive back from Texas A&M. Kevin would start at corner as a rookie, was a prominent contributor on two of the Super Bowl champions (he was injured in 1995) and had a solid nine year career for the Cowboys. As a side note, Kevin was from Orange, Texas, which is very nearby to Port Arthur. At number twenty-four in the first round the Cowboys selected Robert Jones, a linebacker from East Carolina. Robert started at middle linebacker as a rookie, was named the NFC rookie of the year, and had a ten year NFL career. In the second round at number thirty-seven the Cowboys selected Darren Woodson. We previously discussed Woodson's incredible Cowboy career.

1992 draft

Round	Pick	Position	Player name	University
1	17	DB	**Kevin Smith**	Texas A&M
1	24	LB	Robert Jones	East Carolina
2	36	WR	Jimmy Smith	Jackson ST
2	37	DB	**Darren Woodson**	Arizona ST
3	58	DB	Clayton Holmes	Carson-Newman
3	82	T	James Brown	Virginia ST
4	109	G	Tom Myslinski	Tennessee
5	120	DB	Greg Briggs	Texas Southern
5	121	G	Rod Milstead	Delaware ST
6	149	TE	Fallon Wacasey	Tulsa
9	248	DB	Nate Kirtman	Pomona-Pitzer
9	250	DB	Chris Hall	East Carolina
10	275	G	John Terry	Livingstone
11	302	WR	Tim Daniel	Florida A&M
12	317	DB	Don Harris	Texas Tech

In addition to the three starters that the Cowboys added with the 1992 draft, the Cowboys further added depth to their tremendous defense by obtaining defensive end Charles Haley in a trade from San Francisco. The Cowboys gave a second and a third round draft pick for the volatile, but extremely athletic and effective pass rushing specialist. Clearly the league did not realize what was happening in Dallas prior to the 1992 season. In retrospect the fans really did not know either. Jimmy claims that he did know. That must have been a really good feeling.

Jimmy and Jerry's young Cowboys started the 1992 season at home against the defending Super Bowl champion Washington Redskins. They ambushed the Redskins with their aggressive pressure defense, holding Washington to 75 yards rushing and 185 net passing yards. The Cowboys rushed for 175 yards and scored touchdowns running, passing and on a punt return. It was a complete win for the young Cowboys over the Super Bowl champs, 23-10. It was a sign of things to come.

The Cowboys would go on to win the NFC East Conference with an overall record of 13-3. Emmitt Smith was the leading rusher in the NFL in 1992 with 1,713 yards. Emmitt fumbled only four times in 373 carries. That is one fumble in ninety-three carries, which is about one fumble in five games; remarkable! The Cowboys had the overall number one defense in the league (yards/game allowed). They mauled the Philadelphia Eagles in the Divisional round at home, 34-10. Then they had to go to San Francisco for the NFC Championship game against the 14-2 49ers. The 49ers had

Steve Young, Jerry Rice, Ricky Watters and the number one offense in the NFL. The 49ers also had the league's number three ranked defense. Finally, the 49ers had a decided home field advantage, and they were favored to win the NFC Championship game over Dallas.

There was tremendous history overshadowing the 1992 NFC Championship game between Dallas and San Francisco. Ten years earlier the 49ers had ended the Cowboys decade long run of NFC dominance, when Joe Montana hit Dwight Clark with "The Catch" to win the 1981 NFC Championship. San Francisco went on to win four Super Bowls in the 1980s, while the Cowboys franchise deteriorated, culminating in the 1989 arrival of Jerry Jones and Jimmy Johnson.

In the first quarter the Cowboys recovered a fumbled punt at the San Francisco 22 yard line. Dallas drove to the 49ers one yard line, where they reached fourth down. They kicked a field goal to take a 3-0 lead. San Francisco returned the ensuing kickoff 50 yards to the Dallas 48. They drove to the Dallas one yard line, where Steve Young snuck in to give the 49ers a 7-3 lead.

In the second quarter a Dallas drive was stopped and they had to punt. San Francisco drove in to Dallas territory, but the drive stalled, and the 49ers missed on a 47 yard field goal attempt. Then Dallas responded with a sustained drive that culminated in a four yard touchdown run by Emmitt Smith to tie the game 10-10. That would be the half time score.

Dallas received the second half kickoff, and they drove 78 yards, capped off by a three yard touchdown run by Darryl Johnston, to take a 17-10 lead. The drive included a spectacular leaping catch by Alvin Harper for 38 yards over Eric Young. Later in the third quarter San Francisco added a field goal to cut the Dallas lead to 17-13, where the score remained heading to the fourth quarter.

In the fourth quarter Dallas put together another sustained ball control drive that resulted in a 16 yard touchdown pass from Troy Aikman to Emmitt Smith, to give Dallas a 24-13 lead. Midway through the fourth quarter Steve Young was pressured and he threw an interception that was caught by the Cowboys Ken Norton Jr. Dallas then drove to the San Francisco seven yard line where they faced a fourth down and one yard to go, leading 24-13. Rather than kicking a short field goal, Jimmy Johnson gambled for the knockout blow and went for the first down. But San Francisco's defense stopped the running play for no gain and took over on downs. The 49ers then drove 93 yards for a touchdown to cut the Cowboys lead to 24-20 with 4:22 remaining in the game.

At this point the 49ers crowd was roaring, and they were anticipating a 49ers come-back win on their home turf over the young and inexperienced Cowboys. On first down from their 21 yard line, Jimmy Johnson did not want to just try to run out the clock, because the 49ers were capable of scoring quickly and taking the lead, if Dallas could not convert for a first down. Even though his prior possession fourth down gamble had back-fired on Dallas, Jimmy remained aggressive in his play calling. So on first down Troy Aikman, seeing a blitz, threw a ten yard quick slant pass to Alvin Harper. The 49ers cornerback slipped on the muddy field and Harper turned up the field and raced down the sideline for seventy yards to the San Francisco nine yard line, to the dismay of the shocked San Francisco crowd. Two plays later Troy Aikman passed to Kelvin Martin who managed to dive across the goal line for the touchdown. The extra point was blocked, however Dallas had stretched the lead to 30-20 with just three minutes remaining. On the ensuing desperation drive, Steve Young was intercepted by James Washington to seal the final score; Dallas 30 – San Francisco 20. There had been another "changing of the guard", a decade later, on the Candlestick Park field. This time Dallas was the young, up and coming team of destiny. The Cowboys post-game locker room celebration was made infamous by a film clip of an overjoyed Jimmy Johnson exclaiming *"how 'bout them Cowboys!"*.

The Cowboys were champions of the NFC, and they earned a spot in Super Bowl XXVII against the AFC champion Buffalo Bills. The Bills had lost two consecutive Super Bowls, to the New York Giants 20-19 in 1990, and to Washington 37-24 in 1991. The bad luck Bills timing was unfortunate, as they made their third straight Super Bowl appearance against the young, powerful, and confident Cowboys.

Buffalo got off to a good start in the first quarter of Super Bowl XXVII. Dallas was forced to punt from their fifteen, and the Bills blocked the punt. The ball went out of bounds at the Cowboys sixteen yard line. Buffalo got a tough one-yard touchdown run by Thurman Thomas to take a 7-0 lead.

On the next Buffalo possession Cowboys safety Kenny Gant blitzed and hit Jim Kelly as he threw. The errant pass was intercepted by James Washington. Troy Aikman finished a Cowboy drive by hitting Jay Novacek for a twenty three yard touchdown pass to tie the game 7-7. After the kickoff, and with Buffalo at their own nine yard line, Jim Kelly dropped back to pass. Charles Haley sacked Kelly and the ball popped up in to the air. Dallas defensive tackle Jimmie Jones caught the ball and dove in to the end zone for a Cowboy touchdown, and a 14-7 lead. Dallas had scored two touchdowns in sixteen seconds.

In the second quarter Buffalo got a forty eight yard pass and run from Jim Kelly to Andre Reed to reach the Dallas five yard line. On third and goal from the one, Cowboys linebacker Ken Norton Jr drilled Kenneth Davis for no gain setting up fourth and goal. Buffalo "went for it" on fourth down, and Jim Kelly's pass was intercepted by Cowboy safety Thomas Everett. On the next Buffalo possession, still trailing Dallas 14-7, Jim Kelly was hit by Ken Norton Jr while attempting to throw, and suffered a knee injury. Kelly was replaced by the very able Frank Reich. Buffalo managed a field goal to cut the Dallas lead to 14-10.

Dallas then went on a long drive that was finished off by a beautiful nineteen yard touchdown pass from Troy Aikman to a streaking Michael Irvin. Dallas lead 21-10. Then disaster ensued for Buffalo, as Leon Lett stripped the ball from Thurman Thomas, and it was recovered by Jimmie Jones. Dallas quickly converted the turnover into points, as Troy Aikman again hit Michael Irvin, this time for a twenty three yard touchdown pass, to open the Dallas lead to 28-10. Dallas had again scored back-to-back touchdowns, this time within eighteen seconds. Dallas held a commanding halftime lead.

In the third quarter Dallas got a field goal to extend their lead to 31-10. Buffalo then got a forty yard touchdown pass from Frank Reich to Don Bebe. On the play Reich clearly stepped over the line of scrimmage as he made the throw (a penalty), but the officials missed the call, and the Dallas lead was cut to 31-17, going into the fourth quarter.

Early in the fourth quarter Dallas had possession at the forty four yard line. With a well-protected pocket to throw from Troy Aikman dropped back, and he threw deep down the right side line and hit Alvin Harper in step for a fifty six yard touchdown pass. When he crossed the goal line Harper ran across the end zone and dunked the football over the goal post. Dallas had an insurmountable 38-17 lead. On the next possession Frank Reich was hurried by the Cowboys unrelenting pass rush, and his pass was intercepted by safety Thomas Everett, who returned it twenty two yards to the Buffalo eight yard line. Three plays later Emmitt Smith found the end zone and the rout was on, 45-17. Buffalo had the ball at their twenty yard line when Frank Reich was once again hit by the Cowboys and again he fumbled. Ken Norton Jr picked up the rolling football and scrambled fifteen yards for the touchdown to turn the rout into a laugher, with Dallas crushing Buffalo 52-17.

Then came the most infamous play of Super Bowl XXVII. Buffalo had moved the ball across midfield. Frank Reich dropped back to pass and again the Cowboy pass rush mobbed him. Reich was hit and fumbled. Cowboy defensive tackle "the big-cat" Leon Lett scooped up the ball and began rumbling down the right sideline for what appeared to be another Cowboy defensive touchdown. As Leon approached the goal-line, in his excitement he held the ball out to his side in his right hand. Unknown to Leon was that Don Bebe was chasing him. At about the one yard line Bebe caught Leon Lett and he swatted the ball out of Leon's hand. The ball went out of bounds in the end zone, giving Buffalo a touchback, and robbing Leon Lett of Super Bowl touchdown glory. Poor Leon...everyone remembers that unfortunate and comical moment, rather than his dominant play throughout the game, when he was stopping the run and pressuring the quarterback. Leon Lett was a relentless force in Super Bowl XXVII.

The Cowboys would force nine turn-overs from which they would score 35 points. They lead 28-10 at half-time and ran away to a 52-17 win. Troy Aikman was fittingly named Super Bowl MVP. Emmitt Smith became the first NFL rushing title winner to also win the Super Bowl in the same year. The Cowboys defense was so dominant that Troy Aikman outrushed Thurman Thomas, 28-19. The Cowboys had their third Super Bowl win in franchise history and the first in the Jerry Jones era. The architect of the four year turn-around from the league's worst team to the Super Bowl champion was without question Jimmy Johnson. To Jerry Jones credit, he said yes to the moves that Jimmy recommended, which included one of the most questioned, but ultimately one of the most heralded, trades in NFL history.

At the end of the game, on the sideline, Jerry was seen hugging Jimmy and running his hands through Jimmy's disheveled hair, after Jimmy's Gatorade shower. At that moment the Dallas Cowboys appeared to be on the brink of a dynasty. They had the NFL's best quarterback, best running back, the playmaker at wide receiver, a relentless tight-end, an uncontrollable defense, the best coach, and a brash and innovative owner. The Cowboys appeared to be an unstoppable force for years to come.

Jimmy and Jerry's Cowboys went in to the 1993 season as the defending Super Bowl champions, and as the favorite to repeat. You wouldn't think that the 1993 draft would really matter, considering the depth of the 1992 Dallas Cowboy roster. However, Jimmy Johnson drafted nine players between the second and eighth rounds in 1993. Five would contribute significantly to the Cowboys success in 1993:

Those five significant draft choices that would have long NFL careers were: Kevin Williams (eight years), Darrin Smith (eleven years), Ron Stone (twelve years), Brock Marion (eleven years) and Dave Thomas (nine years).

1993 draft

Round	Pick	Position	Player name	University
2	46	WR	Kevin Williams	Miami-FL
2	54	LB	Darrin Smith	Miami-FL
3	84	DB	Mike Middleton	Indiana
4	94	RB	Derrick Lassic	Alabama
4	96	G	Ron Stone	Boston Coll.
6	168	LB	Barry Minter	Tulsa
7	196	DB	Brock Marion	Nevada-Reno
8	203	DB	Dave Thomas	Tennessee
8	213	LB	Reggie Givens	Penn St.

The Dallas Cowboys had two previous chances, but had never won back-to-back Super Bowls in their history (1972 and 1978). In 1993 they would get another chance. However the Cowboys started the 1993 season without one of the "triplets". Emmitt Smith was in a contract hold-out, as Jerry Jones tried to make the case that Emmitt should not get the same contract that Thurman Thomas had just been given by the Buffalo Bills ($13.5 million for four years). Jerry's offer was $10.5 million for four years. Emmitt was a restricted free agent, and that may have made Jerry think that he had some leverage in the negotiations. So Emmitt said "no-thanks", and he held out.

The Cowboys were soundly beaten in the first game by the Washington Redskins, 35-16. In week two the Cowboys had a rematch of the Super Bowl with the Buffalo Bills. The Cowboys were terrible offensively, committing turnovers, and they lost to the Bills at Texas Stadium, 13-10. No team in NFL history had ever started the season 0-2, and gone on to win the Super Bowl. In the locker room after the Buffalo loss, there was a "blow-up" by the ever vocal Charles Haley, in which Charles made it clear to Jerry Jones that he needed to get Emmitt Smith signed, *immediately*. Four days later Emmitt was signed for four years and $13.6 million. Emmitt would go on to lead the NFL in rushing again in 1993, despite playing in just fourteen games. He would fumble only four times in 283 attempts. Clearly this was a very special running back, who would eventually become the NFL's all-time leading rusher, and a member of the Hall of Fame.

After starting 0-2, but getting Emmitt back, the Cowboys would then win their next seven consecutive games. One of those wins was a rematch of the 1992 NFC championship game with the San Francisco 49ers. The game was a war. Both teams entered with 3-2 records, and were highly motivated to win, notwithstanding who the opponent was that day. Both defenses were good in this game, but the Cowboys were better. Charles Haley had two sacks of Steve Young and the Cowboys had a total of four sacks on the day. Michael Irvin was a beast, with twelve catches for 168 yards, including a thirty six yard touchdown from Troy Aikman in the third quarter that gave the Cowboys the lead that they would not surrender that afternoon. Then came a road trip to Atlanta to face the 3-6 Falcons. The Cowboys played without Emmitt Smith and Troy Aikman due to injuries, and they were awful. They trailed 13-0 at the half, and 27-7 in the fourth quarter. The Cowboys produced only forty eight yards rushing and only 230 yards of total offense.

After the road loss to Atlanta the Cowboys had to play a Thanksgiving Day game four days later against the 8-2 Miami Dolphins. Weather was a factor in the game as Dallas had an unusual snow storm. The Dolphins were good that day, playing without the injured Dan Marino. Keith Byars had a seventy seven yard touchdown run in the first quarter followed by a "snow angel" enactment. The Cowboys lead 14-7 at the half. However, they could not generate any sustained offense in the second half. The Cowboys lead the Dolphins 14-13 with under a minute to play in the fourth quarter. The Dolphins got in to position to attempt a forty one yard field goal with just seconds left. The kick was blocked, however the ball's trajectory after the block was down the field toward the goal line. With the clock running down and nearly every Dallas Cowboy defender waving their arms to stay away from the ball, the Cowboys Leon Lett lumbered down the field. He slid in to the ball rather than covering it, or diving upon it, which shoved it free and the Dolphins immediately pounced upon it. This gave Miami possession inside the Cowboys five yard line, and a second chance at the field goal. The short kick was good, and the Cowboys had lost two consecutive games and were 7-4 for the season. Back-to-back Super Bowls were again in question. And poor old Leon Lett had added another infamous blunder to his otherwise stellar playing career resume.

The Cowboys would then win the next four games with very little drama to set up what would be an intense and climactic final game of the regular season. In a schedule makers dream matchup, the Cowboys would play at the NY Giants, with both teams entering the game with 11-4 records. The winner would take the NFC East title, and home field advantage in the playoffs. What a game it was. Troy Aikman completed 24 of 30 pass attempts with one touchdown and no interceptions. Emmitt Smith was relentless, and the undisputable difference in the game, with 32 carries for 168 yards. But that isn't the whole story. Emmitt took a brutal hit late in the first half that sent him to the locker room with a right shoulder injury. Team doctors diagnosed a first-degree separation of his right shoulder. For the "layman", this means that it literally hurt, and I mean a lot of discomfort, for Emmitt to just get up off of the field after the hit. Walking to the sideline, he appeared as if his right arm was just hanging off of his body. They say that he was given an injection for the pain at halftime. But this was the kind of injury from which it hurts like hell just to hold your arm up. Most players would have taken their pads off, put their arm in a sling and watched the rest of the game from the sideline as a spectator. And that would be perfectly understandable, and acceptable. But Emmitt played through this injury, and not in a "decoy" role. Emmitt was a warrior in a heavy-weight fight.

The Cowboys lead 13-0 at the half, however the Giants were up to the task in the second half, and after four quarters of the sixteenth regular season game, the NFC East was still undecided. The score was 13-13, and these two great rivals were going to over time. Anyone who saw this game live will never forget what they saw. Even Cowboy hating Giants fans had to admire the heroic effort that they saw that day from Emmitt Smith. In overtime the Giants got the ball first, and on their home field they appeared to be in good shape as they carried the momentum from their second half come-back. However, an illegal block penalty dug a hole that they couldn't overcome and the Giants were forced to punt. When the Cowboys took their only possession of the overtime period, Emmitt Smith touched the ball on nine of the 11 plays in the drive, converting 41 of the 52 yards that they drove in to position for Eddie Murray's field goal attempt. Murray converted on the 41 yard kick to win 16-13, and the Dallas Cowboys were NFC East champions and controlled the home field advantage throughout the NFC playoffs.

The divisional playoff game was anticlimactic when compared to the Cowboys accomplishment of finally earning the NFC East championship in the season ending win over the Giants. Dallas faced Green Bay at Texas Stadium on January 16 in the divisional round. The Cowboys were in control, leading 17-3 at the half, and 27-10 in the fourth quarter, and the game was never really in question.

In the NFC championship game it was a rematch with the San Francisco 49ers. Unlike the prior season the Cowboys had the home field advantage this time. On the Thursday evening before the Sunday game with San Francisco, Jimmy Johnson made an appearance on a sports talk-radio show in Dallas. During his dialogue Jimmy stated *"you can put it in three-inch headlines; we will win the ball game"*. Now that got all kinds of attention all over the league. What an audacious statement for the head coach to make. You have to love that Jimmy Johnson. But Jimmy's Cowboys backed him up emphatically. The Cowboys took the opening kickoff and drove seventy five yards for a touchdown and a 7-0 lead. After San Francisco tied the score 7-7, the Cowboys scored three unanswered touchdowns to take a 28-7 lead at the halftime break. Troy Aikman was knocked out of the game in the third quarter with a concussion, however the Cowboys maintained control throughout the second half and the game was never in question. The Cowboys lead 35-14 after three quarters, and won 38-21. The Cowboys would, after all, get a chance to win back-to-back Super Bowls for the first time in their history.

The unfortunate Buffalo Bills would make their fourth consecutive Super Bowl appearance against the deeply talented, but now veteran and supremely confident Dallas Cowboys. How could the Cowboys not be favored in this Super Bowl rematch? They had destroyed the Bills twelve months earlier in the big game, converting nine turnovers in to thirty five points in a 52-17 blowout. The Bills came in to the game with real determination to change history. After the two teams exchanged field goals in the first quarter the Cowboys held a slim 6-3 lead. In the second quarter the Bills used effective running by Thurman Thomas and efficient short passing by quarterback Jim Kelly to drive to the Cowboys four yard line. From the four, Kelly handed off to Thomas, who made a nifty move near the line of scrimmage to avoid a tackle and then scampered untouched in to the end zone. The Bills lead 10-6, and would add a field goal to lead the Cowboys at halftime 13-6.

Any thoughts of the Bills really holding their lead, or otherwise finding a way to defeat these Cowboys disappeared within one minute of the second half kickoff. On a running play by Thurman Thomas, Leon Lett forced a fumble and the ball bounced free of the pile and was picked up by Cowboy safety James Washington, who then weaved his way forty six yards through the dismayed Bills, to the end zone for a Cowboy touchdown. The Cowboys had tied the game 13-13 and stunned the Bills and their fans. Then the Cowboys climbed on to the strong back of Emmitt Smith, who carried the ball seven times for sixty one yards in a sixty four yard drive, including a fifteen yard touchdown scamper to put the Cowboys ahead 20-13 midway through the third quarter.

Early in the fourth quarter Jim Kelly was intercepted by James Washington who returned to the Buffalo 34 yard line. On fourth and goal from the one, Jimmy gambled and Emmitt rewarded him with the touchdown plunge to put Dallas ahead 27-13. Eddie Murray added a short field goal with 2:50 remaining and the Dallas Cowboys defeated Buffalo 30-13 to win Super Bowl XXVIII. It was the Cowboys fourth Super Bowl win in franchise history. Emmitt Smith had thirty carries for 132 yards and two touchdowns, and was named the Super Bowl MVP. Buffalo joined Minnesota as the second NFL team to lose in all four Super Bowl appearances.

The Dallas Cowboys Super Bowl XXVIII win gave them their first back-to-back championships in their illustrious history. They also had one of the youngest teams in the NFL, with unquestionably the most talented player personnel, as well

Emmitt Smith, Super Bowl XXVIII MVP

as the best coaching staff. What could possibly stop this great franchise from dominating the NFL for years to come? This was the nightmare that the rest of the NFL was contemplating in January 1994.

You would think that Jerry Jones would do anything necessary to continue the winning and preserve the perch atop the NFL that the Dallas Cowboys had reached in 1992-1993. Unfortunately for Cowboy fans, that is not what happened. Having said that, Jerry Jones deserves credit for the part that he played in returning the Cowboys to greatness in the early nineties. Jerry is largely responsible for taking the Cowboys from worst to first in just four years. It was Jerry Jones who selected Jimmy Johnson. When no one other than Jimmy's parents in Port Arthur, Texas believed that Jimmy was the man to turn the Cowboys franchise around, Jerry Jones was the one who proclaimed that Jimmy Johnson was worth *"five first round draft picks"*.

Jerry Jones was also to blame for the sudden end to the Jimmy Johnson era with the Cowboys. Make no mistake about this, when Jimmy left the Cowboys, the team began to deteriorate. To be fair, there would have been some decline in the talent level even if Jimmy had remained, due to the new salary cap and free agency rules. However, without Jimmy's player personnel knowledge to make the selections in the draft, Jerry Jones was exposed as a novice NFL talent evaluator, when not being advised by a talented player evaluation and selection expert.

What would follow would be a two decade long roller coaster ride of watching our Cowboys go up and down, and then ultimately watching Jerry finally "figure it out".

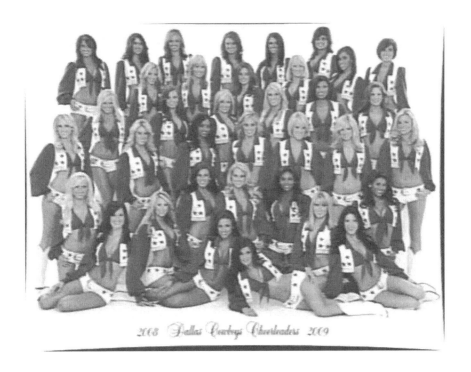

2008 Dallas Cowboys Cheerleaders 2009

The World Famous Dallas Cowboy Cheerleaders

Dallas Cowboys, Americas Team Is Back

Chapter Two

From Greatness To Mediocrity

On January 30, 1994 the Dallas Cowboys won Super Bowl XXVIII, their second consecutive NFL championship. The Cowboys were on top of the NFL world. They had the youngest and most talented roster in the league. They also had the best coaching staff in the league. The rest of the NFL was trying to figure out, how do you beat these Dallas Cowboys? The Cowboy fans were also on top of the world, enjoying the two straight Super Bowl victories, and anticipating the continued winning and the realistic opportunity for more championships, and possibly a dynasty. Unfortunately, Jerry Jones gave the rest of the teams of the NFL a gift that they could have never expected, when he paid Jimmy Johnson to leave the Dallas Cowboys. It would be the beginning of the end for Cowboy greatness at the time.

Apparently there had been indications for those on the "inside" of the NFL world, and for those who closely cover it, that for some time there had been a brewing level of discontent that was building momentum, between Jimmy Johnson and Jerry Jones. The discontent was apparently about Jimmy Johnson's recognition as the architect of the Cowboys rebuilding and their on-field success. Jerry Jones was unhappy with the fact that he was left out from the recognition as being one of the key contributors who were really responsible for the Cowboys achievements on the field. It was not enough for Jerry that he was the man who had bought the floundering franchise, and had made the choices and the investments that ultimately lead to the incredible and quick success. Jerry wanted more than the personal satisfaction of accomplishment, and the financial success. He wanted to be a part of the daily story of the team management, and the well documented camaraderie that Jimmy had with his coaching staff.

On March 29, 1994 the official announcement was made that Jimmy Johnson had resigned as the head coach of the Dallas Cowboys, and that he had been released from the remaining five years on his contract with the team. Then, on March 30, 1994 the Cowboys held the infamous press conference in which Jerry Jones sat next to Barry Switzer and announced that Barry was the new head coach of the Cowboys. Do you remember it? I will never forget it. Barry had his arm around Jerry, so awkwardly as if they were "buddies" in a bar recounting old times. I remember when Barry loudly exclaimed "we've got a job to do, and we're gonna do it baby!". The look on Jerry's face appeared to be one of discomfort, or embarrassment. It was comical. Unless you were a loyal OU fan, or a friend or family member of Barry Switzer, you had to be either a little embarrassed, or worried for the Cowboys on that day. Ultimately the league would get the last laugh, but not for a while longer. The

Cowboys did still have the great team that Jimmy Johnson had built, and that had just won back-to-back Super Bowls.

The 1994 draft would be the first that Jerry Jones would maneuver without the guidance of the departed Jimmy Johnson. With the exception of one outstanding offensive lineman and a marginal defensive end, the draft was weak. It was a sign that Jerry had been wise to hire Jimmy, and that the Cowboys General Manager was exposed without his player evaluation expertise.

1994 draft

Round	Pick	Position	Player name	University
1	23	DE	Shante Carver	Arizona St.
2	46	G	Larry Allen *	Sonoma St.
3	102	T	George Hegamin	N. Carolina St.
4	109	WR	Willie Jackson	Florida
4	131	LB	DeWayne Dotson	Mississippi
6	191	DB	Darren Studstill	W. Virginia
7	216	DE	Toddrick McIntosh	Florida St.

* Larry Allen *HOF*

The 1994 regular season would be among the best in Dallas Cowboys history in terms of regular season success. The Cowboys would go 12-4 and would once again win the NFC East, for the third consecutive season. They charged out to a record of 8-1. However, they lost at San Francisco 21-14 to drop to 8-2, in a game in which they uncharacteristically had three turnovers and were out-rushed by the 49ers. Unlike the

1992 and 1993 seasons which were relatively injury free, the Cowboys suffered significant injuries in 1994. Erik Williams had a serious car accident and was lost for the season. Troy Aikman was knocked out of the game in week eight and did not play at all in the Thanksgiving Day game. Emmitt Smith suffered a pulled hamstring near the end of the season, that hindered his level of performance in the playoffs.

The 1994 Thanksgiving Day game was very memorable. The Cowboys played the Green Bay Packers without Troy Aikman, and without his backup Rodney Pete, due to injuries. Third string quarterback Jason Garrett aroused memories of Clint Longley from 1974, as he rallied the Cowboys to 36 points in the second half and a 42-31 win. The Cowboys were 10-2 after November, however they were only 2-2 in the month of December and conceded home field advantage to the 49ers. That would prove costly.

In the divisional playoff round the Cowboys drew the Green Bay Packers again. The Cowboys dominated the Packers, leading 28-9 at halftime and ultimately winning easily 35-9. The Cowboys would then face the 49ers on the road for the NFC championship, and a chance at a rare "three-peat". It was the third consecutive year that the Cowboys and the 49ers met for the NFC championship. The Cowboys won the first two meetings, once in San Francisco and then in Dallas.

The 13-3 49ers had played their entire season in preparation for this game, and they were ready for the Cowboys. The 49ers had added free agents Deion Sanders and Ken Norton Jr (Norton from the Cowboys) to strengthen their defense. Their defense would be instrumental in taking control of the game early. On the Cowboys first possession, Troy Aikman attempted a pass in the right flat to Kevin Williams. Eric Davis pulled off of his coverage of Michael Irvin and jumped the route, intercepting the pass and returning it forty four yards for a touchdown. Was the play poorly designed? Would Jimmy Johnson have put the offense in that alignment? It was a great read and reaction by Eric Davis. However, I have to wonder if Jimmy's game preparation and resulting play calling would have been different.

Down 7-0, on their next possession Troy Aikman completed a deep in-route to Michael Irvin. However, in the process of the tackle Eric Davis stripped the ball free and caused a fumble, which the 49ers recovered on the Cowboys forty yard line. The 49ers drove to the Cowboy twenty nine, then Ricky Watters made a catch and run for the touchdown and a 14-0 lead just 4:40 in to the game. On the ensuing kickoff Kevin Williams fumbled and San Francisco recovered. The 49ers drove inside the Cowboys five, and William Floyd scored the touchdown to make it San Francisco 21-0 with 7:30 left in the first quarter. It was a devastating and irreparable start to the game for the Cowboys.

During the rest of the game the Cowboys were very valiant. They twice cut the lead to ten points. Troy Aikman was a warrior in the pocket. Michael Irvin had a monster day with twelve catches for 192 yards and two touchdowns. Michael Irvin *owned* Deion Sanders that day. The only stop that Deion could get on Irvin was on an obvious pass interference that was not called. But Jerry Rice also owned Larry Brown, and he kept the 49ers separated from the Cowboys comeback. With five minutes to play in the game Michael Irvin beat Deion Sanders again, down the left sideline. Troy Aikman threw a perfect pass. However Deion Sanders hooked Irvin with his left arm in an obvious pass interference that would have given the Cowboys possession at the 49ers five yard line, down 38-28 with five minutes left. The pass interference penalty was not called. That was the last chance for Dallas and they lost the NFC championship game 38-28.

That was a devastating loss because it prevented the potential three-peat, which the Cowboys almost certainly would have accomplished. The AFC champion was San Diego, which would have been no match for the Cowboys. San Francisco easily defeated San Diego 49-26 in Super Bowl XXIX.

With the start of the NFL salary cap in 1994, drafting strategies became more important for highly talented teams, because those teams would be forced by the cap to make choices and to let some talented players go due to high contract offers from other teams. So, replacing talent through the draft became the difference maker in the new era of the salary cap. In 1995 the Cowboys got very little usable talent from their ten draft picks.

1995 draft

Round	Pick	Position	Player name	University
2	46	RB	Sherman Williams	Alabama
2	59	TE	Kendell Watkins	Miss St.
2	63	G	Shane Hannah	Mich St.
3	92	DB	Charlie Williams	Bowling Green
4	110	TE	Eric Bjornson	Washington
4	129	DB	Alundis Brice	Mississippi
4	130	LB	Linc Harden	OK St.
5	166	WR	Edward Hervey	USC
5	168	LB	Dana Howard	Illinois
7	236	DE	Oscar Sturgis	N. Carolina

The Cowboys did not have a first round pick that year, and they did have what should be considered a big miss in the second round. At pick number forty six the Cowboys selected Sherman Williams. Four spots later the Philadelphia Eagles picked Bobby Taylor (cornerback – Notre Dame). Taylor played for the Eagles for nine years, and was a very solid NFL cornerback.

The Cowboys roster was still relatively loaded for the 1995 season, and "the triplets" were coming back healthy and hungry to avenge the 1994 NFC championship game loss to San Francisco. Their free agency losses prior to 1995 were Alvin Harper, James Washington, Mark Stepnoski and Jim Jeffcoat. Then in the first regular season game against the NewYork Giants, which the Cowboys won 35-0, cornerback Kevin Smith tore his achilles tendon. This caused the Cowboys to enter a bidding war for free agent cornerback Deion Sanders. The Cowboys signed Deion for $35 million over seven years, with $13 million paid at signing.

The Cowboys raced out to an 8-1 record. Then they faced the defending Super Bowl champion San Francisco 49ers at Texas Stadium. The 49ers came in to the game with a record of only 5-4. The Cowboys now had Deion Sanders at cornerback and everyone else was relatively healthy. It was revenge time for the Cowboys! However, the 49ers defense knocked Troy Aikman out of the game in the first quarter, and San Francisco lead 31-7 at the half. They would go on to beat Dallas 38-20. The Cowboys and their fans were stunned; they had now lost three consecutive meetings with San Francisco. The Cowboys won their next two games to improve to 10-2 and were looking good to win home field advantage throughout the playoffs. Then they lost to Washington and Philadelphia to drop to 10-4, and were trailing in the fourth quarter against the Giants. Dallas rallied to beat New York on a late field goal to avoid their third consecutive loss. The Cowboys hammered the Arizona Cardinals 37-13 in their season finale, while the 49ers lost to Atlanta to fall to 11-5, breaking the 49ers six game winning streak, and handing the Cowboys (12-4) home field advantage throughout the NFC playoffs.

In the divisional round the Cowboys drew the Philadelphia Eagles. The game was never really in question. The Cowboys lead 17-3 at the half, and were ahead 30-3 in the fourth quarter before Philadelphia finally found the end zone. Dallas won the game by a final score of 30-11. In the NFC championship the Cowboys faced Green Bay, which had defeated the defending Super Bowl champion San Francisco 49ers in the divisional round. The Packers were game, and they made the Cowboys work. The Cowboys lead 24-17 after a very exciting first half. However, the Packers lead 27-24 going in to the fourth quarter. The Cowboys defense took over in the fourth quarter and Dallas scored two unanswered touchdowns to win 38-27. Troy Aikman had two touchdown passes to Michael Irvin, and Emmitt Smith had 150 yards rushing and three touchdowns. Leon Lett had an interception of a screen pass. While this Cowboys team was two years removed from Jimmy Johnson's presence, they were still talented enough to win the NFC Championship, and earn a Super Bowl berth for the third time in four seasons.

The Cowboys would play the Pittsburgh Steelers in Super Bowl XXX. This was significant to Cowboy fans because Dallas was 0-2 against the Steelers in their Super Bowl history (1975 and 1978). The Steelers on the field in 1995 were a worthy opponent. They had started the season 4-4, then had won seven consecutive games, and fell short of eight in a row only due to a season finale loss at Green Bay. The Steelers had the third ranked defense in the 1995 NFL regular season.

In Super Bowl XXX the Dallas Cowboys controlled the game early. On their opening drive they got a twenty yard completion to Michael Irvin and a twenty three yard run by Emmitt Smith. The drive resulted in a forty two yard field goal by Chris Boniol, and a 3-0 lead just three minutes in to the game. After forcing the Steelers to punt the Cowboys used a forty seven yard completion from Troy Aikman to Deion Sanders to propel a drive that moved Dallas to a first and goal at the Pittsburgh three yard line. Aikman executed a perfect play action fake to Emmitt Smith to the right side, while Jay Novacek came free across the field to the left side, and Aikman lofted a perfect pass for the three yard touchdown to give Dallas a 10-0 lead late in the first quarter.

Jay Novacek (TE), Troy Aikman's "safety valve" (Dallas Cowboys, 1990-1995)

Early in the second quarter the Cowboys had another possession in which they drove into Steelers territory, and Aikman hit Michael Irvin for a twenty four yard touchdown pass. The touchdown was called back for an offensive pass interference penalty (a questionable call) against "The Playmaker".

Michael Irvin in Super Bowl XXX against the Pittsburgh Steelers

The Cowboys would have to settle for a thirty five yard field goal by Boniol and a 13-0 lead with six minutes remaining in the first half. After the teams exchanged punts the Steelers took possession with four minutes remaining in the half at their forty six yard line. During the ensuing drive the Steelers would convert a fourth down, and overcome two ten yard sacks. They drove to the Cowboys six yard line with seventeen seconds remaining in the half, after Steelers quarterback Neil O'Donnell hit Ernie Mills for a seventeen yard completion on a critical third and thirteen from the Dallas twenty three. O'Donnell then hit Yancey Thigpen for a touchdown on the next play to make the score 13-7 at the half. Steeler fans were believing and Cowboy fans were wondering.

In the third quarter the teams traded possessions, then with eight minutes remaining, Pittsburgh had the ball at midfield when Neil O'Donnell attempted a pass that was intercepted by Larry Brown, and he returned the interception forty four yards to the Steelers eighteen yard line. Two plays later Emmitt Smith scored from the one and the Cowboys increased their lead to 20-7. The game would move to the fourth quarter with the same score. On the first possession of the fourth quarter, Pittsburgh used the strong running of big power back Bam Morris to drive to the Cowboys nineteen yard line. On third and eight Tony Tolbert sacked Neil

O'Donnell. The Steelers wisely kicked a field goal to cut the Cowboys lead to 20-10 with eleven minutes to play. Bill Cowher's coaching staff recommended that he call for a surprise on-side kick, and Cowher concurred. The Cowboys were unsuspecting, and the Steelers Deion Figures recovered the kick untouched at the Pittsburgh forty eight yard line. Now inspired by the bold call, Pittsburgh took five minutes to methodically drive the fifty two yards in nine plays. The drive was capped off by Bam Morris three yard run untouched in to the end zone to cut the Cowboys lead to 20-17 with six minutes remaining in the game. Super Bowl XXX was now in question.

After the kickoff, Dallas faced a second and nine at their thirty five when Troy Aikman was sacked for a nine yard loss. The Cowboys had to punt, and the Steelers took possession at their thirty two with 4:15 remaining in the game. The Steelers had a chance to rally and beat the Cowboys in the Super Bowl again (70's flash back)! On second and ten from their thirty two, Neil O'Donnell attempted a pass on which his receiver cut a different direction and his pass went directly to Cowboys cornerback Larry Brown. Brown returned his second interception of Super Bowl XXX to the Steelers six yard line. On second and goal from the four yard line Emmitt Smith scored off right tackle and the Cowboys lead 27-17 with 3:43 left in the game. The Cowboys defense held the Steelers and the Cowboys ran out the clock. The Dallas Cowboys were champions of Super Bowl XXX, for an unprecedented third Super Bowl win in four seasons. It was Dallas fifth Super Bowl win in franchise history, which in 1995 was the most Super Bowl wins by any NFL team. Pittsburgh and San Francisco had four Super Bowl wins each at that time.

The fun, dominant, and dynamic period of the early nineties Dallas Cowboys ended when the 1995 Cowboys walked off the Sun Devil Stadium field in Tempe, Arizona. The Cowboys run of greatness that was started by Jerry Jones and engineered under the drafting and player development of Jimmy Johnson, ended when the Super Bowl XXX clock ticked 0:00 on January 28, 1996. The Cowboys were then two years removed from Jimmy Johnson's game planning, player selection, discipline, game day preparations, and talent evaluation. The Cowboys would move on in to the salary cap era lead by a General Manager still unproven in draft assessment, and the bizarre head coach Barry Switzer. We all know that ultimately did not work out well for our Cowboys.

Let's take a step back and look at how the Cowboys went from being on top of the NFL world in 1993, to then sliding into a period of mediocrity, lead by an undisciplined head coach and an over-confident owner who was operating with less support than he had during the first five years of his ownership.

Numerous media stories have been written about this. They all point to the same theme. Jerry Jones bought the Cowboy franchise and he hired Jimmy Johnson to rebuild the football team. From the many public stories that were published, and from reading Jimmy's book "Turning The Thing Around", it is pretty clear that when Jerry bought the team, he hired Jimmy Johnson to be more than just the head coach. Jimmy was also to be the player personnel director, although he wasn't formally given that title. Jerry had his hands quite full in the early days of his ownership running the financial operations of the franchise. I think that Jerry makes it clear that Jimmy was more than just a coach, with his proclamation that "Jimmy Johnson was worth five first round draft picks".

Jimmy has stated publicly many times, and also referenced in his book, that he was given total responsibility over the football operations in his contract. That included personnel, coaches and the draft. Jimmy makes it clear that it was this defined responsibility that allowed him to turn the team around so quickly. What changed things between Jerry and Jimmy were success and time, as well as the fact that Jerry probably allowed his ego to get the best of him. When the Cowboys became world champions in 1992, there were a lot of stories written about how the Cowboys had gotten so much better. Those stories focused on Jimmy Johnson and his staff. The stories were not about Jerry Jones, and how he was turning the franchise into a huge financial success. Over time that became a source of personal irritation, and ultimately some level of jealousy for Jerry Jones.

There is a good summary of the ultimate break-up of Jerry Jones and Jimmy Johnson courtesy of Sports Illustrated from April 1994. The story illustrates just how childish, immature and ego driven the interaction was "behind the public's view", between Jerry Jones and Jimmy Johnson during 1992 and 1993. This story is from the day before the 1992 NFL draft. The Dallas Cowboys "inner-circle" of Jimmy Johnson, Jerry Jones and Bob Ackles, formulated a trade to offer to the Cleveland Browns. Late that day, after Jerry had left the office, Cleveland coach Bill Belichick called to say that he would do the deal, and the Cowboys announced it. On draft day Jerry came to the office upset that he hadn't been called when the deal was confirmed, and he asked to see Jimmy. Their meeting apparently carried on until, with only five minutes left before the start of the draft, Jerry told Jimmy, "you know the ESPN camera is in the draft room today. So whenever we're about to make a pick, you look at me, like we're talking about it." In other words, Jerry wanted Jimmy to make him appear as if he was a draft day "player", even though Jerry wasn't in fact the one making the picks.

Jimmy stormed out of his meeting with Jerry and walked, not to the draft room, but to his office. When Dave Wannstedt went to tell Jimmy to hurry to the draft room, Johnson bitterly responded, "Let Jerry handle the draft. He knows all about it." Johnson gave in, but he stewed about Jones all day.

Apparently Jimmy Johnson told this story to a table of former Cowboys staff, including Bob Ackles, Dave Wannstedt, and Norv Turner, during a party at the NFL meetings in March 1994. While Jimmy was recounting the story, Jerry Jones approached the table with a drink in his hand, and proposed a toast. Jerry Jones later said that he doesn't remember having made the remark about ESPN to Jimmy. "But if that's the story they were telling when I approached their table," he said, "now I know why they all looked so sheepish." When Jones made his toast, the group, which included two people whom Jones had fired, reacted very coolly, and Jones was not invited to join the table. The snub led to Jones's widely reported remark later that night that he might get Switzer to coach the Cowboys.

Jones claimed that for two or three years he had a list of replacements in mind for Johnson. Worn down by his deteriorating relationship with Jones, Johnson said that he had all but vowed to quit after the 1993 season but had changed his mind over the winter. And even though the events in Orlando pushed both men to the breaking point,

Johnson and Jones came close on the morning of their break-up (March 29, 1994) to agreeing that Johnson would coach one final season.

According to Sports Illustrated, Johnson had been goading Jones since late in the 1993 season. Four days before Dallas played the New York Giants for the NFC East title, Johnson told ESPN that he might consider an offer to coach the expansion Jacksonville Jaguars. Jones, upset at Johnson's ill-timed remark, told the press that Jones, and only Jones would decide Johnson's coaching future. This made the strong-willed Johnson furious. On the team's charter flight home after the win over the Giants, Johnson walked up to Jones and said, "By the way, I'm the one who's going to decide how long I coach here." When Johnson was told in Orlando that Jones was threatening to fire him and replace him with Switzer, everything began to unravel. Johnson and Jones exchanged volleys in the press and then met on March 28 to sort out their future. "We came up with five options," says Johnson. "Number one, fire me, which we eliminated. Number two, I quit, which we eliminated. Number three, I continue to work under my existing contract, which we eliminated. Number four was to settle the contract and part. The fifth was to put all our efforts into one year. I even said I'd change the language in my contract, [which specifies] that I have sole control of all personnel moves. Then after one year I'd be free to go where I wanted."

That night Johnson went home to think about the final two options. He talked to Troy Aikman, who urged him to stay. The next morning, before leaving for the office, Johnson was leaning toward giving the thing one more try. Once in the office, though, Johnson saw the front page of the Fort Worth Star-Telegram. The headline read, JERRY TO JIMMY: COMMIT OR QUIT. Johnson was livid. He regarded the Fort Worth paper as Jones's mouthpiece, and the headline did not convey the tenor of the meeting that he had with Jones, not by a long shot. "I said to myself, I'm so tired of this," says Johnson. He walked into Jones's office and told him, "It's time." Jones agreed, and they worked out a deal whereby Jones would tear up the last five years of the contract. Johnson was a free man, with a bonus. "I want to thank you for everything you've done for the Cowboys," Jones told him. "How does two million dollars sound?" "Jerry," Johnson said, "you don't have to do that." "Hey, I want to do it," Jones said. "You deserve it." Johnson was thrilled with the deal. "I didn't want to be like Joe Gibbs, who still doesn't know if he can get out of his Washington contract," he says. "And I didn't really want a financial settlement. I just wanted to be a free agent."

Ok now, let's be honest, and before I say this let me say to Jimmy, I love you man. I am a Port Arthur guy, a graduate of Thomas Jefferson. So take this gently, please: Jimmy was childish too. I mean, the feud about "Jones deciding Johnson's coaching future"? Really? Of course Jerry has the power to fire Jimmy. He owns the Cowboys! But I guess that hurt Jimmy's pride, and based on his success he really didn't have to put up with that non-sense. As a Cowboy fan it is just really disappointing that because these two men behaved the way that they did, the early 90's championship run appears to have ended before it should have. History tells us that kind of success does not occur often. When it does it should be protected. In this case, it was not.

There have been numerous interviews, and various stories written about those interviews, in recent times about the "break-up" of the Cowboys brain trust in 1994. One really telling article was published by the Dallas Morning News in November 2012. Apparently Jimmy Johnson had an opportunity to react to comments made by Jerry Jones, following the Cowboys loss to the Atlanta Falcons on November 4, 2012. Jimmy said he wasn't interested in creating controversy, but that he wanted to set the record straight about his role with the Cowboys in the years that he had coached the team. "The time that I was with the team, I had complete and total responsibility over the football operation," Johnson said in a telephone interview from his home in the Florida Keys. "That meant personnel, the draft, coaches, including the strength coach. Everything. It was always in my contract."

Jerry Jones puts a different spin on the issue of the GM: "When I bought the team, the night I bought it, I said I would be doing what I'm doing and that's GM the team and making the final decisions on personnel," Jerry Jones said. "That's the way it's always been done. We've won three Super Bowls doing it that way, so I'm going to do it again." Jones spin on the Cowboys history indicates that he is taking full credit for the dominant performance of the 1992 – 1995 teams, notwithstanding the lack of success in the years after Jimmy Johnson left Dallas.

The GM statement by Jerry is somewhat revisionist history in the sense that while Jerry was in fact the GM in 1989-1993, he was receiving personnel advice from the very competent Jimmy Johnson. It is undeniable that GM Jones benefitted from the advice of his head coach. The player selections that were "recommended" by Johnson allowed the Cowboys to win "those three Super Bowls" (1992, 1993 & 1995).

Johnson, who coached two of those three Super Bowl teams that beat the Buffalo Bills in 1992 and 1993, and who has been widely credited for assembling the talent that went on to win a third Super Bowl against the Pittsburgh Steelers with Barry Switzer as the Cowboys head coach, agreed that Jones held the title of "general manager". However, Johnson adds that "When we signed that first contract, Jerry said, 'I'll be in charge of the finances, you'll be in charge of the football,' we'll make history,". Jones responded in a statement: "I came into the NFL as the owner and general manager of this team, and one of the first decisions I made in the role of GM was to hire Jimmy as head coach," Jones said. "Jimmy and I worked well together. We had great communication, and I have always appreciated what he has done for the organization. I wanted all the input in the world from Jimmy on personnel. "During Jimmy's tenure, the authority to hire the players was with the GM. But it was agreed that we wouldn't bring a player into the organization that he didn't approve of. We were a team and it worked very well. In our unique circumstances, where the owner and the GM were the same person, in the case of a disagreement — which we never had — the owner had the ultimate authority."

Johnson said Jones wanted more credit when he realized the business end of the Cowboys was not as glamorous as the day-to-day football operation. "In the third or fourth year, Jerry said, 'I want to be a part of this. Nobody cares how much money I make, they want to know about a second-string guard," Johnson said. Johnson said when the

Cowboys traded with Atlanta for defensive tackle Tony Casillas in training camp before the 1991 season, he was surprised to hear Jones taking credit. Johnson said when he told Jones about the trade, the owner was not familiar with Casillas, who had played at the University of Oklahoma and been the second pick of the 1986 draft. "I was steamed," Johnson said.

Johnson said when he negotiated subsequent contracts with Jones, the Cowboys owner was "always very adamant" that clauses detailing Johnson's control be removed. "It was always a sticking point with Jerry," Johnson said. "I would never agree."

So to be fair, I will say that both Jerry Jones and Jimmy Johnson are responsible for the early end of the highly successful Cowboys GM and head coach pairing of the early 90's. The drop-off in success for the Dallas Cowboys after Jimmy Johnson left is pronounced. From 1989 through 1993 the Cowboys had a playoff record of 7-1, and won two Super Bowls. They lost the NFC Championship in 1994, then won Super Bowl XXX in 1995. Then from 1996 through 2013 Dallas won just two playoff games, and both were wildcard games. For a life-long Cowboy fan, enduring eighteen seasons with only two wildcard playoff wins has been humbling.

1996 draft

Round	Pick	Position	Player name	University
2	37	DE	Kavika Pittman	McNeese
2	49	LB	Randall Godfrey	Georgia
3	67	C	Clay Shiver	Fl State
3	94	WR	Stepfret Williams	La Monroe
3	95	DT	Mike Ulufale	BYU
5	167	LB	Alan Campos	Louisville
6	207	DB	Wendell Davis	Oklahoma

The Cowboys draft of 1996 was not very productive. They had no first round draft pick due to previous trade activity. However, in the rebuilding years Jimmy had been productive in most rounds of the draft. The lack of a pick in the first round was not the downfall of this draft. In the second round the Cowboys took defensive end Kavika Pittman. Pittman would make the roster and play for the Cowboys, however he was not particularly an impact player. Denver selected eventual Pro-bowl defensive back Tory James seven picks after the Cowboys selected Pittman. Also in the second round, the Cowboys drafted Randall Godfrey, who did turn out to be a very productive player, and their best pick of this draft. The Cowboys had three picks in the third round, and basically got nothing from them. Players that the Cowboys could have drafted but missed in the third round include: Donnie Abraham, (cornerback) drafted by Tampa Bay; Terrell Owens, (wide receiver) drafted by San Francisco; and John Runyan, (offensive tackle) drafted by Houston. The lack of success in the 1996 draft was an unfortunate indication of drafts to come for GM Jerry Jones.

The Cowboys went in to the 1996 season as the defending Super Bowl champions, with a veteran and very talented starting lineup on both sides of the ball. However, several bad things happened over the course of the season to weaken the team. First, the Cowboys went in to the season opener with Michael Irvin on a five game suspension due to an off season incident that resulted in his arrest. Not having the "play maker" hurt the Cowboys offense. Jay Novacek had retired after the 1995 season, so Michael Irvin was Troy's "go-to" receiver. Without Irvin, the Cowboy offense was crippled. The Cowboys lost three of the first four games. In a loss to Chicago, the Cowboys did not score a touchdown, and in a loss to Buffalo they only scored one touchdown. Emmitt Smith was injured in the game one loss to Chicago, and the injury would limit his effectiveness early in the year. Charles Haley suffered a serious back injury and would miss the majority of the season. Leon Lett would be suspended due to a violation of league drug policy. In general the Cowboys lineup had been depleted of the depth that they had enjoyed in 1992 and 1993, as a result of losses to free agency that began in 1994, and because of the unproductive drafts after Jimmy Johnson left.

After beginning the season 1-3, the Cowboys won four games in a row. They went in to a big game at San Francisco at 5-4, with the 49ers at 7-2. The Cowboys had lost their last three meetings to San Francisco, since Barry Switzer had become the head coach. They managed to grind out an overtime win 20-17, which helped propel them to finish the season on a 5-2 run, and win the NFC East again. They would play in the wild card game in the playoffs, against the Minnesota Vikings. Minnesota was a weak wildcard opponent. The Vikings had to win three of their last four games to get to 9-7, and sneak in to a wild card spot. The Cowboys dominated the Vikings from the start, at one point leading 30-0, and ultimately winning 40-15. This win was no indication of the Cowboys ability to compete against a quality NFC playoff opponent.

Next the Cowboys faced the surprising Carolina Panthers. In just their second year in the league, the Panthers had gone 12-4 to win the NFC West, and claim home field advantage in the divisional playoff round. Carolina had a top ten defense in yards allowed, and second ranked in the NFL in points allowed. The Cowboys were hoping to advance for a chance to play Green Bay (the Packers had a first round bye) in Lambeau Field for the first time in the playoffs, since the famous "Ice Bowl" game (1967). On the second play of the game the Cowboys Michael Irvin was tackled from behind and landed awkwardly, driving his right shoulder in to the turf, and breaking his collar bone. With Irvin out of the game, Troy Aikman had no "go-to" receiver to rely on. The Cowboys reverted to their problems seen early in the season when Michael Irvin had been suspended. They were ineffective in the red zone, having to settle for field goals on three out of four trips. Without Michael Irvin, this game was effectively lost in the first quarter.

The Cowboys defense also had problems as they were missing heroes of prior year's playoff success, including Charles Haley and Leon Lett. Because the Cowboys had very little depth on defense even before those two monumental losses, the younger Panthers offense was able to consistently run the ball in the second half, and to produce enough to put the Cowboys away 26-17. The post Jimmy Johnson era Cowboys had fallen another step further away from their former greatness. The 1996 season was the beginning of the slide into mediocrity. With Jimmy gone, there simply was no one in the Cowboy organization with the ability to rebuild the roster through the draft.

Due to the continued losses to free agency, as well as aging starters, the Cowboys had several needs in the 1997 draft. The needs included the offensive line, the defensive line,

1997 draft

Round	Pick	Position	Player name	University
1	22	TE	David LaFleur	LSU
3	65	LB	Dexter Coakley	Appal St
3	83	G	Steve Scifres	Wyoming
3	94	DB	Kenny Wheaton	Oregon
4	101	DT	Antonio Anderson	Syracuse
4	127	WR	Macey Brooks	James Madison
4	129	RB	Nicky Sualua	Ohio St
7	224	DB	Omar Stoutmire	Fresno St

wide receiver and tight end. The Cowboys drafted tight end David Lafleur in the first round (with Troy Aikman's "blessing"). In the third round at number 65 the Cowboys took Dexter Coakley (linebacker). Aside from these two players, and the seventh round pick Stoutmire, the 1997 draft was a bust, and in a year when the Cowboy roster was in serious need of rebuilding.

The Cowboys went in to the 1997 season hopeful to improve on the 10-6 1996 season. They got off to a real good start, opening with a 37-7 win at Pittsburgh (it's always great to win at Pittsburgh!) and going 3-1 in the first month. Then the deeper weaknesses of the aging team began to surface. The offensive line that had been such a strength in the Super Bowl years (1992-1995) was now growing old, slow, and basically weak "up the middle". Mark Tuinei and Nate Newton were aging, and Nate was also really "out of shape". The new center, Clay Shiver was being over-powered and could not provide the run support or pass protection that was required by the Cowboys offensive scheme. As a result Emmitt Smith's production declined and Troy Aikman faced more pressure and more blitzing schemes. On the defensive side of the ball the defensive line wore down as the year progressed due to a lack of depth. Without the pass rush of prior years the secondary was put under added strain. Deion Sanders was great, however Kevin Smith was picked on, and he was just not the same after his achilles injury in 1995. The Cowboys fell from 3-1 to 4-4 at mid-season. It would not get better from there. The Cowboys lost at home on Thanksgiving Day (they had been 6-1 on Thanksgiving in the 90's) and closed the 1997 season losing five straight games, to finish at 6-10.

Barry Switzer resigned as the Cowboys head coach in January 1998. Barry was a popular figure to a lot of fans, but in reality he was a "has-been", and he added nothing to the Cowboys once Jimmy's roster began to decline due to age and free agency. Barry was the first of a series of poor decisions that Jerry Jones made. After Switzer's resignation there was a lot of discussion regarding the lack of discipline that plagued the Cowboys while Switzer was the head coach. The lack of discipline was the fault both of some of the players, and the head coach Barry Switzer.

Hall of Famers -- Super Bowl Champions

Dallas Cowboys, Americas Team Is Back

Chapter Three

The End For The Triplets

Jerry Jones started his search for a new head coach in January 1998 with a focus on three candidates. He interviewed George Seifert, the former head coach of the San Francisco 49ers, Sherman Lewis, the Green Bay Packers offensive coordinator, and Terry Donahue, the former head coach at UCLA. Apparently the Terry Donahue conversations went as far as discussing money and head coaching control. But Jerry surprised everyone by choosing Chan Gailey, previously the offensive coordinator for the Pittsburgh Steelers.

In making the announcement Jerry Jones defined the reasons why he liked and had chosen Chan Gailey: he was previously a head coach (Troy University; and Birmingham-World Football League); he was a former quarterback (University of Florida); ten years as an NFL assistant coach; and "high energy". I suspect that the unspoken reasons for the hire were (1) there was little chance that Chan Gailey would embarrass Jerry or the Cowboys, as Gailey had a strong moral background, and (2) he was relatively cheap, accepting a contract of $2.5 million for five years. Gailey was an offensive focused coach, having been an NFL offensive coordinator. The Cowboys offense was in need of improvement after the disaster of 1997.

The other new coaches announced in 1998 were Wade Phillips in Buffalo, Jim Mora in Indianapolis and John Gruden in Oakland. As for Wade Phillips, he will be discussed in detail later in this book. Jim Mora worked out well for the Colts. And then there is John Gruden. Well, I am glad that Jerry didn't consider him, because in my opinion he is over-rated, and over-priced. Gruden would have never worked with the veteran Cowboys. So in retrospect I really don't have a big problem with the Chan Gailey pick for head coach. What continued to be missing was a player personnel resource, for player evaluation and draft advising.

1998 draft

Round	Pick	Position	Player name	University
1	8	DE	Greg Ellis	N. Carolina
2	38	T	Flozell Adams	Michigan St.
4	100	DT	Michael Myers	Alabama
5	130	LB	Darren Hambrick	S. Carolina
5	138	T	Oliver Ross	Iowa St.
6	188	DB	Izell Reese	Ala-Birmingham
7	223	RB	Tarik Smith	California
7	227	G	Antonio Fleming	Georgia
7	237	TE	Rodrick Monroe	Cincinnati

Dallas went in to the 1998 draft with needs in the offensive line, the defensive line and at wide receiver. These needs are illustrated by the Cowboys 1997 performance: the Cowboys offense had been ranked number twenty two in the league in 1997, and their big problem was getting to the red zone, but not being able to score touchdowns; Troy Aikman was sacked thirty three times in 1997; for reference, Troy was sacked only fourteen times in 1994; the Cowboy defense was ranked number one against the pass in 1997, but number twenty four against the run. Opponents did not have to pass much on the Cowboys, when they could run at will.

Coming off the 6-10 record of 1997 the Cowboys had the eighth pick in the first round. The 1997 draft was one of Jerry's better drafts, as the Cowboys got production from the first four players that they selected. However Jerry got nothing from the lower rounds of the draft, so the Cowboys continued to miss on about half of their draft picks.

The Cowboys won the first game of the 1998 season, thumping the Arizona Cardinals 38-10. In the second game the Cowboys traveled to Denver to play the defending Super Bowl champions. Denver was in championship form and the Cowboys weaknesses were exposed. Denver scored five first half touchdowns, and the Cowboys could not stop the running of Terrell Davis. To make matters worse, Troy Aikman was lost to a fractured collar bone. He was replaced by Jason Garrett. Denver won easily 42-23. The Cowboys went 3-2 with Garrett replacing Aikman, and they went into their bye week with a record of 4-3.

The Cowboys got Troy Aikman back and won their next four games to improve to 8-3 going in to the Thanksgiving Day home game. The Cowboys faced the Minnesota Vikings. The Vikings came in to the game 10-1, and they were on their way to a 15-1 regular season. They had Randall Cunningham at quarterback and their sensational rookie wide receiver Randy Moss. The Cowboys were without the injured Deion Sanders, so the secondary was shorthanded, and Randy Moss had vowed to make the Cowboys pay for picking Greg Ellis over him in the first round of the 1998 draft. The Vikings torched the Cowboys weakened defense as Minnesota receivers were literally running free throughout the Dallas secondary. Randy Moss had three catches for 163 yards, all for touchdowns. Randall Cunningham threw for 359 yards and four touchdowns. Troy Aikman valiantly threw for 455 yards, but the Vikings beat the Cowboys 46-36. The Cowboy defense could not stop the relentless Vikings, as they gave up 470 yards of total offense on a national television broadcast.

The 8-4 Cowboys went to New Orleans to play a 5-7 Saints team that was on its way to finishing the season losing seven out of nine games. But the Cowboys "laid an egg", as they rushed for eight yards in the game (eight yards – not a misprint) and had only 182 total yards. The next week the Cowboys went to Kansas City where their weak run-stopping defense was again exposed, when Bam Morris rushed for

137 yards, and the Chiefs beat the Cowboys 20-17, dropping them to 8-6.

The Cowboys would close the 1998 regular season by beating 3-11 Philadelphia and 6-9 Washington at home, to finish at 10-6 and win the NFC East. However, the Cowboys were exposed as inconsistent offensively during the final month of the season. Was it the age of the club's veterans that was a burden at season's end? Or was it the play calling of Chan Gailey, who couldn't seem to decide if he wanted to be aggressive or conservative? Gailey was both the head coach and the offensive coordinator, and he called the offensive plays.

The Cowboys made the 1998 playoffs as NFC East champions, and hosted the NFC wild card game against the Arizona Cardinals, a team that they had defeated 38-10 and 35-28 in the regular season. However, there were two completely different teams on the field in Texas Stadium on January 2, 1999. This game was shocking and numbing for Cowboy fans, who still saw this team as the great Cowboys that had the triplets. In the first quarter Jake Plummer hit Frank Sanders with a fifty nine yard pass to the Cowboy fourteen yard line. Two plays later Plummer beat an all-out blitz with a shovel pass that went twelve yards for the touchdown. Arizona 7 – Dallas 0. The Cardinals added a field goal for a 10-0 half time lead.

The Cardinals opened the third quarter with a seventy four yard run by Adrian Murrell. Deion Sanders delayed the touchdown by running Murrell down from behind. However, it set up a short touchdown pass from Plummer to Larry Centers, and the Cardinals lead the Cowboys 17-0. The lead would go to 20-0 before the Cowboys finally scored a touchdown with four minutes left in the game. The Cardinals would win 20-7, for the franchise' first playoff game win since 1947. It was a big upset.

Troy Aikman commented on the sideline throughout the game that he had no receivers open. Troy was sacked four times in the game, and intercepted three times. Emmitt Smith rushed for seventy four yards. The Cowboys produced a total of 260 yards of offense. It was another weak offensive showing, a common theme in the latter half of the season. This wildcard loss was caused by a repeat of the same problems that caused the three straight losses in late November and early December. The offensive line was weak up the middle, and the Cowboy offense could not convert in the red zone. The defense could not stop the run. The cause of these problems was a lack of talent, which was the outcome of poor results in multiple drafts.

The Cowboys of 1998 just did not have the caliber of talent as compared to the glory years of 1992-1995. The offensive line was not as strong. The defensive line was weak against the run and had no depth. The receivers aside from Michael Irvin, were Patrick Jeffers and Billy Davis (journeymen). There was no serious threat to stretch the field, so Irvin was double covered. David Lafleur was not on par with the retired Jay Novacek, so Troy Aikman did not have a reliable outlet in pressure situations as he had in prior years, and many times Troy could not find an open receiver. This caused the offensive inconsistency seen in 1998.

1999 draft

Round	Pick	Position	Player name	University
1	20	DE	Ebenezer Ekuban	N. Carolina
2	55	G	Solomon Page	W. Virginia
3	85	LB	Dat Nguyen	TX A&M
4	118	WR	Wayne McGarity	Texas
4	132	DE	Peppi Zellner	Fort Valley St
6	193	WR	Martay Jenkins	Neb. Omaha
7	229	TE	Mike Lucky	Arkansas
7	243	G	Kelvin Garmon	Baylor

The Cowboys had clearly defined weaknesses that were in need of being addressed in the 1999 NFL draft. Again it was the offensive line, the defensive line and the need for a big play threat wide receiver. Ebenezer Ekuban was a rational choice at number twenty. In the second round at number fifty five, the Cowboys picked an offensive guard, and there were two guards chosen within five picks who had far better NFL careers. After the Cowboys picked at number eighty five, San Francisco picked a defensive end at number eighty nine and Green Bay selected a defensive tackle at number ninety four that produced more than the Cowboys got from Dat Nguyen. After these three marginal picks, the 1999 Cowboys draft resulted in five more draft selection misses. Of note is the fact that the Cowboys picked a wide receiver at number 118 in the fourth round, and again at number 193 in the sixth round. Neither player did anything significant for the Cowboys. The Green Bay Packers selected Donald Driver (wide receiver) in the seventh round at number 213 in 1999. Donald Driver played in the NFL through the 2012 season, and produced 10,137 yards and sixty one touchdowns. It is fair to say that a lot of teams missed on Donald Driver. Clearly Jerry Jones was continuing to experience a lengthy and painful learning curve with regard to player evaluations for the draft, after Jimmy Johnson's exit from the Cowboys in 1994.

The 1999 season began with a road game at Washington. The Redskins are a division rival. It is always great to win in the Nation's Capital. Going to the fourth quarter of the first regular season game, the Redskins were leading the Cowboys 35-14, however Troy Aikman, Emmitt Smith and Michael Irvin rallied the Cowboys for three fourth quarter touchdowns to tie the game and send it to overtime. The Redskins could do nothing with the first possession in overtime. The Cowboys got the ball and faced a third and two at their own twenty four yard line. The Redskins bought a great play-action fake to Emmitt, and Troy threw a perfect pass in stride to Rocket Ismail and he ran away untouched for the seventy six yard winning touchdown, and Dallas won in overtime in a thrilling comeback. The 1999 season started 1-0. The Cowboys won the next two games convincingly over Atlanta and Arizona to go 3-0.

Game four of the 1999 NFL regular season may be the saddest, and most repugnant NFL game that I have ever witnessed, with regard to the shocking and detestable behavior of the Philadelphia Eagles fans. On October 10, 1999 in the first quarter of the game, Michael Irvin was injured on a play, and while he lay injured on the field, many of the Eagles fans cheered loudly when he remained sprawled on the field after the play. Even worse, there was a second loud cheer by the Eagles fans when the paramedics wheeled a stretcher out onto the field for Irvin. What was not immediately known, but must have been apparent to those on the field at that time, was that Michael had sustained a critical injury that was of a career ending nature. As Michael was placed on the stretcher and wheeled off of the field, the Eagles crowd once again cheered loudly, but not in the sportsmanlike manner that crowds typically give out of respect for the injured player. Even the Eagles players talked after the game about how embarrassed they were for their fans behavior. With Michael Irvin out of the lineup the Cowboys offense bogged down, as it had in the prior year when Irvin was out for an extended period of time. The 0-4 Eagles generated just enough offense to defeat the Cowboys 13-10, and gave Andy Reid his first win as the Eagles head coach.

The next week the Cowboys went to New York to face the 2-3 Giants. With no Michael Irvin, the Cowboys offense would again be significantly weakened. The Giants knew that from studying the early part of 1998 when Irvin was suspended, and from the previous week in Philadelphia. The Giants defense held Emmitt Smith to 26 yards on 22 carries. The Cowboys lost for the second week in a row 13-10.

The Cowboys would go on to lose four games in a row and fall to 4-4 at mid-season. The Cowboys struggled for the balance of the year, having to win their final game to even their record at 8-8. The Cowboys qualified for the wild card game and were matched with the Minnesota Vikings. The Cowboys defense allowed Robert Smith to rush for 140 yards, and Randy Moss caught a 58 yard "hail Mary" touchdown pass with one minute to go in the second quarter. The Cowboys offense was simply incapable of overcoming the Viking offensive production, and Minnesota ended the Cowboys season 27-10.

After the season Michael Irvin and Daryl Johnston each announced their retirement as a result of career ending injuries that they suffered early in the 1999 season. With Michael Irvin's retirement came the literal end of "the triplets". That was very sad because they provided several years of dominant performances, and of course three memorable Super Bowl championships.

Jerry's Chan Gailey experiment came to a sudden end when Jerry dismissed the head coach with three years left on his contract. Gailey was criticized for his play calling and his offensive style, which was inconsistent and relatively unproductive for Dallas. Gailey's philosophy was to confuse the defense, by frequently changing the personnel on the field, as well as the alignments, for example sometimes having an empty backfield, and using running backs as receivers. In the running game he emphasized getting outside rather than running between the tackles. Running between the tackles was the strength of Emmitt Smith. Emmitt's style and physical attributes were not suited to running "outside".

It certainly did not help Chan Gailey that the offense was without Michael Irvin for nearly half of 1998, and for most of the 1999 season. The Cowboys also did not get much production from the tight-end, as they had in previous years before Jay Novacek retired. The bottom line is that Chan

Gailey was a good man, and he tried hard, but he inherited the declining Cowboys when the roster was in the free-fall from greatness due to age, injuries and salary cap losses.

Jerry took a mere two weeks to decide that we was promoting Dave Campo from defensive coordinator to head coach, to replace Chan Gailey. Jerry Jones had replaced three head coaches in six seasons. Campo had come to Dallas with Jimmy Johnson from The University of Miami in 1989. During his announcement of Campo's promotion, Jerry Jones stated "it reduces the transition"; "Dave will be overseer and ultimate decision maker". The term "overseer" was a reference to the role of new head coach Dave Campo, however, the "ultimate decision maker" was at that time yet to be defined.

Campo would have his work cut out for him, as the Cowboys had led the NFL in penalties and penalty yardage in 1999, and were 1-8 on the road. Campo stated "I want to run on throwing downs and throw on running downs; I want us to attack and be aggressive; my number one objective is to develop an attitude on this team." Campo was given a more generous contract than Gailey, as it was reported to be for five years at $800,000 to $1 million per season.

After settling the coaching situation to his satisfaction, Jerry Jones got busy working on the "needs" of the Cowboys roster. The needs for the 2000 Cowboys were significant. On offense, in 1999 the Cowboys could not run the ball when they "had to" particularly against good defenses. The offense ranked 24th in the league in passing yards, and was unable to convert for touchdowns in the red zone. The combination of those three factors resulted in the Cowboys not being productive against the better teams in the league, thus their record of 8-8, and a playoff game loss in which the game was never really in question. On defense they ranked eighth in the league overall, however if you look at their games against the better teams (which is who you play in the playoffs) the Cowboys were weak up the middle against the run, and were vulnerable to the big pass play. The Minnesota playoff loss was a perfect example: they were torched by the running of Robert Smith, and could not defend the big play threat of Randy Moss.

The Cowboys made several personnel moves in early 2000. There were several free agent signings, one big trade, and of course the draft.

First let's discuss the trade. Jerry traded the Cowboys first round picks in the 2000 and 2001 drafts to the Seattle Seahawks, for wide receiver Joey Galloway. This trade was made in reaction to the retirement of Michael Irvin. The reason for the trade was sound. The Cowboys offense clearly bogged down during 1998 and 1999 when Michael

Irvin was not on the field. There were two problems with this trade. Joey Galloway was the wrong player to pick to replace Michael Irvin, and two first round draft picks was too much to give for Joey Galloway. Joey Galloway was 5 ' 11", 195 pounds, and he was a speed receiver, not the physical possession receiver that the dominant 6' 2", 210 pound Michael Irvin had been. Irvin had long arms and huge hands, and he used his big frame for leverage to gain position on defensive backs. Joey Galloway never possessed the physical attributes of Michael Irvin. So from that aspect alone the trade was miss-guided, and it was evaluated as such at the time (see Sports Illustrated – Peter King).

One of the Cowboys major offensive weaknesses in 1998-1999 was the lack of a physical "possession" receiver, and Joey Galloway would not be the answer. The two first round draft picks were too much to give for an average sized speed receiver, who by the way, was in a contract hold-out with Seattle at the time. Jerry was apparently focused on one player, rather than trying to find the right fit for the Cowboys need. Jerry's tunnel vision made him willing to over-pay to get Galloway. So the bottom line is that Jerry Jones chose the wrong player, and he compounded the mistake by over-paying for Galloway. That would cost the Cowboys because of the extra draft pick, and because Galloway did not solve the possession receiver production problem.

Jerry made several free agent moves, primarily to address the Cowboys needs at cornerback resulting from the subtraction of Kevin Smith (retired) and the necessary salary cap move to cut Deion Sanders. Darren Woodson talked his good friend Phillipi Sparks out of retiring, and Sparks signed a two year deal with the Cowboys to help at cornerback while the newly drafted rookies were "brought along". The Cowboys also signed free agent cornerback Ryan McNeil, a seven year NFL veteran. Jerry also signed a veteran wide receiver, James McKnight, who had spent his first five seasons with Seattle. McKnight was another speed receiver.

Jerry in his own way attempted to address the needs for improvement and depth through the trade and free agent signings. Then came the 2000 draft. Clearly, cornerback was Jerry's first priority, but his approach was quantity and not necessarily quality. The Cowboys did not have a first round pick in the 2000 draft due to the Joey Galloway trade.

2000 draft

Round	Pick	Position	Player name	University
2	49	CB	Dwayne Goodrich	Tennessee
4	109	CB	Kareem Larrimore	W. TX A&M
5	144	RB	Michael Wiley	Ohio St
6	180	CB	Mario Edwards	Fl. State
7	219	LB	Orantes Grant	Georgia

In the second round at number forty nine the Cowboys selected 5' 11" cornerback Dwayne Goodrich. Goodrich played in sixteen games over three seasons, producing eight tackles with no interceptions. Goodrich was a miss. (Goodrich NFL career was cut short by his arrest and conviction on charges of vehicular homicide) Given the Cowboy defense's weakness in run stopping from the prior year, it is notable that just six picks after the Cowboys took Goodrich, the Vikings selected defensive tackle Fred Robbins, who was a strong middle run stuffer and produced good middle pass pressure as well. Robbins went on to have a ten year NFL career with thirty five career sacks.

In the fourth round at number 109 the Cowboys took 5'11" cornerback Kareem Larrimore, and he played in nineteen games over two seasons with seventeen tackles and no interceptions. Larrimore was a miss. In the fifth round at number 144 the Cowboys selected a running back from Ohio State. Wiley did nothing for the Cowboys in two years. Five picks after the Cowboys selected Wiley, the Green Bay Packers took Kabeer Gbaja Biamila, a defensive end from San Diego State. All Biamilia did was rack up 74.5 career sacks in an eight year NFL career. At number 153 Kansas City took Dante Hall, wide receiver from Texas A&M, who had a ten year NFL career and was a spectacular return specialist. Finally, if running back was the fifth round priority, Sammy Morris of Texas Tech was available to the Cowboys at 144, and he went on to a ten year NFL career, as a backup and role player.

In the sixth round at number 180 the Cowboys selected 6' 0" 200 pound cornerback Mario Edwards. Edwards would play relatively well for the Cowboys in 2001, and he was a starter in 2002 and 2003. Oh by the way, at pick number 199 in the sixth round, the New England Patriots got a quarterback from Michigan, named Tom Brady. But who knew, right?

The Cowboys last selection in the 2000 draft was a 6'0" 228 pound linebacker at number 219. He would play sparingly for two years and recorded eight tackles (total). In comparison, at number 224 the Green Bay Packers selected offensive tackle Mark Tauscher from Wisconsin, and he would have a solid ten year NFL career, in which he appeared in 132 games.

Jerry's player personnel work in preparation for the 2000 season was poor, and the results of the 2000 season substantiate this evaluation. Jerry's big trade was a bust because he traded for the wrong type of receiver, given the role that he was trying to replace in the Cowboy's offense (Michael Irvin). His free agent signings of Phillipi Sparks and Ryan McNeil were acceptable stop gap measures, and they played relatively well for the Cowboys for a couple of seasons. The 2000 draft has to be considered a complete disaster. The Cowboys got one player who was marginally productive (Mario Edwards). However, the other four draft picks were wasted. NFL teams are built and maintained through effective drafting. Without effective drafting a roster will deteriorate. The difference between the winners and the losers in the NFL is the ability to evaluate talent and make the right draft selections.

The Dallas Cowboys 2000 season began inauspiciously, and was an omen of things to come. I remember this game well, because I was there. The temperature was 105 degrees at game time. It was scorching hot down on the field in Texas Stadium. The Eagles surprised the Cowboys with an on-side kick on the opening kickoff, which they recovered. They quickly drove 58 yards in eight plays to take a 7-0 lead. It was 14-0 at the end of the first quarter. Troy Aikman was sacked three times in the first quarter. In the second quarter, Troy under jail break pressure, threw an interception that was returned for a touchdown and Philadelphia lead 21-0. On the fourth sack of the day by the Eagles, Troy sustained a bad concussion and he left the game. The Eagles lead at half time 24-6. In the fourth quarter the Eagles had built their lead to 41-6, before the Cowboys scored a touchdown and added a two point conversion. To add "injury to insult", late in the game Joey Galloway sustained a torn ACL that ended his season before the first game was over. It was a very bad day, a terrible start to the season and unfortunately, an indication of how bad this Cowboys team had become. The final score was 41-14.

It was apparent that there had been a changing of the guard in the NFC East, after years of Cowboy dominance, and the Eagles former futility. Now the Eagles had the innovative and aggressive head coach Andy Reid, and their new star quarterback Donovan McNabb. On this day the Cowboy offense produced 167 total yards in the game. The Cowboy defense gave up 306 rushing yards to the Eagles. Weakness against the run was not a new theme for the Cowboys.

In game two the Cowboys traveled to Arizona to play the Cardinals. The Arizona Cardinals of 2000 would turn out to be one of the worst teams in the NFL. The Cowboys would play this game without Troy Aikman (concussion) and of course without Joey Galloway. The backup quarterback for Dallas in 2000 was the former Eagle, and Viking Randall Cunningham. The Cowboys had to feel better about themselves in this game, as they lead the Cardinals 7-3 after one quarter, and 21-13 at the half. The Cardinals pulled to within 24-23 in the third quarter. The Cowboys extended their lead to 31-23 midway through the fourth quarter. However, the Cowboy defense continued to show its weaknesses. With the Cowboys leading 31-26, Arizona got the ball at their own fifteen yard line with about six minutes left to go, and they drove the 85 yards, with Jake Plummer hitting Frank Sanders for the final seventeen yards, to give the Cardinals the win over the Cowboys 32-31. The Cowboys were 0-2.

The Cowboys offense was better against Arizona than in the Philadelphia game, however the achievements of the day came against what would be the NFL's 30th ranked defense. The Cowboy defense had just been plundered for 32 points by what would be the 2000 NFL's 24th ranked offense. This was a bad Cowboy team. The 2000 Dallas Cowboys record would never get to .500 and they would finish the season at 5-11. Troy Aikman would suffer another concussion in week 15 against the Redskins, after which he would never play again. In the 2000 season the Cowboys were 0-8 against playoff teams, and in those games they were outscored 202-76.

As a Cowboy fan, if you had not admitted to yourself that "it was over" for the Cowboys, then the end of Troy Aikman's career had to be the serious wake-up call to that fact. Troy had a contract option for the 2001 season that was at the Cowboy's option, that would have paid him $70 million over seven years, with $7 million paid in a signing bonus. That contract had huge salary cap implications for the club. So given Troy's numerous injuries and concussions in 1999-2000, the club declined the option and released Troy Aikman on March 7, 2001. Troy briefly considered free agency, but on April 9, 2001 he held a press conference at Texas Stadium and announced that he was retiring from the NFL.

Troy Aikman's career was outstanding. In 12 seasons for the Dallas Cowboys he had an overall win-loss record of 94-71, and a playoff record of 11-4. During the dominant period of 1992 through 1995, Troy's record as the starting quarterback was 46-14, with a playoff record of 10-1. He quarterbacked three Super Bowl wins in three tries, and was the 1992 Super Bowl MVP. Quarterbacks as talented, disciplined and efficient as Troy Aikman are rare in NFL history. Troy is not ranked as high as many quarterbacks in NFL history because he did not have gaudy numbers in terms of completions, total touchdown passes, or total passing yards. But Troy played at a time when running the football was a priority. Troy was a master game manager, and he was handing off to the NFL career leader in total rushing yardage. Troy's accuracy and efficiency made the running game with Emmitt Smith ever more threatening, because defenses could not key on Emmitt, for fear of Troy passing to Michael Irvin, Alvin Harper or Jay Novacek, as he did so many times for key first downs or game breaking big plays.

With Troy's retirement, that was it. The Cowboys former greatness was officially over. It did not take long for Troy to find employment, as the Fox network wisely signed him on as a color analyst for their NFL television coverage. One year later, Troy would become the number one color analyst on the Fox NFL broadcast team, matched with Joe Buck.

On April 3, 2001 the Cowboys announced that they had signed veteran quarterback Tony Banks to a one year $500,000 contract; a low cost, no risk deal with upside if Banks played well for the Cowboys. It appeared that Jerry had a plan! Jerry Jones quote upon signing Tony Banks was, "he's been out only two games in his entire career to injury," Jones said. "Yet he potentially has his career ahead of him". Jerry continued, "in other words, to get that experience we didn't totally accept that we'll have a QB that is an interim stopgap, if you will". More from Jerry, "We've got an opportunity for the curtain to go up here for Tony Banks, and in so doing, reward the Cowboys and our fans as well." Jerry had signed a five year NFL veteran to lead the team, while he looked through the draft, and possibly watched for another free agent or a trade opportunity to upgrade later if the opportunity arose. But for the time, the Cowboys had signed a guy with NFL experience and some legitimate NFL talent and ability. But for some unknown reason, Jerry did not stick with the plan.

In August 2001 after just two pre-season games, the Cowboys abruptly cut Tony Banks (the "curtain fell"). Why did Jerry cut Tony Banks after just two pre-season games? Did Jerry have a better replacement for Tony Banks? Well, it does not appear that he did. Was there another quarterback lighting it up in the pre-season, with upside to be the future of the franchise at its most important position? Aside from the rookie quarterback just drafted (we will cover the 2001 draft next) the backup quarterbacks were journeyman Anthony Wright and former Arkansas Razorback Clint Stoerner. It is not clear why Jerry cut Tony Banks. Maybe it was just a little bit of "Jerry being Jerry". It did not make much sense at the time.

The 2001 draft is a nominee for the worst draft in the Jerry Jones era. History shows that most teams in the NFL consistently get some value in the first four rounds of the draft, and then there are some misses, and some lucky finds in the later rounds of the draft (rounds 5 - 7). It would be very unusual for a good NFL General Manager to finish a draft and then to ultimately have nothing to show for it. (the entire draft, all seven rounds) But that is exactly what the 2001 Dallas Cowboy draft resulted in. Nine picks, and absolutely nothing of any real NFL value.

The Cowboys did not have a first round pick in the 2001 draft because Jerry had traded it to Seattle for Joey Galloway in 2000. The Cowboy's draft needs were extensive, and included the offensive line, defensive line, linebacker and

2001 draft

Round	Pick	Position	Player name	University
2	53	QB	Quincy Carter	Georgia
2	56	DB	Tony Dixon	Alabama
3	93	DT	Willie Blade	Miss St
4	122	LB	Markus Steele	USC
5	137	C	Matt Lehr	Va. Tech
6	171	DT	Daleroy Stewart	S. Miss.
7	207	DE	Colston Weatherington	C. Mo. St
7	240	DT	John Nix	S. Miss
7	242	T	Charron Dorsey	FSU

quarterback. After watching the first round, the Cowboys had two picks in the second round at number fifty three and number fifty six. At number fifty three Dallas selected Quincy Carter, quarterback from the University of Georgia. Most of the pre-draft projections had Quincy Carter going in the fourth or fifth round. This was Jerry Jones pick. Clearly it was a reach, and Jerry would have to answer for the outcome of the selection.

Quincy Carter was a reach at number fifty three, and ultimately he was a failure. Carter was to the NFL what he was in college. He had the physical tools. He was big and fast and mobile. He had moments of brilliance that made you think that he could be great. But he was so inconsistent that he would hurt his team with his performance. This was his record as a college quarterback. In his three years with Dallas he threw twenty nine touchdown passes, but thirty six interceptions. Ultimately he would be overcome by off the field problems. In comparison, seven picks later at number sixty the Tennessee Titans picked Andre Dyson, a cornerback who had twenty two interceptions in seven NFL seasons. The Titans found value in the second round, as you would expect of a competent NFL GM.

At number fifty six the Cowboys selected a defensive back from Alabama. Tony Dixon played for the Cowboys for three years and produced one interception. He also had the physical tools, but just didn't have "the head for the NFL game". He was not a difference maker. Thirty-one NFL teams had an opportunity to select Tony Dixon before the Cowboys, but they didn't. Five picks later at number sixty one the Detroit Lions selected a big defensive tackle (Shaun Rogers) from Texas who could stop the run, and he had 37.5 sacks in his NFL career. Rogers had a massive rookie season. He could have helped the Cowboys 31st ranked run defense. Good draft evaluation is the difference between winning and losing, in the NFL.

In the third round at number ninety three the Cowboys selected defensive tackle Willie Blade from Mississippi State. He played for the Cowboys for one year and was generally ineffective, and then he was waived. (a third round pick, wasted when there were many needs) In the fourth round at number 122 the Cowboys picked Markus Steele, a linebacker from USC. Steele was with the Cowboys for three years. His second and third seasons were unproductive and thereafter he was waived. Very disappointing for a fourth round pick.

In the fifth round the Cowboys picked Matt Lehr, a center from Va. Tech. Lehr was with the Cowboys through 2004, and he was the starting center in the 2003 season. The four picks from the sixth and seventh rounds were so bad that there is nothing to discuss about them. Ultimately, not one of the nine players drafted by the Cowboys in 2001 were considered to be a productive use of the draft choice. The entire 2001 Dallas Cowboys draft was a failure. It has to be considered one of the worst drafts in the Dallas Cowboys team history.

The 2001 Dallas Cowboys regular season was, and I am being kind, a disaster. Here are some telling statistics: the Cowboys offense ranked thirtieth in the league in points scored; the Cowboys committed thirty four turnovers in sixteen games (that is bad); the Cowboys scored only eight rushing touchdowns in sixteen games (that's very bad); the Cowboys scored twenty two total touchdowns in sixteen games; the Cowboys defense ranked twentieth in the league. With the thirtieth ranked offense and the twentieth ranked defense, the Dallas Cowboys compiled a regular season record of 5-11. It was a bad year, made worse by the fact that the Cowboys General Manager still had a lot to learn about evaluating NFL talent.

After cutting the veteran Tony Banks in the pre-season the Cowboys announced that Quincy Carter would be the starting quarterback to open the season. In the season opener the Cowboys offense produced eight first downs, 127 total yards, three turnovers and scored just six points. Quincy Carter was injured and would miss two months of the season. In his absence the Cowboys saw a lot of Anthony Wright, and some Clint Stoerner. The results were awful and the team started the season 2-5. It could have just as easily been 1-6 or 0-7. So Jerry, being Jerry, made another move. He signed the unemployed, 1998 draft bust quarterback Ryan Leaf. This was a "hey, let's try this" move.

Ryan Leaf had been selected number two overall, in the 1998 draft by San Diego, after the Colts took Peyton Manning. His three years in San Diego were filled with injuries, interceptions, losses and just bad behavior. In San Diego Ryan Leaf was 4-14 as a starter, and he threw 33 interceptions, against 13 touchdown passes. His completion percentage was 48 percent. San Diego while not good at that time, was better without Ryan Leaf (10-20, 33% winning percentage) than they were with him starting at quarterback (4-14, 22%). After Leaf was cut by San Diego, Tampa Bay signed Leaf to see if they could have better luck. Tampa's approach was to bring him along slowly, and to allow him to learn their offense. They also wanted to help him with his injured wrist. The Tampa doctors suggested surgery. So the team asked him to accept a lower base salary and a lower spot on the roster while he recovered from his injury in 2001. Ryan Leaf refused the cut in pay, so Tampa Bay cut him. So Ryan Leaf came to Dallas in October 2001 to quarterback The Dallas Cowboys.

The results were predictable. With Leaf at quarterback the Cowboys went 0-4. Leaf threw three interceptions against one touchdown pass, and compiled 494 passing yards in four games. His performance was so bad that, as soon as Quincy Carter was cleared from his injury recovery, he was installed as the starter. The Cowboys went 3-3 in the final six games of 2001 and finished 5-11 for the second consecutive season.

2002 draft

Round	Pick	Position	Player name	University
1	8	DB	Roy Williams	Oklahoma
2	37	G	Andre Gurode	Colorado
2	63	WR	Antonio Bryant	Pittsburgh
3	75	DB	Derek Ross	Ohio St
4	129	FB	Jamar Martin	Ohio St
5	168	DB	Pete Hunter	Va Union
6	179	C	Tyson Walter	Ohio St
6	208	WR	Deveren Johnson	Sacred Heart
6	211	TE	Bob Slowikowski	Va Tech

Leading in to the 2002 season the Cowboys faced the same problems that had plagued them basically since 1999. The offense was ranked thirtieth in the NFL in 2001. The defense was weak against the run and was vulnerable to the big pass play. They needed help in the offensive line, at wide receiver, they did not have a quarterback, and they needed defensive linemen who could stop the run and pressure the quarterback. You might say, "other than that they were ok". That is funny now, but it wasn't then.

In 2002 the Cowboys owned the eighth pick in the draft. There was a decent amount of talent in this draft The Dallas Cowboys defense was ranked thirtieth in the NFL the prior season, and one of their biggest weaknesses was stopping the run. Jerry's pick at number eight in the first round was Oklahoma safety Roy Williams. Everyone has an opinion on that pick. Roy Williams was a star at the college level, but he was exposed in the NFL because he was not effective against the pass.

Given what the Cowboys glaring need was at that time, there were two players that were available to the Cowboys at number eight, whom I am sure that you have heard of. At number eleven, the Indianapolis Colts selected defensive end Dwight Freeney. Freeney has 111 career NFL sacks. At number fifteen the Tennessee Titans selected defensive tackle Albert Haynesworth. He was a solid force in the middle for the Titans and he had thirty one career NFL sacks. Roy Williams was a good NFL player and he had a seven year career with Dallas. But was he a difference maker? No, he was not. There were difference makers available in the 2002 draft, at the number eight draft position. Given what the Cowboys needs were, the Cowboys missed on this pick.

In the second round the Cowboys selected Andre Gurode, an offensive guard from Colorado. Gurode was a good player for the Cowboys. He split time at center and at guard during his Cowboys career between 2002 and 2010. He was a good value for the second round pick used on him. Later in the second round the Cowboys picked wide receiver Antonio Bryant from the University of Pittsburgh. Bryant had a lot of talent and physical ability, but he would ultimately become a behavior problem, and would be traded away in 2004.

The rest of the players selected by the Cowboys in the 2002 draft are not worth further discussion here. What is worthy of further discussion is that this would include the third through the six rounds, and a total of six draft choices. While the Cowboys missed on these six draft choices, other NFL teams were finding value in those rounds. In the third round at number ninety one, The Philadelphia Eagles picked running back Brian Westbrook. Emmitt Smith was entering the last year of his contract in 2002, so choosing a quality backup was a relevant consideration. Westbrook had an eight year NFL career, producing over 10,000 yards from scrimmage. (Dallas did not re-sign Emmitt after the 2002 season) Derek Ross, chosen by Dallas at number seventy five was released after two years. At pick number 146, Seattle chose defensive tackle Rocky Bernard, who played in the NFL for ten years and had thirty three career sacks. The 2002 draft was another costly learning experience for Cowboys GM Jerry Jones, while the better NFL teams took productive NFL players in the middle and late rounds of the draft. This is what separates the good teams from the average in the NFL.

Jerry made a couple of free agent moves prior to 2002 to try to improve the team. He signed defensive tackle La Roi Glover, who had previously played for New Orleans. Glover was a very good defensive tackle, and he played well for the Cowboys. He would compile twenty one sacks in his four years with the Cowboys. But he was an expensive free agent. A good draft choice could have saved the Cowboys a lot of salary cap money here (remember Shaun Rogers at number sixty one in the second round in the 2000 draft?; or Albert Haynesworth who was available in the first round at number eight in 2002?)

The other prominent free agent signing by the Cowboys prior to 2002 was quarterback Chad Hutchinson. As a 6' 5", 225 pound 1995 high school graduate, Hutchinson was drafted in the first round of the Major League Baseball draft by the Atlanta Braves. However Hutchinson chose to take a scholarship to Stanford to play football (quarterback) and baseball (pitcher). After two years at Stanford, Hutchinson decided to move on to professional baseball. In four years in the minor leagues, between A ball and up to AAA, as a pitcher, Hutchinson compiled a record of 17-25 with a 5.63 ERA. If you are not a baseball fan, that is not real good. Based on his statistics of ten strikeouts per nine innings, but seven walks per nine innings, and his 5.63 ERA, it appears that Hutchinson was more of a strong armed "thrower", and not so much a good "pitcher". He eventually made a brief appearance with the St Louis Cardinals as a relief pitcher. It did not go well. So Chad Hutchinson decided to give the NFL a try.

The Cowboys apparently outbid the Chicago Bears and Washington Redskins for Hutchinson. He signed with the Cowboys for seven years, with three million dollars paid at signing. According to Jerry Jones the Cowboys had a two year plan to allow Hutchinson to migrate back to football after his baseball career, and that Quincy Carter would be the starter going to training camp. I suppose that Hutchinson was a reasonable, relatively low risk gamble for a future quarterback. But his signing had to be a non-verbal admission by GM Jerry Jones that his reach in the 2001 draft for Quincy Carter had indeed been a big mistake.

The 2002 season began with the anticipation that Emmitt Smith was less than 1,000 yards from breaking Walter Payton's all-time NFL rushing record of 16,726 yards. Aside from that excitement, the season was another big disappointment. It started with a humiliating loss to the newest NFL franchise, the Houston Texans, in their first ever NFL game. In game eight, with a record of 3-4 on the season, the Cowboys faced the 1-5 Seattle Seahawks at Texas Stadium. Emmitt Smith broke Walter Payton's all-time NFL rushing record in this game, at home in front of the Cowboy fans. That was appropriate. However the Cowboys went on to lose that game to the previously 1-5 Seahawks. It was befitting of the season, and the Cowboys went on to finish 5-11 for the third consecutive year. It would be Emmitt's last season with the Dallas Cowboys.

December 29, 2002 was Emmitt Smith's last game played for the Dallas Cowboys. It was also the final game of Dave Campo's coaching tenure with the Cowboys. Campo was dismissed by the Cowboys on December 30, 2002. The story after Campo's dismissal was that he was the first Cowboy head coach with a losing record, and the first Cowboys head coach to fail to make the playoffs during his tenure. Dave Campo had seven starting quarterbacks during his three years as the Cowboys head coach. That was the result of Jerry Jones continuing GM learning curve.

The Dallas Cowboys in 2002 were three years removed from their last playoff appearance. They were six years removed from their last playoff game victory. They were a decade removed from Jimmy Johnson's departure from the franchise. Jerry was still going through a difficult process of learning how to be an effective NFL General Manager.

Dallas Cowboys, Americas Team Is Back

Chapter Four

Bill Parcells
Jerry Reels In The Big Tuna

On January 1, 2003 the National Football League was focused on the playoffs. Twelve teams and their fans had the dream of reaching, and possibly winning the Super Bowl. But not in Dallas. The Cowboys had just finished their third consecutive 5-11 season. Jerry Jones had fired his fourth head coach in fourteen seasons, the day after the final game of the season. Dallas fans at that time had no reason to be optimistic about the Cowboys future. The Cowboys had no great young players to build around, and based on the draft results of 1995 – 2002, there was no reason to expect that the draft would yield the answer for future improvement.

Then came Thursday January 2, 2003. Jerry Jones hired the great Bill Parcells as the new head coach of The Dallas Cowboys. Jerry made some statements regarding the hiring of Parcells that seemed to indicate that he may be giving Parcells some authority with regard to player personnel selection. Parcells certainly had a successful history to indicate that this would be the right thing to do. But after the post Jimmy years of 1994-2002, could this be too good to be true? This is what Jerry said in the press conference announcing Parcell's hiring: "It's rare to have the opportunity to attract perhaps the most qualified coach in our sport. If you sense that opportunity, then you want to grab it," Mr. Jones said. *"You do this because this franchise has five Lombardi trophies. You do this because of the national and international recognition that this franchise receives, but most of all, you do it because we want to win".* "I stood at this podium almost fourteen years ago (1989) and I said that we must win. We will win. *Winning is the name of the game.*" Well hallelujah Jerry, that all makes perfect sense! And now you have backed up your well stated logic, with a hiring that actually makes winning possible again!

With that statement, and the fact that Bill Parcells had in fact signed a four year contract worth seventeen million dollars, Dallas Cowboy fans actually had hope for a realistically brighter future. There was reason to believe that the team could be rebuilt because now there was a seriously experienced football professional on staff, with a proven record of NFL success, both as a coach and as a team builder.

Parcells had a monumental task to rebuild the 2003 Dallas Cowboys. The 2002 Cowboys offense had ranked thirty first out of thirty two NFL teams, and the defense had ranked eighteenth. Emmitt Smith had just finished the last year of his contract, so a decision needed to be made regarding his future with the team. They did not have a viable NFL quarterback. Parcells made a statement on the day that his hiring was announced, that in retrospect was prophetic, when he said "perhaps my quarterback is already here. If not, then we'll make every effort to get one."

Parcells brought in some free agent talent that he was familiar with, and that he knew that he could rely on to upgrade the team, and to provide leadership. Richie Anderson was a veteran fullback that had played for Parcells when he coached the NY Jets. He also signed Terry Glenn, a speedy wide receiver that he had coached while with the New England Patriots. Also, after the 2003 draft the Cowboys signed an unknown free agent quarterback from Eastern Illinois University, named Antonio Ramiro (Tony) Romo.

2003 draft

Round	Pick	Position	Player name	University
1	5	DB	Terence Newman	KSU
2	38	C	Al Johnson	Wisconsin
3	69	TE	**Jason Witten**	Tenn
4	103	LB	Bradie James	LSU
6	178	DB	BJ Tucker	Wisconsin
6	186	WR	Zuriel Smith	Hampton
7	219	G	Justin Bates	Colorado

The Cowboys owned the fifth overall pick in the 2003 draft. With that pick they selected cornerback Terence Newman from Kansas State. Newman would remain with the Cowboys through 2011. In the second round the Cowboys selected Al Johnson, an offensive guard from Wisconsin.

In the third round the Cowboys selected Jason Witten, tight end from Tennessee. This is perhaps one of the top two draft picks of the Bill Parcells era (Demarcus Ware the other). In the fourth round the Cowboys selected Bradie James, a linebacker from LSU. James would become very productive when the Cowboys later converted to a 3-4 defense. The Cowboys did not have a fifth round selection. The sixth and seventh round picks had no impact for the Cowboys. The 2003 draft overall was relatively good and produced some immediately usable NFL talent. It was a night and day improvement from the drafts of the prior five years. With the draft and the free agent signings the Cowboys had added six new players to the roster that were significant talent upgrades. And Parcells was right. The Cowboys did have their quarterback. They just didn't know it yet.

Now it was time to find out just how much Bill Parcells could improve the team on the field. Parcells began by installing a rigorous off-season program emphasizing discipline, conditioning and mental preparation. Parcells is known for being a disciplinarian, and for being "edgy" even when things are going well, to keep his players sharp

In the first game of the 2003 regular season the Cowboys were home to the Atlanta Falcons. The Cowboys lost the game 27-13, but what was worse than the loss was the way the Cowboys performed. They were sloppy and undisciplin-ed. There were seven penalties, two turnovers, three sacks allowed and the Cowboys only converted five of thirteen third downs. Not the kind of performance that a bad team can afford. Quincy Carter completed fifteen out of thirty two passing attempts, with an interception and also lost a fumble. Again, not a good performance.

Parcells got his first win as the Cowboys head coach on a Monday night in New York against the Giants. It was a crazy and high scoring game. Both quarterbacks had an interception that was returned for a touchdown. The Cowboys lead 20-7 at the half, and 29-14 early in the fourth quarter. But the Giants torched the Cowboys defense in the fourth quarter, and they took a 32-29 lead with just eleven seconds left to play in the game. It seemed that the Cowboys would fall to 0-2. But the Giants made a huge kicking game error. On the kickoff, an attempted squib kick that was intended to run the clock down, went out of bounds. This gave the Cowboys the ball at their forty yard line. They only had time for one play, and they needed to get as close to the Giants thirty yard line as possible, to have a chance for a game tying field goal. Quincy Carter somehow hit Antonio Bryant with a pass to the Giants thirty four yard line. Cowboys kicker Billy Cundiff then kicked a game tying fifty two yard field goal. Cundiff eventually won the game in overtime with another field goal.

After improving to 1-1 with the thrilling and nationally televised win over the Giants, the Cowboys won six of the next seven games to get to 7-2 at mid-November. Down the stretch the Cowboys went just 3-4. The offense scored ten points or less in three of the four losses. Turnovers, and specifically interceptions, were a major problem. The Cowboys finished the season 10-6, for second place in the NFC East. Dallas qualified for the wild card playoff round.

Dallas played at The Carolina Panthers in the wildcard game. Carolina was 11-5 in 2003 and champions of the NFC South Division. The Cowboys had beaten Carolina in Dallas during the regular season, 24-20 when the Cowboys defense held Carolina to just 244 total yards. The wild card game however would have a dramatically different outcome. The Cowboys were never really "in this game". The Panthers jumped on them early, and lead 16-3 at the half, 26-3 early in the fourth quarter, and won running away by a final score of 29-10. The Cowboys offense was manhandled by the Carolina defense, producing just ten first downs, seventy two yards rushing, 132 net passing yards, and Quincy Carter was sacked three times. Carolina would be the eventual NFC champion, and would lose to New England in Super Bowl XXXVIII.

Bill Parcells first year as the Cowboys coach had been a success and had produced improvement beyond expectations. But the challenges ahead were still substantial. The Cowboys offense finished the 2003 season ranked 21st in the league in average points scored per game. They clearly needed a bona-fide NFL quarterback in order to have a consistent chance of winning. The good news was that the defense had improved significantly, and had finished the year ranked second in the league in points allowed, and first in the league in yards allowed. Bill Parcells still had challenges remaining, but he also had some good things to build on.

In the 2004 off-season one of the top concerns for Bill Parcells and the Cowboys was the situation at quarterback. Quincy Carter had been the starter in 2003, but Carter had continued to demonstrate periods of inconsistency, and was prone to turnovers. There were also some indications of problems off the field regarding substance abuse.

On March 15, 2004 the Cowboys traded a third round draft pick to the Houston Texans for the rights to Drew Henson, who had played college quarterback for the University of Michigan. The Texans had drafted Henson in the sixth round of the 2003 draft, however Henson had opted to sign an MLB contract with the New York Yankees. Henson developed to the AAA level with the Yankees, however his progress as a major league hitter flattened out at the AAA level and he retired from baseball to revive his football career.

Henson had played quarterback for Michigan as a backup to Tom Brady in 1998-1999, and then as a starter in 2000 as a junior. He passed for 56% completions, with twenty two touchdowns and seven interceptions in twenty five games. The Cowboys signed Henson to a contract that paid him the league minimum salary, however gave him the opportunity to earn $3.5 million from incentive bonuses.

Later in March 2004 the Cowboys traded wide receiver Joey Galloway to Tampa Bay in return for wide receiver Keyshawn Johnson. Johnson had previously played for Bill Parcells, with the NY Jets. Johnson was the big possession receiver that the Cowboy's system needed, and Johnson was happy to reunite with Parcells. This trade was an unspoken admission that Jerry Jones trade for Joey Galloway in 2000 had been a mistake.

2004 draft

Round	Pick	Position	Player name	University
2	43	RB	Julius Jones	Notre Dame
2	52	T	Jacob Rogers	USC
3	83	G	Stephen Peterman	LSU
4	121	DB	Bruce Thornton	Georgia
5	144	TE	Sean Ryan	Boston College
7	205	DB	Nate Jones	Rutgers
7	216	WR	Patrick Crayton	NW OK St
7	223	DB	Jacques Reeves	Purdue

In April the Cowboys participated in the 2004 NFL draft. As had become a custom for Jerry Jones, the Cowboys traded out of their first round pick (number twenty two) in order to add picks in the second and fifth rounds, and in the first round in 2005. Had the Cowboys drafted at number twenty two in 2004, running back Steven Jackson was available, however he would go to the St Louis Rams. With their first pick in 2004, in the second round at number forty three, the Cowboys selected running back Julius Jones from Notre Dame. Jones would play four seasons for Dallas, with flashes of brilliance, but ultimately was plagued by injuries and was not re-signed by the Cowboys after his contract expired. At number fifty two in the second round the Cowboys selected an offensive lineman from USC, Jacob Rogers. Rogers was a decorated offensive lineman at USC and in the Pac-10, unfortunately injuries cut short his Cowboys NFL career.

In the third round at number eighty three the Cowboys selected Stephen Peterman, an offensive guard from LSU. He was a starter on the LSU national championship team of 2003. He was plagued by injuries while with Dallas and was released after the 2005 season. In the fourth round at number 121 the Cowboys selected defensive back Bruce Thornton from Georgia. His career with the Cowboys was injury plagued and he was released after 2004. In the fifth round at number 144 the Cowboys selected Sean Ryan, tight-end from Boston College. He was a backup, primarily as a blocking tight-end in 2004 and 2005. He was traded in August 2006.

The next pick was in the seventh round at number 205, where the Cowboys selected Nate Jones, a defensive back from Rutgers University. Jones played for the Cowboys on special teams and as a backup defensive back through 2007. At number 216 in the seventh round the Cowboys selected Patrick Crayton, a wide receiver from Northwest Oklahoma State. Crayton was "found gold" from the seventh round. He played six seasons for the Cowboys, and played in eighty two games producing twenty three touchdowns and a fifteen yards-per-catch average. The Cowboys final pick in the 2004 draft was Jacques Reeves, a defensive back from Purdue. He would play for the Cowboys through 2007.

The Cowboys signed quarterback Vinny Testaverde in June 2004 to add experienced depth at quarterback, and to add a legitimate mentor for newly signed rookie quarterback Drew Henson. Announcing his signing, the Cowboys stated that Testaverde would compete for the starting job in the 2004 training camp. Meanwhile Tony Romo handled the role of holder for field goals and point-after kicks.

During the 2004 training camp, and with no warning, on August third the Cowboys abruptly cut the team's starting quarterback, Quincy Carter. There was speculation that Carter had failed a drug test, and that as a result he had been dismissed from the team. Carter had apparently been under previous league supervision for positive drug testing. While Carter denied the drug testing rumor, later events involving Carter after football indicate that this was likely the case in August 2004. So the Cowboys would start the 2004 season with a forty year old quarterback, backed up by two inexperienced rookies.

In the first game of the 2004 season Dallas played at Minnesota. The Cowboys defense was abused by the Vikings for 415 yards and thirty five points. The Cowboys had nine penalties for 119 yards and lost two fumbles. Minnesota won 35-17. In the second game, at Texas Stadium, the Cowboys survived a penalty and turnover plagued game by both teams, and managed to beat Cleveland 19-12 to even their record at 1-1. The Cowboys third game of 2004 was a Monday night matchup at Washington featuring the coaching rivalry of Joe Gibbs versus Bill Parcells. Going into this game, Bill Parcells coached teams had won eleven out of seventeen, and six consecutive against Joe Gibbs. Additionally, the Cowboys had won twelve of the last thirteen games played against the

Washington Redskins. Parcells continued his advantage over Joe Gibbs as the Cowboys won 21-18 in a game in which Washington rallied in the fourth quarter and just ran out of time. Mark Brunell burned the Cowboy secondary for 325 yards. But the Cowboys managed five sacks, employing an aggressive blitzing defense. The Cowboys were 2-1, and had an early season bye week.

After the bye week the Cowboys defense was repeatedly exposed, as they lost six of seven games and fell to 3-7 on the season, by surrendering an average of 370 yards of total offense, and thirty three points per game. In four of the six losses Dallas lost by twenty or more points. Meanwhile the offense averaged 2.5 turnovers per game. Not a good combination. In the week ten loss to Baltimore, Vinny Testaverde was injured in the fourth quarter and Drew Henson entered the game. On his first play from scrimmage he fumbled while scrambling and the Ravens recovered at the Cowboys one yard line, scoring on the next play.

Drew Henson got the start at quarterback the next week on Thanksgiving Day, due to the Testaverde injury. Henson completed just four out of twelve passes in the first half, and he had an interception returned for a touchdown by Chicago. Henson was benched by Parcells at halftime, despite the Dallas fans booing the insertion of Vinny Testaverde in the third quarter. Julius Jones had a great game on national television, while going against his older brother Thomas, the running back for Chicago. Julius rushed for 150 yards on thirty three carries, including two touchdown runs. The Cowboys won the Thanksgiving Day game 21-7, to improve to 4-7 on the season. The Cowboys defense held the anemic Bears to 140 total yards, and no offensive scoring in the game.

Vinny Testaverde finished the season at quarterback for the Cowboys. Dallas would go 2-3 in their last five games and finish the season at 6-10. While the season was not successful in terms of the record and missing the playoffs, the team had made progress under Parcells which would yield benefits later. They had dismissed the troubled Quincy Carter, and while they still did not have their quarterback of the future identified, they had largely determined that Chad Hutchinson and Drew Henson were not the answer. The future quarterback was on the roster, watching, waiting and holding for extra points and field goals.

On December 29, 2004, Darren Woodson announced his retirement from the Dallas Cowboys and from professional football. Woodson had missed the 2004 season due to back surgery. He had been drafted in 1992 and played for the Cowboys through the 2003 season. *Woodson was the Dallas Cowboys all-time leading tackler.* This fact had been over-shadowed because he had broken the record in the same game (against Seattle on December 6, 2004) in which Emmitt Smith became the NFL's all-time leading rusher. Woodson is considered to be the best strong safety in Dallas Cowboys history. He had the size and physicality to stop the run. He also had the speed, quickness and athletic ability to defend against the pass. He was used against the slot receiver frequently, which was a luxury afforded the Cowboy defense over the years, not typically available from a strong safety. Darren Woodson was a great player on the field, but he had also been a good citizen off the field and represented the Cowboys admirably with his personal life.

In the off-season prior to the 2005 campaign Parcells and the Cowboys made moves to further improve the team on the field. In February 2005 the Cowboys signed Drew Bledsoe to address the immediate need at quarterback. In March the Cowboys signed free agent cornerback, Anthony Henry, to help shore up the secondary, and they signed defensive tackle Jason Ferguson, to anchor the nose tackle in a conversion to the 3-4 defense.

Then came the draft in late April. Because the Cowboys had traded out of the first round in 2004, they had two of the first twenty picks in the first round in 2005. Uncharacteristically for Jerry Jones, the Cowboys used both picks, rather than trading one or both for more picks later. Perhaps Bill Parcells

2005 draft

Round	Pick	Position	Player name	University
1	11	LB	**DeMarcus Ware**	Troy
1	20	DE	Marcus Spears	LSU
2	42	LB	Kevin Burnett	Tennessee
4	109	RB	Marion Barber	Minnesota
4	132	DE	Chris Canty	Virginia
6	208	DB	Justin Beriault	Ball State
6	209	T	Rob Pettiti	Pittsburgh
7	224	DE	Jay Ratliff	Auburn

influenced a more reasoned approach to this draft. With the eleventh selection in the first round, the Cowboys took defensive end DeMarcus Ware from Troy University. This is arguably the best draft pick of the Bill Parcells era (Jason Witten – 2003?) and post Jimmy Johnson. Ware had 117 sacks in nine seasons. At number twenty the Cowboys selected Marcus Spears, a defensive lineman from LSU. Spears played for the Cowboys through 2012 before becoming a salary cap casualty. At number forty two in the second round the Cowboys selected Tennessee linebacker Kevin Burnett. Burnett played for the Cowboys through 2008, recording one interception and four sacks primarily in a reserve role. The next pick was in the fourth round at number 109 and the Cowboys selected Marion Barber III, a running back from Minnesota. Barber had a relatively productive time with the Cowboys through 2010. At number 132 in the fourth round the Cowboys selected Chris Canty, a defensive lineman from Virginia. Canty would play for the Cowboys through 2008 before moving on in free agency.

In the sixth round at number 208 the Cowboys selected Justin Beriault, a safety from Ball State. A recurring knee injury ended his football career in 2006. At number 209 the Cowboys selected Rob Petitti, an offensive lineman from Pittsburgh. Petitti played one season for the Cowboys, and was then released. With the 224th overall pick in the seventh round the Cowboys selected Jay Ratliff, a defensive lineman from Auburn. Ratliff played for the Cowboys through 2012, and is a four time pro bowler, from the seventh round of the draft. The 2005 draft was the best draft of the Bill Parcells era.

On April 26, 2005 the Cowboys signed free agent corner-back Aaron Glenn after his release by the Houston Texans, to help shore up a pass defense that had been ranked 21st in the league in 2004, having surrendered 31 touchdown passes. Bill Parcells made the decision to convert the defense to the 3-4 alignment for the 2005 season.

The 2005 Cowboys were in their third year under Bill Parcells. The Cowboys of 2003 (Parcells year one) had gone 10-6 and had made the playoffs, however as playoff teams go, that was a very weak team and they were eliminated immediately in the wildcard round. In 2004 the record had fallen to 6-10, however the roster was improved over 2003, and major weaknesses had been identified and were being addressed. The 2005 outlook was hopeful.

The opening game of the 2005 season was on the road, at the defending AFC West champion San Diego Chargers. One of the weaknesses of this Cowboy team was exposed in this game. New quarterback Drew Bledsoe was sacked four times during the game, and was pressured consistently. Dallas rushed for 109 yards, with a 3.3 yards per rush average. The offensive line was less than impressive. The Cowboys scored a touchdown with three minutes remaining in the game to take the lead 28-24. The defense then surrendered a ten play, sixty two yard drive that ended, when the Cowboys Aaron Glenn made a game saving interception in the end zone, on a tipped pass, with thirty seconds remaining. It was a good road win for the Cowboys, against a good NFL team.

Game two was a Monday night meeting with the Washington Redskins, at Texas Stadium. The Cowboys had the lead 13-0 with four minutes to play. Washington quarterback Mark Brunell then went in to desperation mode, and he torched new Cowboys cornerback Aaron Glenn for touchdown throws of thirty nine and seventy yards, both to Santana Moss. The Redskins stunned the Cowboys on national television 14-13.

In game three the Cowboys traveled to San Francisco to play the 49ers, who were coming off of a 2-14 record in 2004. This was a game that Dallas was expected to win. The Cowboys trailed 31-19 in the fourth quarter, however Drew Bledsoe rallied the offense to two touchdown drives, the last coming with under two minutes to play, to pull out a 34-31 win and improve their record to 2-1.

Game four of 2005 was at 0-3 Oakland, a team that was 5-11 the prior year. Oakland had a Cowboy nemesis in the person of Randy Moss. Moss hauled in a seventy nine yard pass on Oakland's second play. Thereafter the Cowboy safeties played deep to prevent the big pass play, and this opened up the running game for the Raiders. The Raiders lead 19-13 with four minutes to play. Bledsoe drove the Cowboys to the Raiders five yard line with two minutes to play. However, the Raiders stopped the Cowboys there and ran out the clock for the win, to drop the Cowboys to a disappointing 2-2.

The Cowboys would go on to win five of the next six games and improve their record to 7-3, going in to the traditional Thanksgiving Day game. On Thanksgiving Day they hosted the Denver Broncos. Denver was 10-6 the prior year, and was on the way to a 13-3 regular season record for 2005, and would play in the AFC championship game against Pittsburgh. The Broncos were 8-2 coming in to this game.

The nationally televised game was a back and forth affair, with the Cowboys tying the score on a Drew Bledsoe to Jason Witten touchdown pass early in the fourth quarter. Dallas Billy Cundiff had missed a thirty four yard field goal attempt with 7:46 remaining in the fourth quarter, and the game ended regulation tied, and went to an overtime period. Denver won the coin flip and took the first possession. Ron Dayne broke a 55 yard run, which set up a 24 yard game winning field goal.

After the Thanksgiving Day overtime loss dropped Dallas record to 7-4, the Cowboys wilted down the stretch to fall to 9-7 for the year, and Dallas missed the playoffs. The 2005 Cowboy defense had improved over the 2004 team. The offense had shown some signs of explosiveness, but lacked consistency. Parcells first three seasons with the Cowboys had a 25-24 record, which was a vast improvement over the 15-33 record of the three seasons before his arrival. More importantly, Parcells was incrementally improving the roster through the draft.

2006 was the final year of Bill Parcells four year contract with the Cowboys. Parcells had his finger print on this Cowboys team, with his transformations of the roster including Drew Bledsoe, Julius Jones, Marion Barber III, Terry Glenn, Patrick Crayton, Jason Witten, DeMarcus Ware, Marcus Spears, Jay Ratliff, Chris Canty and the yet unknown undrafted free agent quarterback, Tony Romo. Parcells had also installed the 3-4 defensive scheme. The Cowboys were much improved from when Parcells arrived. The outlook for the 2006 Cowboys was very positive.

Bill Parcells was not finished adding to the Cowboys roster. On March 18, 2006 the Cowboys announced the signing of wide receiver Terrell Owens, who had been released after two tumultuous seasons in Philadelphia. Then on March 24, the Cowboys signed kicker Mike Vanderjagt. Other 2006 free agent signings included linebacker Akin Ayodele, offensive lineman Jason Fabini, and offensive lineman Kyle Kosier.

2006 draft

Round	Pick	Position	Player name	University
1	18	LB	Bobby Carpenter	Ohio State
2	53	TE	Anthony Fasano	Notre Dame
3	92	DE	Jason Hatcher	Grambling St
4	125	WR	Skyler Green	LSU
5	138	DB	Pat Watkins	Florida St.
6	182	DT	Mont Stanley	Louisville
7	211	T	Pat Mcquistan	Weber St
7	224	C	EJ Whitley	Texas Tech

Then came the draft in April 2006. In the first round at number eighteen Dallas picked linebacker Bobby Carpenter of Ohio State. He would become a draft bust and was eventually traded for another draft bust from St Louis (Alex Barron). Perhaps Parcells was biased on the Carpenter draft choice by the fact that his father (Rob Carpenter) had played for Parcells with the Giants. At number fifty three in the second round the Cowboys took a tight end from Notre Dame, Anthony Fasano. He would play for the Cowboys for two seasons before being traded to the Miami Dolphins in 2008 along with Akin Ayodele, for a fourth round pick.

In the third round at number ninety two the Cowboys selected defensive lineman Jason Hatcher from Grambling. Hatcher was a good defensive tackle for the Cowboys, and he started all sixteen games in 2012, and had a break-out season in 2013 in the final year of his contract. In the fourth round at number 125 the Cowboys selected LSU wide receiver Skyler Green. He would make the practice squad in 2006. In the fifth round at number 138 Dallas picked Florida State safety Pat Watkins. He would play for Dallas through 2009, with four interceptions and contributions on special teams.

In the sixth round at number 182 Dallas selected Montavius Stanley, a defensive tackle from Louisville. Stanley did not make the 2006 roster. In the seventh round the Cowboys selected Weber State offensive lineman Pat McQuistan at number 211, and Texas Tech offensive lineman E.J. Whitley at number 224. McQuistan would play for Dallas through 2009. Whitley did not make the roster.

The 2006 draft was the least productive of the four Parcells drafts, as third round pick Jason Hatcher was the only long term and significant addition from this draft. After the draft, the Cowboys signed four undrafted free agents: Miles Austin (wide receiver); Stephen Bowen (defensive lineman); Sam Hurd (wide receiver); and Oliver Hoyte (fullback). Bowen would contribute to the defensive line rotation through 2009, and Austin would become a starter at wide receiver. These undrafted free agent signings helped supplement an otherwise weak draft.

In the 2006 season opener the Cowboys played at Jacksonville. The Cowboys started strong and lead 10-0 after the first quarter. However, penalties and turnovers allowed Jacksonville to tie the game at the half, and the Jaguars scored the tying touchdown with less than thirty seconds remaining in the half, after a Drew Bledsoe interception. Jacksonville adjusted their defense to control Terrell Owens in the second half, and Bledsoe was pressured, sacked twice and threw two more interceptions. Jacksonville opened a 24-10 lead in the third quarter and held on to win 24-17.

Game two was a Sunday night national TV broadcast in Dallas against Washington, which had swept the Cowboys in 2005. There would be no sweep in 2006. The Cowboys defense sacked Mark Brunell six times and held Washington to 245 total yards. Terry Glenn caught six passes for ninety four yards and one touchdown, and Drew Bledsoe threw for two touchdowns with no interceptions. The Cowboys won 27-10 to even the record at 1-1. However, they lost new receiver Terrell Owens for an estimated two to four weeks due to a broken finger. The Cowboys had their bye week after game two.

Game three, after the bye week, was at the Tennessee Titans. Terrell Owens played just two weeks after having surgery on his broken finger. Owens drew double coverage, which opened the field for Terry Glenn, who had five catches, and two were for touchdowns. Julius Jones rushed for 122 yards and one touchdown. The Cowboys had 396 total yards, and only one turnover. Dallas won 45-14 to improve to 2-1.

Game four was at Philadelphia, and this was Terrell Owens first game back there since signing with the Cowboys. However, Owens would not be the story of this game. The Eagles defense constantly blitzed Drew Bledsoe, sacking him seven times and forcing three interceptions. Donovan McNabb exposed the Cowboy safeties for touchdown passes of forty and eighty seven yards. Philadelphia had 406 yards of total offense, 354 of it passing yards. However, after a long pass interference penalty, the Cowboys were trailing 31-24, and had the ball first and goal to go on the Philadelphia seven yard line with thirty seconds remaining in the game. Shockingly, Drew Bledsoe was intercepted in the end zone, and Lito Sheppard returned the interception 102 yards for a touchdown, sealing the game, and the final score at 38-24. The Cowboys fell to 2-2.

Game five was at home against the Houston Texans. The Cowboy defense held Houston to 232 yards, did not allow a touchdown and forced two turnovers. The Cowboys offense had 170 yards rushing, thirty five minutes in time of possession and no turnovers in the game. Terrell Owens had three touchdown catches. Of note, Parcells inserted backup quarterback Tony Romo in the game late in the fourth quarter. Romo had completions of thirty three yards to Sam Hurd, and a two yard touchdown pass to Terrell Owens. Dallas beat Houston 34-6, and improved their record to 3-2.

Game six was a Monday Night Football matchup at home against the New York Giants. Both teams came in to this game with a record of 3-2. New York got a fifty yard touchdown pass from Eli Manning to Plaxico Burress three minutes in to the game for a 7-0 lead. The Giants added a safety on a sack of Drew Bledsoe for a 9-0 lead. New York added a field goal in the second quarter to go up 12-0. Bledsoe then lead the Cowboys on an eighty yard drive, that included completions to Terrell Owens of thirty one and seventeen yards. After a pass interference call put the ball at the Giants one yard line, Bledsoe snuck in for the touchdown to cut the lead to 12-7. Later in the second quarter Tiki Barber fumbled after being violently hit, and the Cowboys recovered at the Giants fourteen yard line with 3:32 left in the half. The Cowboys moved to the NY Giants four, and had a first and goal, at the two minute warning. After no gain on first down, Bledsoe's second down pass attempt was intercepted by Sam Madison. The Giants ran out the first half clock and held a 12-7 halftime lead.

Apparently the late second quarter interception by Drew Bledsoe was more than Bill Parcells could tolerate. When the Cowboys offense took the field in the third quarter, it was with the unheralded backup Tony Romo at quarterback. On Romo's first play from scrimmage he was chased from the pocket and pursued by Michael Strahan. Romo attempted a pass intended for Anthony Fasano, but the ball was tipped by Strahan, and was then intercepted by Antonio Pierce and returned to the Cowboys fourteen yard line. It took the Giants three plays to score, and increase their lead to 19-7. After the kickoff, Tony Romo drove the Cowboys to the Giants thirty two yard line. Unfortunately the Cowboys failed to convert on a fourth and two, when a wide open Terrell Owens dropped what should have been an easy catch. The

Giants then methodically drove sixty eight yards for another touchdown, and opened up a 26-7 lead.

Tony Romo tried to rally the Cowboys in the fourth quarter, but mistakes and penalties, as well as strong play by the Giants defense resulted in the Giants building an insurmountable lead, and New York prevailed 36-22. Parcells would make no definitive comment during the post-game interviews, about who his quarterback would be the following week.

Bill Parcells did later name Tony Romo as the starter for the next game at the Carolina Panthers (4-3). Carolina scored first in the game with a sixty two yard drive, aided by a twenty yard pass interference penalty, to lead Dallas 7-0 late in the first quarter. Three plays after the ensuing kickoff Tony Romo was intercepted at the Dallas thirty five yard line, and it was returned to the Cowboys twenty four. The Panthers scored on the next play to take a 14-0 lead. In the second quarter Romo drove the Cowboys forty seven yards in nine plays, the final three yards on a pass to Jason Witten for the touchdown, and the Cowboys cut the lead to 14-7. Late in the second quarter Romo drove the Cowboys to the Panthers twenty with thirty seconds left in the half. On fourth and one Mike Vanderjagt kicked a thirty eight yard field goal to cut the lead to 14-10, at the half.

Neither team was able to score in the third quarter. In the fourth quarter Romo drove the Cowboys seventy one yards to the Carolina six, however the drive stalled there. Vanderjagt kicked a chip shot field goal to cut the Carolina lead to 14-13. On the ensuing kickoff Carolina fumbled and Dallas recovered at the Panthers fourteen yard line. Julius Jones covered the fourteen yards on the next play, and the Cowboys were successful on a two point conversion to take a 21-14 lead. The teams swapped punts, and then Cowboys safety Roy Williams intercepted Jake Delhomme at the Carolina thirty two yard line. Five plays later Marion Barber III scored and the Cowboys extended their lead to 28-14 with 2:20 left to play.

On Carolina's second play after the kickoff, Delhomme was sacked and fumbled, and the Cowboys recovered at the Carolina nineteen yard line. It took only two carries by MB III to find the end zone, and provide the final score of Dallas 35 - Carolina 14.

In the seventh game of the 2006 season, the Tony Romo era had begun. Romo completed twenty four out of thirty six pass attempts in the game for 270 yards, with a touchdown and one interception. His mobility, athleticism and passing accuracy made him the clear choice over the aging and immobile Bledsoe. Parcells had made his decision. The Dallas Cowboys quarterback of the future was Tony Romo.

Among many other personnel improvements by Parcells in his four years in Dallas, this would be his Cowboys legacy. Romo had been an undrafted free agent signee, as distant as fourth on the depth chart when Parcells arrived. But Romo was never cut and Parcells had never exposed him to other teams. And now he was the Dallas Cowboys starting quarterback.

The Cowboys were 4-3 and next faced the Redskins on the road. The Cowboys were leading in this game 19-12 heading in to the fourth quarter. Then the "twilight zone" took over. Washington scored a touchdown one minute in to the fourth quarter to tie the score 19-19. The teams exchanged several punts, and then Washington started a drive at their own forty five yard line with 3:41 left in the game. Mark Brunell drove the Redskins to the Dallas thirty one yard line with just thirty seconds remaining. On fourth and six, the Redskins lined up for what appeared to be the potential game winning field goal from forty nine yards. But Nick Novak missed the kick wide right, so the Cowboys took possession at their thirty nine yard line. Tony Romo completed two quick passes to move the ball to the Washington forty five yard line with eighteen seconds left. Romo then found Jason Witten for a twenty eight yard completion to the Washington seventeen yard line with only six seconds remaining. The Redskins fans were stunned, and hushed.

The Cowboys lined up for a thirty five yard field goal attempt by Mike Vanderjagt. Nine times out of ten, with the strength and accuracy of NFL kickers, this is a win for Dallas. Now enter: The Twilight Zone. The field goal attempt was blocked by Washington's Troy Vincent, and then it was picked up by Sean Taylor, and he ran to the Dallas forty four yard line, as regulation time expired. It appeared that overtime would be necessary. However, there was a yellow flag on the field. The Cowboy's Kyle Kosier was flagged for a face mask penalty during the return. Because the game could not end on a penalty, the penalty was enforced and Washington was given one play with no time left on the clock. The penalty mark-off placed the ball at the Dallas 29 yard line. Nick Novak had missed just moments earlier from 49 yards, however this time his kick was good from 47 yards, and the Redskins had a shocking 22-19 win, to drop the Cowboys to 4-4. Ironically, the crazy ending may have never occurred had the Cowboys kicked the extra point after their first touchdown instead of going for the two point conversion, which failed. Had the Cowboys been leading 20-19 when they got the ball with thirty seconds remaining in the game after Novak missed the 49 yard attempt, they would have simply run out the clock and won the game. However, "hindsight is 20/20". Do you want to question Bill Parcells about this? I don't think that I do. Enough said.

Tony Romo was now established as the Cowboys starting quarterback. The Cowboys were 4-4 at the mid-point of the season, which was disappointing in light of the pre-season expectations for the team. However, the Cowboys would go on a four game winning streak to improve to 8-4 with four games remaining. They first won at Arizona 27-10, as Tony Romo completed twenty out of twenty nine attempts, with two touchdowns and no interceptions. The Cowboys defense forced three turnovers, and improved to 5-4.

Next they faced undefeated Indianapolis (9-0), with Peyton Manning. The Colts scored a touchdown to go ahead of Dallas 14-7 with five minutes left in the third quarter. The Cowboys responded with a sixty eight yard drive, with forty six yards rushing, that consumed eight minutes. They were aided by one defensive holding penalty, and Marion Barber scored to tie the game 14-14 with 11:30 remaining. The Cowboys defense forced a three and out and the Colts had to punt. The Cowboys started at their twenty yard line. Romo had completions of nineteen and thirty three yards to Terry Glen to move the ball to the Colts twenty. He then completed a short pass to Julius Jones, who turned it in to a fifteen yard gain to the Colts one yard line. MB III scored the touchdown to put Dallas ahead 21-14 with 6:04 remaining. Peyton Manning then drove Indianapolis to the Cowboys eight yard line, where they faced a third down and two yards for a first down. The Cowboy defense forced two incompletions to take over on downs with 3:05 to play. The Cowboys gained two first downs and ran out the clock, handing the Colts their first loss, and improving to 6-4.

Next, the Cowboys hosted the 3-7 Tampa Bay Buccaneers. Tony Romo threw for 306 yards and five touchdowns. The defense forced two turnovers and held Tampa to 211 total yards. The Cowboys won 38-10 to improve to 7-4. Dallas then traveled to New York to face the Giants, who had hammered the Cowboys six weeks earlier in Dallas. The Giants came in to this game on a three game losing skid. However, New York improved their play against the Cowboys. In the fourth quarter the Giants drove sixty three yards to score a touchdown and tie the game 20-20 with just 1:12 remaining in the game. After the kickoff, Jason Witten got open deep and Romo found him for a gain of forty two yards. The Cowboys newly signed kicker Martin Gramatica, kicked a forty six yard field goal, his third of the game, with six seconds remaining, to give the Cowboys the win 23-20. The 8-4 Cowboys were in first place in the NFC East and were well positioned for the stretch run to the playoffs. Tony Romo was now 5-1 as the Dallas Cowboys starting quarterback.

On a Sunday night nationally televised broadcast, the Cowboys hosted the 8-4 New Orleans Saints, coached by

Bill Parcells protégé Sean Payton. The Cowboys started the game with a defensive stop and a New Orleans punt. Two plays later Julius Jones ran seventy seven yards for a touchdown and a 7-0 lead. Thereafter, it was all Saints, as New Orleans scored three unanswered touchdowns in the second quarter for a 21-7 halftime lead. The Saints ran it up to 42-17 in the third quarter, and then coasted in for the win. The Cowboys were soundly beaten in every phase of the game.

The Cowboys recovered the next week at Atlanta. Tony Romo threw two touchdown passes to Terrell Owens, including a fifty one yarder. Demarcus Ware had a forty one yard interception return for a touchdown. Tony Romo was twenty two of twenty nine passing, and the Cowboys defeated Atlanta on the road 38-28.

Dallas was 9-5 with two games to play, and still in first place in the NFC East. Next for the Cowboys was a rematch with Philadelphia, who had beaten Dallas in week five 38-24. The Eagles came in to this rematch one game behind the Cowboys in the NFC East. However, the Eagles were on a three game winning streak. Their winning streak would continue. The Eagles dominated both sides of the line of scrimmage completely. Philadelphia had 204 yards rushing and controlled the ball with thirty seven minutes in time of possession. The Eagles defense held Dallas to 201 total yards, sacked Romo three times, and forced three turnovers. The Eagles prevailed 23-7, to drop the Cowboys to 9-6 and take over first place in the NFC East.

The Cowboys had at least a wild card playoff spot clinched going in to the final regular season game. The final game would be at home against the 2-13 Detroit Lions. This may possibly be the game that made Bill Parcells want to retire from coaching for the last time. For a playoff bound team, the Cowboys were simply awful against the lowly Lions. The defense surrendered 306 yards passing, four touchdown passes and thirty nine points, against the number twenty two ranked offense in the NFL. Tony Romo was sacked four times, by the number thirty ranked defense in the league. The Cowboys lost three fumbles. The Lions beat the Cowboys at Texas Stadium 39-31, and the regular season ended 9-7. While this was a disappointing end, the Cowboys did qualify for the playoffs, and they would play in a wild card game, against the Seahawks on the road in Seattle.

Seattle was the defending NFC Champion, as they had played in the 2005 Super Bowl, which they had lost to the Pittsburgh Steelers, 21-10. Seattle had "backed in" to the 2006 playoffs, similar to the Cowboys, having lost three of their last four games against bad teams. Seattle had won the weak NFC West with a record of only 9-7. They were the lowest seed of the three Division champions. This was a very winnable playoff game for the Cowboys, even as a road wild card team. The Cowboys had played against a stronger schedule than Seattle had in 2006, in compiling their 9-7 record.

The game started out ominously for Dallas when Martin Gramatica sent the opening kickoff out of bounds, giving Seattle the opening possession at their forty yard line. Matt Hasselbeck drove Seattle to the Cowboys twelve yard line, helped by a thirty six yard completion to Bobby Engram. The Cowboys forced a fourth down at the five, and Seattle settled for a field goal (Seattle 3 – Dallas 0). The Cowboys ensuing drive produced two first downs, and then Dallas was forced to punt. Seattle took over at their own twenty with 7:22 left in the first quarter. On first down Matt Hasselbeck's pass was intercepted by Anthony Henry, giving Dallas possession at the Seattle forty three yard line. Tony Romo completed a fourteen yard pass to Terrell Owens, but the Cowboys drive stalled at the Seattle thirty two. Martin Gramatica kicked a fifty yard field goal to tie the game 3-3, and that completed the first quarter scoring.

After a Dallas punt ended their first possession of the second quarter, Seattle took over at their thirty four yard line. The Seahawks were helped by two Dallas defensive penalties, both of which provided first downs, and they drove to the Dallas twelve yard line. With 8:28 remaining in the second quarter the Cowboy defense stiffened, and Seattle kicked a thirty yard field goal to take the lead 6-3. After the two teams exchanged punts, Dallas took over at their own twenty four with 5:14 remaining in the half. On a third and six at the thirty nine, Romo hit Patrick Crayton for eighteen yards to the Seattle forty three yard line. Later the Cowboys faced a fourth down and two at the Seattle thirty five. Romo then hit Jason Witten for thirty two yards to the Seattle three, setting up a first and goal with twenty four seconds left in the half. On a first down pass play, Mark Columbo was called for offensive holding, moving the Cowboys back to the thirteen yard line with eighteen seconds remaining. On the next play, Tony Romo found Patrick Crayton for a thirteen yard touchdown pass, and the Cowboys lead the Seahawks at half time 10-6.

Dallas got the first possession of the second half, but went three and out. After the punt, Seattle started at their thirty eight yard line. Matt Hasselbeck used several runs by Shaun Alexander, some short passes, and a thirteen yard pass completion to Jeremy Stevens to reach the Cowboys fifteen yard line. On first down Hasselbeck found Jeremy Stevens for the fifteen yard touchdown pass to give Seattle the lead 13-10 with 6:08 remaining in the third quarter.

Seattle would enjoy their new lead for about thirteen seconds. On the ensuing kickoff, Miles Austin, an undrafted rookie free agent, found a seam and exploded to a ninety three yard kickoff return for a Cowboys touchdown. Qwest Field was in shock. It was the first kickoff return for a touchdown in a playoff game in The Dallas Cowboys storied playoff history. The Cowboys regained the lead in a lightning strike, 17-13.

The teams exchanged punts, with the Cowboys punt coming on the first play of the fourth quarter, and still leading the Seahawks 17-13. On first down from the Seattle thirty one, Matt Hasselbeck attempted a long pass that was defended (tipped) by Terrance Newman, and was intercepted by Cowboys safety Roy Williams. Dallas took possession at their forty three yard line with 14:41 left to play. An illegal use of hands penalty backed-up Dallas to their thirty three yard line. But the Cowboys overcame the penalty with a sixteen yard completion to Terry Glenn. Then, five straight runs by Julius Jones, including one for eighteen yards, moved the Cowboys to a third and one to go at the Seattle ten yard line, with 10:59 remaining. On third down the Seahawks defense stuffed MB III for a one yard loss, forcing a fourth down decision. Parcells chose the safe play, and Martin Gramatica kicked a twenty nine yard field goal to extend the Cowboys lead to 20-13 with 10:15 remaining in the game.

After the kickoff Seattle started the possession at their twenty seven yard line with 10:19 remaining. The Seahawks play calling indicated a heightened sense of urgency, and their execution indicated a strong desire to win. Hasselbeck completed passes to Bobby Engram of eleven yards, and then thirty yards, to set up Seattle with a first down at the Dallas thirty.

From here until the end of this wildcard playoff game, you really have to wonder if fate had pre-determined the winner of this game.

On first down from the thirty, Hasselbeck went for the home run, with a pass to the deep middle. As Cowboy fans over the years have seen many times, Terrance Newman was flagged for pass interference, giving Seattle a first and goal to go at the Cowboys one yard line. Then it just got crazy! On first and goal Shaun Alexander was hit in the backfield and dropped for a seven yard loss. Second down resulted in an incomplete pass. On third and goal from the eight Hasselbeck hit Jeremy Stevens, and he was stopped at the Dallas two yard line, forcing a fourth and goal. The Seahawks, without taking a timeout to talk it over, elected to go for it on fourth down. Matt Hasselbeck's pass was incomplete, and the Cowboys took over on downs.

With 6:42 left in the game, the Cowboys had a 20-13 lead, and they had the ball. Dallas just needed to move the ball and run the clock. The challenge was that they were on their own two yard line. On first down, the Cowboys play call was for a quick pass to Terry Glenn. However, Glenn fumbled when he was hit with a quick tackle, and the ball rolled out of bounds along the goal line before possession was gained. By fumbling out of the end zone, the Cowboys gave Seattle a safety, and the Dallas lead was cut to 20-15. Now the Cowboys had to "free-kick" the ball back to Seattle.

After the free kick and a good Seattle return of nineteen yards, the Seahawks had the ball at mid field, with 6:17 remaining. After a short completion and two positive yardage runs, the Seahawks had a first down and ten at the Cowboys thirty seven yard line. Again, the aggressive Seahawks went for the home run, and this time Hasselbeck found Jeremy Stevens for thirty seven yards, and the go ahead touchdown. Seattle went for the two point conversion but was denied. With 4:31 remaining, it was Seattle 21 – Dallas 20.

As unfortunate and disappointing as the last two minutes had been for the Cowboys, they only needed a field goal, and 4:31 was more than enough time to drive into field goal position and win this wild card game on the road. After the kickoff the Cowboys had possession at their twenty eight yard line. This drive really wasn't that difficult for Dallas. On first down Romo completes eleven yards to Patrick Crayton. Julius Jones rushes for three yards. Then on second down Romo completes for twelve yards to Terrell Owens to the

Seattle forty six yard line, with 3:02 remaining. At this point, the Seattle fans are freaking out. All the Cowboys need is a field goal. Now the Seattle coaching staff starts thinking of preserving time on the clock so that they can have a chance for a retaliatory field goal attempt. On first down from the forty six Julius Jones bursts up the middle for thirty five yards to the Seattle eleven yard line. There is 2:15 remaining. On first down from the eleven, Julius Jones gets stuffed for no gain. This brings the two minute warning. On second and ten, the Cowboys run MB III for three yards to the eight yard line. Seattle calls their second timeout. On third down and seven to go for a first down, Tony Romo throws complete to Jason Witten to the one yard line, apparently gaining a first and goal to go. However, the play was reviewed, and upon review the placement of the ball was spotted back to the two yard line. That change of spot is critical. It leaves the Cowboys with a fourth and one yard to go. Seattle takes their third timeout. There is 1:19 left in the game.

Let's reset this dramatic moment. The Cowboys are trailing 21-20. They have the ball fourth down and one at the Seattle two yard line with 1:19 left in the game. Extra points and field goals tried from this point on the field in the NFL are successful approximately 97% of the time. So, on the Seattle sideline they are planning for a one minute drive to get in to field goal position to try to deal with a 21-23 deficit. On the

Cowboys sideline, the defense is planning for their strategy to keep the Seahawks aggressive passing game from crossing mid field, and having any shot at a last minute winning field goal.

The Cowboys field goal special team lines up just like they always do, basically for an extra point attempt. The snap comes back as usual. The snap was good. Tony Romo catches the snap, as he normally does. But as he starts to transfer the ball from the catch position to the inverted position for the kicker to strike the ball with his foot,

something went wrong. The ball falls from his usually sure grip. It tumbles to the ground. Gramatica stumbles rather than completing his kicking motion. Romo realizes that the kick is not possible, so he grabs the ball and begins to scramble to his left and then up the field. He could either score the winning touchdown, or reach the one yard line and gain a Cowboys first down. Romo turns up field and crosses the five yard line. He angles to the left side of the field to try to beat the pursuit to the goal line. Unfortunately for the Cowboys, Jordan Babineaux stayed engaged with the play as it developed. Babineaux tracked Romo and made a shoe-string tackle at the two yard line, short of the needed first down yardage. Tony Romo had been holding for the conversions and field goals for as long as he had been with the Cowboys as an undrafted free agent. We had never seen him miss the catch of the snap, or drop the hold. Fate had just chosen this night and this dramatic moment, and fate can be very cruel. This was the second time during the Cowboy's ill-fated 2006 season that a game had ended with a last-second loss from a bizarre kicking game mishap (Washington Redskins, November 6; lost 22-19).

And just like that, it was over. Seattle 21 – Dallas 20. The 2006 season that had started with so much promise and expectation. The season that had deteriorated early with the lagging performance of the aging Drew Bledsoe, but had rebounded with so much promise with the energetic play of the young Tony Romo. Now the original four year contract obligation of Bill Parcells was completed. Parcells had rebuilt the Cowboys roster, and though the 2006 season ended with disappointment, there was promise for the future. But now what would Parcells do? Would he stay and continue the rebuilding process, and possibly take the next step to the potential for being a championship contender?

Fifteen days after the heart breaking, gut wrenching wild card game loss in Seattle, Bill Parcells announced that he was retiring from coaching in the NFL. There would be no contract extension with the Cowboys. But Bill Parcells was leaving the Cowboys in much better condition than when he was hired. When he came to Dallas, Jerry Jones handed him a team that had gone 5-11 for three straight seasons, that was quarterbacked by Quincy Carter, and that had a defense ranked 18th in the NFL. Parcells was leaving the Cowboys with a playoff caliber team, that was quarterbacked by the young gunslinger Tony Romo, and that had a defense that was ranked ninth in the NFL in 2006.

With Bill Parcells gone, Jerry Jones had another coaching decision to make for his rebuilt and playoff caliber team.

Dallas Cowboys, Americas Team Is Back

Chapter Five

<u>Mediocrity – The Wade Phillips Morass</u>

On February 8, 2007 Jerry Jones hired Wade Phillips to be the seventh head coach of the Dallas Cowboys, and the Cowboys fourth head coach in nine seasons. I did not like Jerry's decision in February 2007. I didn't understand why there wasn't any significant criticism from the press about the Wade Phillips hire. But I do know that history has proved my opinion correct, and others, just absent.

At the time, the Wade Phillips announcement was largely considered to be a good hire by the so called "sports media". It was said that Phillips would be a good addition for the Cowboys due to his defensive coordinator experience, and his focus on the 3-4 defensive scheme. I was completely underwhelmed by the hire. The way that I viewed it, Jerry was going in completely the wrong direction. From 2003 through 2006, the Cowboys had benefitted from Bill Parcells strong discipline and solid history of building teams with his effective personnel selection and player development skill. In his tenure with the Cowboys, Bill Parcells had taken a bad roster and he had made it much better.

Wade Phillips two previous head coaching outcomes had been just the opposite of the Cowboy's experience with Bill Parcells. Both in Denver (1993-94) and in Buffalo (1998-2000) his teams had become weaker, not stronger, during his tenure. Wade Phillips was known as an effective defensive coordinator. He was not known for personnel selection, for developing young players or for being a team builder. Furthermore, Wade Phillips head coaching record in the playoffs was 0-3. I would have preferred that Jerry hire either Norv Turner or Jim Caldwell. Both men had significant NFL experience in order to be able to handle the 2007 Cowboys team, and both men had a strong offensive coaching pedigree, which would be well suited to the high powered offense that Bill Parcells had assembled before he retired from the Cowboys.

What compounded the weakness of this hire, was the fact that along with losing the personnel evaluation, and player development expertise of Bill Parcells, Jerry Jones did not add anyone to the organization's staff to replace that expertise that departed when Parcells left. So the Cowboys were right back where they were after Jimmy Johnson left, and prior to Bill Parcells arrival.

Prior to hiring Wade Phillips, Jerry Jones hired Jason Garrett on January 25, 2007. Garrett had been the quarterbacks coach for the Miami Dolphins. Jerry Jones hired Jason Garrett with the intention of naming him the Cowboys new offensive coordinator, and also to consider him with the nine other candidates for the Cowboys head coaching job. Garrett was thought by some, to be one of the bright young offensive coaches in the NFL.

So in February 2007 Jerry Jones had Wade Phillips as his new head coach and Jason Garrett his new offensive coordinator. Now it was time for the Cowboys coaches and front office to begin to prepare for free agent activity, and the April 2007 draft. The first move made in free agency was to sign a big time offensive lineman. Spending big money on an offensive lineman was necessary because of the Cowboys lack of success in drafting offensive linemen. In the five years prior to 2007 (2002-2006), the Cowboys had drafted nine offensive linemen. One was a legitimate starter with a long time Cowboy career (Andre Gurode; 2002-2010). Two others made contributions (Al Johnson and Pat McQuistan). The other six played sparingly, or none at all.

On March 5, 2007 the Cowboys signed offensive tackle Leonard Davis from the Arizona Cardinals. The cost was fifty million dollars over seven years ($18.7M guaranteed). Next on March 6, the Cowboys signed backup quarterback Brad Johnson. Finally, on March 23 the Cowboys signed veteran safety Ken Hamlin from Seattle, to a one year contract for $2.5 million.

The Cowboys began the 2007 draft in the first round at pick number twenty six, and they selected Anthony Spencer, a defensive end from Purdue. This was a very good number one pick, as Spencer has 33 career sacks (eleven sacks in

2007 draft

Round	Pick	Position	Player name	University
1	26	DE	Anthony Spencer	Purdue
3	67	T	James Marten	Boston College
4	103	QB	Isaiah Stanback	Washington
4	122	T	Doug Free	N. Illinois
6	178	K	Nick Folk	Arizona
6	185	FB	Deon Anderson	Connecticut
7	212	DB	Courtney Brown	Cal Poly-SLO
7	237	DB	Alan Ball	Illinois

the 2012 campaign). The Cowboys second pick was at number sixty seven in the third round. The Cowboys selected offensive tackle James Marten of Boston College. This was a wasted pick as Marten could not make the Cowboys roster, and he also failed with the Bears, Raiders and Dolphins. There was value available at pick number sixty seven for the Cowboys, as the Green Bay Packers selected wide receiver James Jones eleven picks later at number seventy eight. Jones has produced thirty seven touchdowns, and 4,300 yards receiving in seven seasons for Green Bay.

In the fourth round at pick number 103, the Cowboys selected University of Washington quarterback Isaiah Stanback. This pick was a "flyer", as Stanback was not considered to be an NFL quarterback. Apparently the Cowboys wanted to use his speed and athleticism as a kick returner. That never really materialized for the Cowboys. In the fourth round at number 122 the Cowboys selected offensive tackle Doug Free (N. Illinois). Free developed into a starter within three years and continues to be a contributor in the Cowboys offensive line.

In the sixth round the Cowboys picked Nick Folk, a kicker, who would have two strong seasons for the Cowboys in 2007-08. Also selected in the sixth round was Deon Anderson (fullback), who served primarily as a backup and special teams contributor (2007-2010). In the seventh round the Cowboys picked two defensive backs, Courtney Brown and Alan Ball. Brown was primarily a backup, but Alan Ball actually started most of the 2010 season at free safety.

The Cowboys 2007 draft should be characterized as very average. The good was the selection of Anthony Spencer (first round) and Doug Free (third round). However, the Cowboys wasted valuable draft picks in both the third and the fourth round, when other teams were finding productive players.

The 2007 regular season campaign would be a testament to the great work done by Bill Parcells during his four years with the Cowboys. Parcells had completely rebuilt the 5-11 team that he inherited in 2003. Now, Wade Phillips would get to coach this elite team, with an explosive offense and an improving defense.

The Cowboys opened the 2007 season at home against the division rival New York Giants. The Cowboys were hopeful to be productive with their high powered offense, and to have an improved defense. The first happened but the latter did not. The Giants burned the Cowboys for a sixty yard touchdown pass on the third play of the game. The Giants had two drives of seventy five yards or more that produced touchdowns. They also took advantage of a Tony Romo interception for another short touchdown drive. The Cowboy defense gave up 438 yards and allowed seven of fourteen on third down conversions. Tony Romo was fifteen out of twenty four passing for 345 yards and he threw for four touchdowns, with one interception. The Cowboys had 142 yards rushing, with a 4.7 yards per carry average. In the end the Cowboys outlasted the Giants with big plays in a high scoring game, 45-35. The game was in question with 3:11 remaining, when Tony Romo hit Sam Hurd on a slant pattern, which Hurd turned in to a fifty one yard catch and run for a touchdown to put the game away.

Games two and three of the Cowboys 2007 season were on the road. Dallas hammered the Miami Dolphins (1-15 in 2007) 37-20, and then defeated the Chicago Bears (7-9) 34-10, to push their record to 3-0. Dallas returned home to blow out St Louis (3-13) 35-7 to improve to 4-0. Then came a very entertaining game at Buffalo in which the Cowboys played very bad early, but were able to ultimately rally and win. Tony Romo threw an interception on the first Cowboy possession that was returned for a touchdown for a 7-0 Buffalo lead. In the second quarter with Buffalo leading 10-7, Dallas had the ball at its own ten yard line. Tony Romo's pass attempt was blocked at the line and was intercepted, and then run in for a touchdown to extend Buffalo's lead to 17-7. Dallas managed a field goal to cut the lead to 17-10 at halftime.

The Cowboys opened the third quarter with a seventy two yard drive that stalled at the Buffalo eleven yard line. The Cowboys kicked another field goal to cut the Buffalo lead to 17-13. On the ensuing kickoff Terrence McGee returned it 103 yards for a Buffalo touchdown, and widened the Bills lead to 24-13. Early in the fourth quarter the Cowboys kicked yet another field goal to cut the lead to 24-16. Late in the fourth quarter, after a Buffalo punt, the Cowboys took over at their own twenty yard line, down by eight. Tony Romo took the Cowboys down the field with nine pass completions, the final completion for four yards to Patrick Crayton for a Cowboy touchdown to cut the Buffalo lead to 24-22 with just twenty four seconds remaining in the game. The Cowboys attempted a two point conversion for the tie, but it failed when Romo's pass to Terrell Owens was defensed as he tried to make the catch. The Cowboys then executed an on-side kick, and Dallas recovered it in a scrum. By rule, Dallas was awarded possession at the Buffalo forty seven yard line (where the ball was first touched). Tony Romo completed two passes that advanced the ball to the Buffalo thirty five yard line with only two seconds remaining on the clock. Nick Folk then lined up to kick a potential game winning fifty three yard field goal. The snap was good. The hold was good. The kick was also good. However, just before the snap Buffalo managed to call a timeout, so the Cowboys had to line up to try the fifty three yard field goal again. Again the snap was good, and again the hold was good, and Nick Folk's kick from fifty three yards was good for the second time. The Cowboys won the game 25-24 on the final play, to improve to 5-0.

The Cowboys next game would be at home against the 5-0 New England Patriots. This game would indicate how the Cowboys matched up with an elite NFL team. New England took an early 14-0 lead in the first quarter. The Cowboys fought back to make it interesting in the second quarter, and early in the third quarter. But the Patriots ran away from the Cowboys in the fourth quarter. Tom Brady completed thirty one out of forty six passes for 388 yards. Brady threw five touchdown passes with no interceptions. The Patriots converted on eleven of seventeen third downs, and were two-for-two on fourth down. Brady and the Patriots owned the Cowboys defense on this day, outscoring Dallas 27-10 in the second half, and 17-3 in the fourth quarter. New England would go on to finish the regular season 16-0.

After the Cowboys rebounded to defeat Minnesota (8-8 in 2007) 24-14, and improve to 6-1 on the season, they traveled to Philadelphia for a Sunday night game against the defending NFC East division champions. Terrell Owens had a big night against his former team, with ten catches for 174 yards including one touchdown. The Cowboy offense was dominant, with 434 total yards and eight out of twelve in third down efficiency. Tony Romo completed twenty out of twenty five pass attempts for 324 yards and three touchdowns. For the Cowboys, a win in Philadelphia is always sweet. This win improved the Cowboys record to 7-1 for the first time since 1995, their last Super Bowl winning season.

The 7-1 Cowboys next traveled to New York for a rematch with the Giants, who had won six consecutive games coming in to this meeting. The Cowboys hurt themselves with undisciplined penalties in the first half, that ended in a 17-17 tie. However, in the second half the Cowboy offense tightened up its performance, and Tony Romo connected with Terrell Owens for touchdown passes of twenty five yards in the third quarter, and fifty yards in the fourth quarter. The Giants could manage only one field goal in the second half, and the Cowboys won 31-20, to sweep the season series. The Cowboys at 8-1 now had a commanding two game lead in the NFC East.

The Cowboys won their next two games at home. First was a 28-23 win over the Washington Redskins, in which Terrell Owens caught four touchdown passes. Next was a Thanksgiving Day matchup with the New York Jets (4-12). The Cowboys won easily 34-3, to reach 10-1 for the first time in franchise history. This set up a showdown the next week against the 10-1 Green Bay Packers.

The Green Bay game was billed as a showdown of NFC leaders with matching 10-1 records. It was also a quarterback matchup between the Cowboys Tony Romo, and the quarterback that he had idolized as a teenager growing up in Wisconsin, and throughout his collegiate years, Brett Favre. Green Bay got the first possession. The Cowboys had stopped the Packers on a third and ten from the Green Bay forty four yard line, when Demarcus Ware sacked Brett Favre. However, Ware was penalized for being off-side prior to the snap, and the Packers converted for the first down. Favre drove the Packers to the Dallas twenty nine yard line, where the drive stalled. Mason Crosby kicked a forty seven yard field goal to give Green Bay a 3-0 lead.

The Cowboys first possession began on their 45 yard line. Romo drove them forty seven yards in seven plays to the

Green Bay eight yard line. On fourth and two the Cowboys kicked a chip shot field goal to tie the game 3-3. The next Green Bay possession was a three-and-out. Following the punt, the Cowboys took over at their thirty six yard line. Dallas drove thirty one yards in eight plays, to the Green Bay thirty three, where they faced a fourth down and eight to go. Nick Folk kicked a fifty one yard field goal to put the Cowboys ahead 6-3, with 3:20 remaining in the first quarter.

The first twelve minutes of this game had been relatively pedestrian, with the two teams producing three field goals. The next eight minutes of regulation time would be completely different. On first down from the Green Bay twenty four yard line, Brett Favre heaved a deep middle pass attempt that was intercepted by Ken Hamlin at the Dallas forty one yard line. Hamlin returned for eighteen yards and was run out of bounds at the Green Bay forty one yard line. On first down, Tony Romo found Terrell Owens for thirty four yards to the Green Bay seven yard line. After a short running play, Romo found Patrick Crayton in the end zone for the touchdown, and the Cowboys lead Green Bay 13-3, with 1:15 remaining in the first quarter.

The first quarter would not end without another touchdown. Green Bay took over at their twenty nine yard line following the kickoff. The Cowboy defense had stopped Green Bay on a third down and six at their thirty three yard line. However,

Dallas was penalized for having twelve men on the field. After the penalty mark-off, on third and one from the thirty eight, Favre handed off to Ryan Grant, who then got away from the Cowboy defense for sixty two yards for the touchdown. The first quarter would end with the Cowboys leading Green Bay 13-10.

After the kickoff the Cowboys had possession at their twenty four yard line. On first down, Tony Romo completed a long pass to Terrell Owens down the deep middle for forty eight yards to the Green Bay twenty eight yard line. On second and eight from the twenty six, Romo connected with Anthony Fasano for the touchdown to give the Cowboys a 20-10 lead.

Green Bay started their next possession at their sixteen yard line. On a second and twelve from their forty three, Brett Favre's pass attempt to Greg Jennings was intercepted by Terence Newman. Following the interception, on first down from the Green Bay forty five, Tony Romo tried a deep pass to Miles Austin. The Packers were called for pass inter- ference and the ball was placed at the Green Bay five yard line. After a false start moved the Cowboys back to the ten yard line, Tony Romo hit Terrell Owens for the touchdown. In a period of just 8:22, encompassing just eight offensive snaps by the Cowboys, Dallas had stretched their lead from 6-3, to 27-10.

When the Packers offense took the field it was with Aaron Rodgers at quarterback. Apparently Brett Favre had been hit during the prior possession and had suffered a shoulder injury, for which he had gone to the locker room to be assessed. The two teams traded punts, and then Green Bay took possession at their twenty six with 5:23 remaining in the half. Rodgers took Green Bay on a seventy four yard drive in eight plays, with the final eleven yards coming on a pass to Greg Jennings, to cut the Cowboys lead to 27-17. This was Aaron Rodgers first career touchdown pass. After the kickoff Tony Romo took a knee to reach halftime.

Dallas started the second half by driving to the Green Bay thirty one, where they faced a fourth and two. The Cowboys went for the first down, but the running play with Julius Jones was stuffed by the Packers defense. The Packers took over on downs at their thirty two. Aaron Rodgers then took Green Bay on a twelve play, sixty nine yard drive that included pass completions of seventeen and twenty two yards. The Cowboys helped the Packers when Greg Ellis was called for a face mask penalty. The drive was capped by a one yard touchdown plunge by Ryan Grant. With 5:15 remaining in the third quarter, Aaron Rodgers had pulled the Packers to within 27-24.

The Cowboys started at their twenty yard line following the kickoff. Tony Romo overcame a third and nineteen hole with a thirty five yard completion to Patrick Crayton. From their forty six yard line the Cowboys then moved to the Green Bay thirty one on a Marion Barber III run that also included a fifteen yard facemask penalty. A pass completion to Terrell Owens followed by a seventeen yard run by Marion Barber III moved the Cowboys to a first and goal at the Green Bay five yard line. On second and goal from the six, Tony Romo tried to hit Terrell Owens, but Al Harris intercepted the pass in the end zone for Green Bay.

The Packers took over at their twenty yard line, trailing 27-24 with 14:08 to go in the fourth quarter. Green Bay converted one first down, but then the Cowboys held them to a fourth and fourteen, at their thirty one. The Packers were forced to punt.

Dallas took over at their twenty five yard line with 12:20 remaining. On first down Romo found Jason Witten for thirteen yards to the thirty eight. On the next play Flozell Adams was called for holding. On second and twenty from their twenty eight yard line, Romo again found Witten for twelve yards to make third down a manageable distance. On third and eight, Romo again found Witten, this time for thirteen yards and a first down at the Green Bay forty seven. On first down, Tony Romo went for it all on a deep throw to Miles Austin. The pass was not completed, but Green Bay was again called for pass interference at the Packers five yard line. Two plays later on third and goal from the four, Tony Romo hit Patrick Crayton for the touchdown to put Dallas ahead 34-24 with 7:51 remaining in the game.

Green Bay took possession at their twenty six after the kickoff. Aaron Rodgers moved the Packers into Dallas territory with a scramble for thirteen yards, and three completions covering another twenty six yards. Then on third and one from the Dallas thirty five, Green Bay ran the ball with Ryan Grant, who in the second quarter had a sixty two yard touchdown run. This time the Cowboys stuffed Grant, forcing a fourth and one at the Dallas thirty five. Green Bay elected to kick the field goal (fifty two yards) to cut the lead to seven, 34-27 with 5:03 remaining.

Miles Austin returned the ensuing kickoff for thirty two yards to the thirty seven yard line. The Cowboys offense then forced their will upon the Green Bay defense. On first down Marion Barber rushed for four yards, and the clock ran. On second and six, Tony Romo passed to Jason Witten who ran for fifteen yards. On first down at the Green Bay forty one, Marion Barber ran for three yards, and Green Bay was penalized for a facemask (fifteen yards). The Packers burned a timeout. On first down at the twenty six, Marion Barber ran for six yards. Green Bay burned another timeout. On second and four Marion Barber got the first down, at the two minute warning. Three more running plays moved the

Cowboys to a fourth and one at the Green Bay seven yard line. Nick Folk then kicked the short field goal to put Dallas ahead 37-27 with 1:03 remaining in the game.

The Cowboys special team did an excellent job on the kickoff return. Green Bay started at their nineteen yard line, down by ten with only fifty nine seconds remaining. Aaron Rodgers managed to complete two passes to move the ball up to the Green Bay forty four yard line. But the Cowboys defense stopped the Packers there, and forced a turnover on downs with just twenty four seconds left in the game. Tony Romo took a knee, and the Dallas Cowboys won for their sixth straight game, and improved their record to 11-1. The Cowboys had a commanding lead for the best record in the NFC, and home field advantage throughout the playoffs, with four games to play.

The Cowboys finished the regular season with a disappointing 2-2 record in the month of December, including a 10-6 loss at home to Philadelphia (8-8) and a 27-6 pasting at the hands of the Washington Redskins (9-7) in the season finale. They did however, finish 13-3, with the best record in the NFC, and with the home field advantage throughout the playoffs. Step one had been accomplished. Now, could Wade Phillips coach this team in the playoffs?

The Cowboys finished the regular season on Sunday December 30. Wade Phillips and his staff knew on that Sunday night that the Cowboys had two weeks to prepare for the winner of the NFC wildcard game between the New York Giants and the Tampa Bay Buccaneers. The Giants had to go on the road to play Tampa Bay. Tampa had won the very weak NFC South division with a record of 9-7, and the Buccaneers had lost three of their last four games. New York went to Tampa Bay having won seven consecutive road games. The Giants lost their first game of 2007 at Dallas, but then won all of their remaining road games in the season.

New York dominated the Buccaneers in the wildcard game, leading 14-7 at the half, then 17-7 after three quarters, and 24-7 in the fourth quarter before Tampa Bay scored late to make it appear closer than it was (24-14 final score). This road win was the Giants eighth consecutive win away from home. Now the Giants would return to Dallas to face the Cowboys for the right to play in the NFC championship game. The Cowboys coaching staff would have a week to prepare for their division rival, whom they had already beaten twice in 2007.

Wade Phillips coached teams have a history of fading at the end of the season. Dallas was 11-1 going in to December in 2007, and they faded to 2-2 to end the season. In three of

Phillip's previous five seasons as a head coach, his teams closed the season by losing at least three games in the critical final month of the season. In doing so those teams had either "backed in" to the playoffs, or missed the playoffs entirely. Wade Phillips playoff record as a head coach was 0-3. This head coaching record, combined with the New York Giants eight game road winning streak during the 2007 season, were ominous indicators of potential trouble for the Cowboys in their Divisional playoff matchup with the Giants, notwithstanding the "home field advantage".

On Sunday January 13, 2008 the Cowboys hosted the NY Giants in the NFC Divisional playoff round at Texas Stadium. New York won the coin toss and elected to receive. The Giants started at their twenty three yard line. The first two plays were runs by Brandon Jacobs, for five, and then ten yards, for a first down at the Giants thirty eight. After an Eli Manning incomplete pass, and a Brandon Jacobs carry for five yards, New York faced a third and five at their forty three yard line. Eli Manning's pass attempt was incomplete, however the Cowboys were flagged for being off-side before the snap, giving the Giants the first down. This was a critical error by the Cowboys defense. Two plays later Eli Manning completed a short pass to Amani Toomer, and he eluded tackle attempts by Ken Hamlin and Anthony Henry, and then streaked fifty two yards for the touchdown. This was the result of the Cowboys penalty that gave New York a second chance on the drive, and because of the very poor tackling by the Cowboys secondary on the touchdown pass play. This was not a good indicator of a well-coached or mentally prepared team (the NFC's number one seed), playing at home in the biggest game of their season. The New York Giants lead Dallas 7-0 just three minutes and ten seconds in to the game. At that point the Giants 8-1 2007 road record had to be weighing on the Cowboys minds.

The Cowboys first offensive possession started at their twenty three yard line. Marion Barber gained five yards, and the Giants were called for a fifteen yard facemask penalty, moving the ball to the Cowboys forty three. Then the Cowboys had a run for no gain, and two Tony Romo incompletions, to bring up a fourth and ten, and force a punt.

The Giants took a fair catch of the Cowboys punt at their ten yard line. Eli Manning mixed in two short passes with four effective running plays to move the Giants to the Dallas forty five yard line, where they faced a third down and two yards to go. Manning handed off to Bradshaw at right tackle, but the Cowboys defense held, and the Giants chose to punt on fourth and one at the Cowboy forty four. A very effective punt pinned Dallas at their four yard line, with 4:53 remaining in the first quarter (NY Giants 7 – Dallas 0).

On first down Marion Barber burst up the middle for six yards to the ten yard line. On second down, Romo and Terrell Owens hooked up for a catch and run for thirteen yards to the twenty three. After a three yard loss on a first down pass play, Marion Barber exploded up the middle for a gain of thirty six yards to the Giants forty four yard line. Tony Romo then hit Patrick Crayton for fourteen yards to the thirty yard line. Next, Romo handed off to Barber who gained another eleven yards to the Giants nineteen. The Cowboys seemed to have the Giants defense off balance. On first down from the nineteen the Cowboys went in to a no huddle line-up, however Mark Columbo was called for a false start. On first and fifteen from the twenty four, Romo handed to Barber and he ran left for twenty yards, down to the Giants four yard line. On first and goal from the four Marion Barber was stopped for a one yard loss, and the first quarter expired. On second and goal at the Giants five, Romo found Terrell Owens for the touchdown to tie the game at 7-7, with 14:56 remaining in the first half. The Cowboys had driven ninety six yards in nine plays, for the tying touchdown.

After the kickoff the Giants took over at their thirty two yard line. Manning completed a pass to Plaxico Burress on first down for five yards. On second down there was a rushing attempt for no gain. On third and five from the thirty seven, Manning's pass attempt was incomplete. However, Greg

Ellis was called off-side, and instead of a fourth down punt, the Giants got a first down by penalty, for the second time. On first down Manning was forced to scramble for a short gain. On second down Brandon Jacobs gained two yards, setting up a third and seven at the New York forty five. Manning was sacked for a ten yard loss and the Giants were forced to punt.

The punt went out of bounds at the Dallas nineteen yard line, but a holding penalty backed the Cowboys up to their ten, with 11:21 remaining in the first half. The Cowboys used six running plays, five by Marion Barber, and a Tony Romo scramble to reach their thirty eight yard line, where they faced a third and seven to go. Romo found Terry Glenn with a short pass, and he broke a tackle to gain eleven yards up to the Dallas forty nine yard line. On a third and seven from the Giants forty eight, Tony Romo hit Terrell Owens for eleven yards down to the Giants thirty seven yard line. After an incompletion and a run for no gain, the Cowboys faced third and ten. Tony Romo was able to complete to Terrell Owens down the deep middle for twenty yards to the Giants seventeen yard line. Julius Jones gained four yards to the thirteen, and the two minute warning stopped the clock. On second and six, Romo completed to Jason Witten who gained eleven yards down to the Giants two yard line (pushed out of bounds). On first and goal Tony Romo's pass attempt to Terrell Owens was incomplete. On second down Marion Barber dove to the one yard line. On third and goal from the one Marion Barber was able to break the plane to score the touchdown, and put Dallas ahead 14-7 with just 0:53 remaining in the half. The Cowboys offense had driven ninety yards in twenty plays and had used ten minutes of the play clock. They were positioned to go in to the half time break with the lead and the momentum.

Ahmad Bradshaw returned the kickoff to the twenty nine yard line, where the Giants set up with just 0:47 left in the half. This is when the playoff legacy of Eli Manning began to emerge from the shadow of his older brother. On second and ten with 0:42 remaining, Manning completed to Steve Smith for twenty two yards to the Dallas forty nine yard line. The Giants called their second timeout (0:34 remaining). On first down, Manning completed to Smith again for eleven yards. In the process of running Smith out of bounds, the Cowboys committed a fifteen yard facemask violation, moving the ball to the Dallas twenty three yard line with 0:28 remaining. On third and ten from the twenty three, Manning found his tight end Kevin Boss for nineteen yards down to the Dallas four yard line with 0:11 remaining in the half. On first down Eli Manning hit Amani Toomer for the touchdown to tie the game at 14-14 at the half. *Eli Manning had taken the Giants seventy one yards, in seven plays, in only forty seconds! Manning still had a timeout left in his pocket.* The Giants had taken back the momentum in a very efficient "two minute drill" to end the half.

After the 14-14 halftime tie, this game would be determined by three possessions, two by Dallas and just one by the NY Giants. The key would be execution, discipline and taking advantage of opportunities; the very definition of the team that is better prepared for an NFL playoff game. On the Cowboys first possession of the second half they started at their twenty two yard line, and they drove to the NY Giants eleven yard line, where they faced a third and seven. Flozell Adams was called for a false start. This is a veteran Cowboy offensive lineman who knows the snap count. This critical penalty now caused the Cowboys to have to convert a third and twelve yards to go, and they could not do it. As a result, the Cowboys were forced to kick a field goal, to lead only 17-14 (and they would never score again).

Another critical mistake occurred with 3:16 remaining in the third quarter, when the Cowboys burned a timeout in a situation that should not warrant a timeout to be called. The Cowboys held the Giants to a gain of five yards on a screen pass, on third down and seventeen to go. The Cowboys did not get their proper personnel on to the field for the punt, so a timeout was called. This limited the number of timeouts available in the critical late moments of the fourth quarter when Dallas was attempting to rally. Again, a big mistake at a critical time in the game, indicating a playoff caliber team that is simply not prepared for the moment. The players are partially to blame, but ultimately the coaching staff is responsible for preventing these kinds of errors.

The Cowboys made another critical mistake with 2:23 left in the third quarter, which lead directly to the Giant's winning touchdown drive. Dallas had converted a second and seven with a ten yard pass completion, but on the play Leonard Davis was flagged for unnecessary roughness, negating the play and causing a second and eighteen, that the Cowboys could not overcome. They were forced to punt from their seventeen yard line. The punt was 45 yards, however it was very returnable. R.J. McQuarters returned the kick twenty five yards to the Dallas thirty seven yard line.

The Giants then methodically drove the thirty seven yards in six plays for the go ahead touchdown. There were no false starts, or personal foul penalties by the Giants; there were no dropped passes, or illegal procedure penalties. The Giants executed when they had the opportunity (good field position) and they took the lead for good 21-17, with 13:22 remaining. The game had been decided.

It all came down to the Cowboys final possession with 1:50 remaining. The field position was very good, with Dallas starting at the Giants forty eight yard line. But the Cowboys had a problem, in that they only had one timeout remaining, because they had wasted one of their timeouts back in the third quarter. Although, remember that Eli Manning drove the Giants seventy one yards in seven plays, in only forty seconds, while only using one timeout on the drive at the end of the first half, when he needed to.

On first down Tony Romo passed short left to Marion Barber who gained nine yards to the Giants thirty nine, but the clock was running. So the Cowboys went no huddle, in the shotgun formation. The play call was a handoff up the middle to Marion Barber, and he was stuffed for a one yard loss. Again, the clock was running. On third and two, Tony Romo found Jason Witten for eighteen yards to the New York twenty two yard line. The Giants called timeout with thirty one seconds left. This timeout call by the Giants was a blessing for the Cowboys.

What happened next just had to make you think, that it just wasn't "going to be", for Wade Phillips and the Dallas Cowboys on this night. On the very first snap after the Giants "gift" timeout, the Cowboys offensive line was called for a false start. The offensive line that knew the snap count, and had the benefit of a timeout to clear their mind and get focused for this critical point in the game, could not get it right. The penalty backed them up to the twenty seven yard line. However, the Cowboys still had thirty one seconds, and a timeout to work with, to go twenty seven yards to win the game. (Again, Eli Manning and the Giants had covered seventy one yards, in seven plays, in forty seconds, at the end of the first half when they had to get it done)

Jason Witten would gain four yards on first down to the twenty three, but could not get out of bounds, so the Cowboys had to burn their final timeout with twenty six seconds remaining. There would be incomplete passes on second and third down. No receivers were open. Tony Romo was pressured. Then on fourth down, Romo was forced into a desperation heave to the end zone that was intercepted. Game over. Giants win 21-17. The New York Giants executed in this divisional playoff game when they had the opportunity to. The Dallas Cowboys did not. It was just that simple. The Giants got their ninth consecutive road win of the season. And it would not be their last. They would go on to win at Green Bay for the NFC championship, and then beat the undefeated New England Patriots to win Super Bowl XLII. The Giants had an amazing 2007 playoff run.

As great as the New York Giants were in this game, it was a very winnable game for the Cowboys. Consider the penalties. The Cowboys had eleven penalties that cost them eighty four yards. This was a game decided by less than a touchdown. If Dallas had half of that penalty yardage back, they probably win the game.

The Cowboys were a poorly prepared team for this playoff game. Wade Phillips and his staff did a bad job. I am not surprised, based on Wade Phillip's well documented head coaching history. They were completely out-coached by Tom Coughlin and his staff. That is unacceptable, because in the NFL there are no second chances.

Consider this: in the two regular season games against the Giants, the Cowboys had scored forty five, and thirty one points, in winning the two meetings. The Cowboys had a lot of "big plays" in those two games. In this playoff game, the Giants changed their strategy in how to defense the Cowboy offense. Rather than the aggressive blitzing pressure defensive scheme, the Giants settled back and took away the big plays. They made the Cowboys play "underneath", which requires a lot of precise and patient execution. The Cowboys were undisciplined. They committed errors that made the Giants task easier. The Giants made the neces-sary adjustments. The Cowboys did not. As a result, the Cowboys lost their sixth consecutive playoff game, and Wade Phillips became 0-4 in the playoffs as a head coach. It was penalties and sloppy tackling, dropped passes and wasted timeouts. A poorly prepared, undisciplined team.

More of the same that had been the case since 1994 when Jimmy Johnson left Dallas.

This game alone (not to mention the rest of the Wade Phillips Cowboy tenure) is validation of my opinion in 2007 when he was hired, that Wade Phillips was not the right choice to coach the Dallas Cowboys. This 2007 team that Bill Parcels had built, had the talent to go to the Super Bowl, and to win it, if they executed. If this team had a coach like Jimmy Johnson or Bill Parcels, to prepare it for the playoff caliber competition, it could have done so. But Jerry Jones made the decision to replace Bill Parcels with Wade Phillips. And the rest, as they say, is history.

2008 draft

Round	Pick	Position	Player name	University
1	22	RB	**Felix Jones**	Arkansas
1	25	DB	**Mike Jenkins**	S. Florida
2	61	TE	**Martellus Bennett**	Texas A&M
4	122	RB	Tashard Choice	Georgia Tech
5	143	DB	**Orlando Scandrick**	Boise State
6	167	DE	Erik Walden	M. Tennessee St.

In the 2008 draft the Dallas Cowboys selected six players. Four years after that draft, only Orlando Scandrick remained with the Cowboys for the 2013 season. With the draft expertise of Bill Parcells gone, Jerry Jones continued to struggle with draft success as he had after Jimmy Johnson left in 1994. Apparently being a good GM in the NFL is a lot harder than it looks.

Following are the players that Dallas drafted, and some of the choices made by other teams behind the Cowboys picks. In the first round at number twenty two the Cowboys selected Felix Jones, a running back from Arkansas. Do you think that the University of Arkansas was the connection here? Immediately after Dallas picked Jones, the Pittsburgh Steelers took Rashard Mendenhall, running back, and he produced 3,500 yards and thirty touchdowns for the Steelers (2008-2012). Immediately after Pittsburgh and just two picks after Dallas picked Jones, the Tennessee Titans picked Chris Johnson, another running back. Johnson became an All-Pro and had 6,890 yards and forty four touchdowns for the Titans in five seasons, compared to Jones 2,725 yards for Dallas.

At number twenty five in the first round, the Cowboys picked defensive back Mike Jenkins. Jenkins did play for the Cowboys through 2012, and he had eight career interceptions. But he is no longer with the Cowboys. Three picks after Dallas took Jenkins, Seattle picked Lawrence Jackson, a defensive end, and he produced 19.5 sacks in four seasons. In the second round at number sixty one the Cowboys drafted Martellus Bennett, a tight end from Texas A&M. He had four average seasons for the Cowboys before signing as a free agent with the NY Giants, and becoming more productive there. Twelve picks after the Cowboys took Bennett, Kansas City selected Jamaal Charles, a running back from Texas. Charles has produced 5,823 yards and twenty nine touchdowns, far more than Felix Jones, whom the Cowboys took in the first round.

In the fourth round at number 122 Dallas selected another running back, Tashard Choice from Georgia Tech. He got very little work by the Cowboys, except in injury replacement situations, during which he performed relatively well. In four seasons with Dallas he had 250 carries, and only three fumbles, a very good ratio. But he was waived by Dallas in 2011, and was signed by Buffalo.

In the fifth round at number 143 the Cowboys selected Orlando Scandrick, a defensive back from Boise State. He is the only player from the 2008 draft that remains with the team. In the sixth round at number 167 the Cowboys selected Eric Walden (linebacker). The Cowboys waived him at the final cut in 2008. Since then he has played three seasons for Green Bay and has nine career sacks. He signed a new contract with Indianapolis. At pick 169, two spots after Dallas, Oakland selected a defensive end, Trevor Scott. He has 16.5 career sacks. Maybe Oakland just got lucky with this pick. It just seems that a lot of other NFL teams "just get lucky" right after the Cowboys make their selections.

The Cowboys made a few free agent moves in 2008. They signed linebacker Zach Thomas (Miami) to a one year contract. He would start fourteen games for the Cowboys in 2008. Then Jerry just got silly. He traded a fourth round draft pick to Tennessee for the very troubled Adam "Pac Man" Jones. He would play in nine games in 2008. He had no interceptions, no sacks, and his punt return average was 4.5 yards. That was a completely wasted draft pick. You might say, it was only a fourth rounder, and the Cowboys were hoping that he could return to his prior level of play. But you can never waste a draft pick in the NFL. Remember Tom Brady? He was selected by New England in the sixth round of the draft. So, no NFL team should ever waste a draft pick, particularly the Dallas Cowboys.

Finally, the Cowboys made a trade with the Miami Dolphins (Bill Parcels) in which the Cowboys received a fourth round draft choice in return for Akin Ayodel and Anthony Fasano. Fasano had been drafted by Dallas two years earlier in the second round. So, either Fasano had been drafted too high in 2006 by Dallas, or the Cowboys just got fleeced by Bill Parcels.

The Dallas Cowboys 2008 season would be their last in Texas Stadium, their home since 1971. Thirty-eight wonderful years in the stadium with the hole in the roof had seen the Cowboys win eight NFC championships, and go on to win five Super Bowl championships. That old stadium had a myriad of memories from Landry, Staubach, Drew Pearson, Dorsett and Lilly in the 1970s, as well as from Jimmy Johnson, Aikman, Irvin and Emmitt in the 1990s.

Dallas began the season 4-1, including a thrilling home win on a Monday night against a very good Philadelphia Eagles team, in a 41-37 shootout. Then they lost back-to-back games, first to the eventual NFC Champion Arizona Cardinals, and then to the 1-4 St Louis Rams. During the week prior to the game with St. Louis, Jerry Jones made a mid-season trade with the Detroit Lions.

On October 14, 2008 Jerry engineered a trade with Detroit to acquire wide receiver Roy Williams. The Cowboys gave Detroit three picks in the 2009 draft (first, third and sixth round) and a 2010 seventh round pick. After the trade, Jerry Jones gave Roy Williams a five year contract extension worth a total of forty five million dollars, of which twenty million was guaranteed.

Jerry traded away too much for a player who just simply did not fit well in the scheme that the Cowboys offense was running. Roy Williams was not productive for the Cowboys. The Roy Williams trade is probably the worst trade in Dallas Cowboys history, just slightly worse than the Joey Galloway trade in 2000 (two first round draft picks for Galloway). For twenty million dollars in 2½ seasons, Roy Williams gave the Dallas Cowboys ninety four catches, for 1,324 yards, and thirteen touchdowns. Roy Williams got the better end of that contract.

If Jerry had not made the trade for Roy Williams, the Cowboys could have added significant new talent with those three 2009 draft picks. With the number twenty pick in the 2009 first round there were three excellent players available: Michael Oher, the offensive tackle (drafted by Baltimore; later signed as free agent by Tennessee Titans); Clay Matthews, Green Bay's pass rushing linebacker; and Hakeem Nicks, the New York Giants wide receiver. Take your pick, any one of those three players would have been better for the Cowboys than Roy Williams. At the number eighty two spot in the third round, the Cowboys could have selected Mike Wallace, the wide receiver drafted by Pittsburgh. Wallace has 5,800 yards and forty seven touchdowns in his career. This is why I said Jerry traded away too much for Roy Williams.

After the loss to the Arizona Cardinals, Dallas played at St Louis (2-14 in 2008). Tony Romo was unable to play against the Rams due to a broken right pinkie finger. His backup Brad Johnson showed that he couldn't "throw a party at Mardis Gras", as he was intercepted three times. Steven Jackson had 160 yards rushing for St Louis. Wade Phillips had no answers as he stood on the sideline with a blank look on his face, and watched the Cowboys get drubbed 34-14.

After falling to 4-3 with the embarrassing loss to St Louis, Dallas won four of their next five games to improve to 8-4, including winning the traditional Thanksgiving Day game. Going in to the final month of the regular season, the Cowboys had an advantage in the standings over Philadelphia (6-5-1) and Washington (7-5) for a wild card playoff spot. The New York Giants had the NFC East lead with a record of 11-1. Going in to December, Dallas controlled their own playoff destiny, and they had two of the four games at Texas Stadium, including the final regular season game before moving to the new stadium.

On December 7 the Cowboys played at Pittsburgh (the eventual 2008 Super Bowl Champion). Dallas was leading the Steelers 13-3 in the fourth quarter, when Pittsburgh began to come back. The Steelers got a forty one yard field goal with 7:15 left to cut the lead to 13-6. The ensuing kickoff went out of bounds giving Dallas the ball at their forty yard line. But on second and nine Tony Romo was sacked, and the Cowboys went three and out. After the Cowboy punt,

Pittsburgh started at their thirty three yard line with 5:10 remaining. Ben Roethlisberger methodically drove the Steelers with four pass completions, mixed with a scramble, and a fourth down quarterback sneak for a first down. The touchdown was a six yard pass to Heath Miller, to tie the game 13-13 with 2:04 remaining.

Following the ensuing kickoff Dallas took possession at their fifteen yard line. After a two yard gain on first down, Pittsburgh called timeout to talk about their defense. There was 1:51 remaining in the game, and the Cowboys were surprised that the Steelers had stopped the clock for them after the short first down gain. On second down Tony Romo attempted a pass to Jason Witten, but there was some miscommunication on the route, allowing the defensive back to undercut the throw and make the interception at the Dallas twenty five yard line. Deshea Townsend then returned the interception nearly untouched to the end zone to give Pittsburgh the win 20-13. The Steelers had scored two touchdowns within twenty four seconds, in the final three minutes of the game to steal the win from the ill-fated Cowboys.

During the prior 13-3 regular season (2007), the Cowboys had slumped to 2-2 in December. Now in 2008 they had started December with a loss after winning four out of five games, including three straight. Dallas next played the 11-2

New York Giants in Texas Stadium in a Sunday night nationally televised game. The Cowboy defense was dominant against the Giants, as they sacked Eli Manning eight times in this game, forced two interceptions and held New York to 218 total yards of offense. Dallas had the ball facing a third and nine at the New York forty nine with 3:10 remaining, when Tony Romo hit Jason Witten for the first down conversion to the Giants thirty eight yard line. On the next play Tashard Choice broke free for the thirty eight yard touchdown run to secure the win for Dallas, 20-8. At 9-5 the Cowboys remained alive for a wildcard playoff spot, but Dallas would have to win their final two games to avoid tie-breakers.

The fifteenth regular season game of the 2008 season would be the final regular season game for the Dallas Cowboys in Texas Stadium. Their opponent would be the 9-5 Baltimore Ravens, who were also fighting for a playoff spot in the AFC. The Cowboys had planned pre-game fanfare and an extensive post-game ceremony to close out the Texas Stadium regular season history. The pre-game mood of the fans was very festive and high-energy. Scenes of the fans in the pre-game tail-gating in the documentary film "America's parking lot" indicated the fans were anticipating a win to further strengthen the Cowboys playoff position. However, the Baltimore Ravens were the team that was more motivated, and better prepared to win this final game ever to be played in Texas Stadium.

Going in to the fourth quarter of this pivotal (to make the 2008 playoffs) and historic (the last game ever in Texas Stadium) game, Baltimore lead Dallas 16-7. The Ravens had been playing with more urgency than the Cowboys through three quarters. On their first possession of the fourth quarter, Dallas put together some good short passes from Romo and some tough running by Tashard Choice against the rugged Ravens defense to get a field goal, and pull within 16-10 with 11:30 remaining. Joe Flacco responded by taking Baltimore on a demoralizing drive that included two third down conversions and one first down by a Dallas off-side penalty, and that resulted in a field goal to push the Ravens lead back up to 19-10 with 6:30 left to play.

On the next possession, Tony Romo completed passes of thirty five yards to Jason Witten, and fifteen yards to Patrick Crayton, with a third down conversion nine yard run by Tashard Choice sandwiched in between, to reach the Baltimore seven yard line with four minutes to play. Tony Romo then lofted a pass into the corner of the end zone that Terrell Owens caught for the touchdown to pull within 19-17 with 3:50 remaining. On the very next play from scrimmage after the kickoff, with the Cowboy defense cheating up to stop the run, Willis McGahee burst straight up the middle and ran away for a seventy seven yard touchdown run. Baltimore 26 – Dallas 17; Texas Stadium was stunned.

Tony Romo urgently drove the Cowboys, starting at their own twenty nine yard line, converting a third and ten with a fourteen yard pass to Jason Witten, and another third and ten with a twenty five yard completion to Patrick Crayton. After a sack buried Dallas in a second and twenty two hole, Romo hit Terrell Owens for twenty yards, and on third and two Tashard Choice got the first down for the Cowboys at the twenty one yard line. Two plays later Romo hit Jason Witten down the middle for a twenty one yard touchdown pass, to cut the lead to 26-24 with 1:36 remaining to play.

The Dallas defense needed to force a punt to give the Cowboys a shot at a game winning field goal. On first down at their own 18 yard line, Le'ron McClain took a handoff at right tackle, broke free and ran away for eighty two yards. It was his career long run and a Texas Stadium record for an opponent. Two shocking one play touchdown drives by the Ravens in the final four minutes. Baltimore 33, Dallas 24. Game over. Texas Stadium was in stunned silence. Fans began to head for the exits, despite the post-game celebration of Texas Stadium, that was yet to come. The tailgate parties outside of the stadium that had been jumping before the game said their good-byes, as this was their last meeting ever at Texas Stadium in Irving.

The 9-6 Cowboys still had "a chance" to make the 2008 playoffs despite the devastating loss to Baltimore. Dallas had a "win and you're in" opportunity in their final game, at Philadelphia. Entering December, Dallas was 8-4 and Philadelphia was 6-5-1. Andy Reid's Eagles had won two out of three in December to get to a "must win" matchup with the Cowboys. *Wade Phillips Cowboys had lost two out of three in December.* During the week leading up to this game, as a Cowboy fan, I had no hope that the Cowboys might win in Philadelphia. With the coaching matchup, the team's respective performances in December, the disappointing way that Dallas had lost to Baltimore, and with the game being played in Philadelphia, my expectation was that Dallas would lose the season finale and would miss the playoffs again.

On December 28, 2008 in Philadelphia at game time the temperature was 65 degrees. At least the weather was in the Cowboys favor. Philadelphia got the first possession of the game. They started with excellent field position at their forty yard line, when the opening kickoff went out of bounds. The Eagles drove twenty two yards to the Cowboy thirty eight, but Brian Westbrook fumbled during a running play and the Cowboys recovered at their twenty five yard line. The Cowboys quickly went three and out, and were forced to punt.

Philadelphia's second possession began at their forty six yard line. The Eagles drove thirty two yards, and then faced a fourth and five at the Dallas twenty two. David Akers kicked a forty yard field goal, and Philadelphia lead Dallas 3-0 midway through the first quarter.

Dallas second possession of the game began at their twenty yard line. Tony Romo took the Cowboys on a fourteen play, sixty one yard drive that consumed eight minutes. A big play in the drive was a third and seven at the Eagles forty one yard line, when Romo went to Jason Witten for seventeen yards to the Philadelphia twenty four. On a fourth and five at the Philadelphia nineteen, Nick Folk kicked a thirty seven yard field goal to tie the game 3-3, at the end of the first quarter.

Philadelphia started the second quarter on their thirty two yard line. On a third and seven during the drive, Donovan McNabb completed a short pass to Ronnie Brown, who turned it into a fifty nine yard catch and run, to the Cowboys six yard line. Two plays later McNabb snuck in from the one, and Philadelphia lead Dallas 10-3 with 12:20 remaining in the first half. Dallas would then have two consecutive three and outs, both of which ended with a fourth and eleven yards to go. In a game that would earn a playoff berth for the winner, the Cowboys offense could not execute.

Philadelphia began their third possession of the second quarter at their twenty nine yard line with 7:22 left in the half. A good mix of McNabb short passes and Brian Westbrook runs moved the Eagles to the Cowboys thirty seven, where they faced a third and nine. DeSean Jackson beat Terrence Newman and McNabb hit him for thirty four yards to the Cowboys three yard line. Two plays later McNabb passed to Correll Buckhalter for the touchdown to put Philadelphia ahead 17-3 with 2:03 remaining in the half. Philadelphia now controlled all momentum in this game. Their offense was imposing its will on the Cowboy defense, and the Cowboys offense had negative two yards of offense in the second quarter, and only fifty nine total yards in the first half.

Adam Jones returned the kickoff to the Dallas thirty six yard line, for good field position with two minutes to go in the half. If Dallas could get some kind of score before the half, it could break the Eagles momentum and re-establish the Cowboys confidence, which at this point was non-existent. Dallas gained a first down and had a second and five at the Eagles forty eight when disaster struck. Tony Romo, under some pass rush duress, under-threw a pass attempt to Roy Williams and it was intercepted by Sheldon Brown, who returned it to the Dallas forty two yard line with 1:04 left in the half.

On third and nine at the Dallas forty one, McNabb passed to Ronnie Brown who got to the Dallas twenty eight for the first down, and then Adam Jones was penalized for a late hit, advancing the ball to the Dallas fourteen yard line. On third and nine at the thirteen, Terrence Newman was flagged for pass interference on DeSean Jackson, giving the Eagles a first and goal at the Cowboys one yard line, with twenty seconds left in the half. With no timeouts left, the Eagles had to pass, and McNabb hit Brent Celek for the touchdown, for a 24-3 Philadelphia lead over the withering Cowboys. But the half wasn't over. And unbelievably, Philadelphia would score one more time.

Adam Jones returned the kickoff to the Dallas thirty one, where he was stripped and Philadelphia recovered the fumble with three seconds left in the half. The Eagles lined up for a field goal, and David Akers made the 50 yard kick to make the half time score Philadelphia 27 – Dallas 3. The Eagles scored seventeen points in the final 2:30 of the half, ten in the final minute. It was a train wreck for the Cowboys.

Dallas received the second half kickoff. They started at their nineteen yard line. Dallas went to the no-huddle, hurry-up offense due to the urgency of a twenty four point deficit. The Cowboys moved to their forty two, where they faced a fourth and one. They went for it on fourth down, and Romo got the first down on a quarterback sneak. On the next play Romo lateraled to Jason Witten, who then threw deep down field to Terrell Owens. The pass was completed for forty two yards to the Philadelphia fourteen yard line. On first down, Flozell Adams was called for a false start, causing a first and fifteen from the nineteen yard line. On second and fifteen, Tony Romo was sacked by Brian Dawkins, and Romo fumbled. The fumble was picked up by the Eagles Chris Clemons, and he raced seventy three yards for a Philadelphia touchdown, which widened the Eagles lead to 34-3 with 11:23 left in the third quarter.

Now in total desperation mode, the Cowboys tried a trick play on the kickoff return. Miles Austin lateraled to Adam Jones trying to catch the Eagles pursuit to one side of the field. But the Eagles were not fooled and Jones was tackled at the Cowboys eleven yard line. Tony Romo completed a pass to Patrick Crayton for twenty two yards to the thirty three. On third and one, Romo completed a deep pass to Terrell Owens for thirty five yards to the Philadelphia twelve yard line.

Then disaster struck the hapless Cowboys, again. On the next play Romo passed complete to Marion Barber, and he got to the Eagles four yard line where he was hit and strip-ped of the ball. Joselio Hanson picked up the fumble, and un-believably he returned it ninety six yards for another Eagles touchdown, the second fumble return for a touchdown for Philadelphia within three minutes. Philadelphia lead Dallas 41-3 with 8:11 left in the third quarter. The game was for all practical purposes, over, with twenty three minutes left to play. Each team added a field goal. The final score: Philadelphia 44 - Dallas 6. Philadelphia made the playoffs in 2008. Dallas did not. It was a humiliating end to an embarrassing month of December, that doomed the Cowboys playoff opportunity. Philadelphia went on to play for the NFC championship, but lost to the Arizona Cardinals.

The final month of the 2008 season is another literal illustration in support of my contention that Wade Phillips was the wrong hire as the Dallas Cowboys head coach in 2007, replacing the retired Bill Parcells. When Wade Phillips was hired, he was lauded for his defensive expertise. Yet in the final two games of the 2008 season, which for more than one reason were "must win" games, the Dallas defense had yielded 691 yards of offense, 402 of it on the ground, and seventy seven points (sixty three yielded by the Cowboys defense). In those two critical games Dallas committed seven turnovers, and fifteen penalties for 132 yards. Wade Phillips and his staff did a poor job of preparing the Cowboys to win against playoff caliber competition. He was out-coached by his adversaries repeatedly. The Cowboys did not deserve to make the playoffs.

Again, Jerry Jones made the decision to replace Bill Parcels with Wade Phillips, and the Cowboys were going backwards as a result of that choice. On top of Wade Phillips being a bad choice for head coach, Jerry continued to produce very amateurish GM results in handling the draft and other player personnel decisions.

The 2009 off-season roster moves continued the dilettante appearance of Jerry Jones as Cowboys General Manager. The 2009 Dallas Cowboy draft has been called by many, probably the worst draft in the entire franchise history. It has also been dubbed "the Special Teams Draft". No NFL team has sufficient depth to commit an entire draft to the special teams. The Cowboys selected twelve players in the 2009 draft, and by the end of 2012, not one single player remained on the Cowboys roster. That is apprenticeship draft results for a GM that is in need of expert advice.

The Cowboys did not have a first round pick in the 2009 draft, because Jerry had traded that away to Detroit for Roy Williams. Recall that if Dallas had still owned that pick in the first round, they could have chosen from Michael Oher, Clay Matthews or Hakeem Nicks. Can you imagine if Dallas would have had Clay Matthews to help DeMarcus Ware and Anthony Spencer terrorize quarterbacks?

Dallas would not have a second round pick either, because Jerry traded that pick away to compile a greater number of picks in the later rounds of the draft. Trading out of the early rounds seems unwise, given Jerry's track record of drafting in the later rounds.

The Cowboys compiled six draft picks in the fifth through seventh rounds that were essentially useless. Compiling late round picks is just not a sound draft strategy, because most drafts are solid only through the first three rounds, and sometimes through four, but only in rare exceptions beyond the fourth round. Anyone who has been involved in the NFL draft at Jerry's level since 1989 should know that. Most NFL executives do know that. Jimmy Johnson used to talk about how thin the NFL draft typically would get after the first few rounds.

There was value in the third and fourth rounds, subsequent to the Dallas Cowboys draft picks in those rounds. The Cowboys could have found significant contributors for the offensive and defensive lines, at defensive back and at wide receiver. Those were all needs in the 2009 draft, at the very least in terms of depth at those positions. Year after year this is the case with Jerry Jones Cowboy drafts. He misses on good players at every level of the draft. This is why the Cowboys have no depth and they are vulnerable to injury as a result. It is also why the Cowboys get into salary cap

2009 Dallas Cowboys draft selections					
Round	Pick #	Position	Player name	University	Status
3	69	LB	Jason Williams	W. Illinois	cut in 2010
3	75	T	Robert Brewster	Ball State	cut in 2010
4	101	QB	Stephen McGee	Texas A&M	cut Sept 2012
4	110	LB	Victor Butler	Oregon State	cut after 2012
4	120	DE	Brandon Williams	Texas Tech	released after 2010
5	143	DB	Deangelo Smith	Cincinnati	waived 2009
5	166	DB	Michael Hamlin	Clemson	cut in 2010
5	172	K	David Buehler	USC	cut after 2011
6	197	DB	Stephen Hodge	TCU	released Nov 2010
6	208	TE	John Phillips	Virginia	not re-signed after 2012; signed with SD
7	227	DB	Mike Mickens	Cincinnati	cut in 2009
7	229	WR	Manuel Johnson	Oklahoma	cut in 2011

trouble, because they have to sign free agents to fill needs that they don't meet with their draft selections.

In 2009 free agent moves, the Cowboys cut Terrell Owens, Roy Williams (safety), Greg Ellis, Adam Jones and Brad Johnson. The Cowboys signed veteran Atlanta Falcons linebacker Keith Brookings. They traded cornerback Anthony Henry to Detroit for backup quarterback Jon Kitna. The cuts had salary cap savings benefits. The signings were necessary to fill spots that were not filled by the draft. These are consequences of unproductive drafting.

The 2009 season was the Dallas Cowboys first in their prodigious new "Cowboys Stadium" in Arlington, Texas. The Cowboys would go 11-5 in 2009 and win the NFC East by virtue of their season series sweep of the Philadelphia

Eagles, which also finished 11-5. The NFC East was weak in 2009, as the NY Giants fell to 8-8, although the Giants managed to sweep their two games against the Cowboys. The Washington Redskins were 4-12. The highlight of the regular season for Dallas was their road win at New Orleans in week 14, when the Saints were 13-0. In the Cowboys season finale they defeated Philadelphia 24-0 in Cowboys Stadium, which gave them the NFC East Division championship, and it assured that Dallas would host a wild card playoff game. Their wildcard opponent would be Philadelphia, for a third meeting in 2009.

The Cowboys dominated the Eagles in this wildcard game, defeating Philadelphia 34-14 for the third time in 2009. I always celebrate beating Philadelphia, and will always hope for failure for the Eagles. This was Dallas first playoff game win since 1996. It also may have been misleading for Jerry Jones and Wade Phillips, because it gave them the illusion that Dallas was actually a playoff level team. The reality was that the 2009 Philadelphia Eagles were not a very good team.

The Cowboys reaction to the Philadelphia wildcard game was indicative of some unfounded overconfidence. Jerry Jones was quoted after the game as saying "the demons are gone!". Keith Brookings was on the sideline near the end of the game mimicking "removing the monkey" from Wade

Phillips back (Phillips had been 0-4 in the playoffs as a head coach).

When Jimmy Johnson was the head coach of the Cowboys, even during 1992-1993 when the team was clearly dominant in the league, Jimmy would not allow the team to become so brash and unfocused. He would focus their attention on preparation for the next opponent, because Jimmy knew that the level of competition goes up as you move deeper in to the playoffs. There was very little concern expressed for the Minnesota Vikings. The Vikings were 12-4 during the regular season, and had a week to rest while the Cowboys prepared for the wildcard game.

The Vikings ambushed the Cowboys in the Divisional round match-up, winning 34-3 in Minneapolis. The Cowboys did not match the Vikings intensity. The Vikings caused two fumbles, an interception, and sacked Tony Romo six times. The Cowboys had only one red zone incursion on the day, resulting in a second quarter field goal. Dallas managed to cross mid-field on three other drives, resulting in two missed field goals, and a sack with a lost fumble.

The 2009 Cowboys had "over-achieved" due to a soft schedule and a weak division. As they continued to move further away from Bill Parcels 2007 exit, the team was continuing to weaken. It would continue to weaken until Jerry Jones can figure out how to rebuild through the draft.

The 2010 Super Bowl (XLV) was scheduled to be played at the new Cowboys Stadium. Prior to the 2010 season there was much speculation and discussion that the Dallas Cowboys could become the first team to ever play in a Super Bowl hosted by its home stadium. Jerry Jones and the Cowboys organization fueled some of this speculation themselves. This speculation was entirely unfounded, given the questionable talent depth of the team entering the 2010 season.

The Cowboys were not active in the 2010 free agent market, primarily due to salary cap constraints. The 2010 draft produced two players with potential to help the team immediately:

2010 draft:

1	24 WR	**Dez Bryant**	Franchised 2015
2	55 LB	**Sean Lee**	signed long term deal 2013
4	126 DB	Akwasi Owusu-Ansah	cut Nov-2011
6	179 T	Sam Young	cut Sept-2011
6	196 DB	Jamar Wall	cut Sept-2010
7	234 DT	Sean Lissemore	traded to SD 2013 for 7th Rd pick

Dez Bryant is a very athletic wide receiver with size and speed. He has been very productive in his first five seasons. Sean Lee has been consistent and productive when healthy, but he was prematurely signed to a long term (six years - $42 million) contract extension in August 2013. Sean Lee missed ten games due to injury in 2012 prior to the signing, and has a history from his college career of being injury prone. That is why Lee dropped to the Cowboys in the second round of the draft. He missed all of 2014 after a preseason knee injury.

Jerry Jones salary cap mismanagement has been well documented. This is an example of why the Cowboys salary cap could not afford to keep DeMarcus Ware in 2014. The other four players that were selected in the 2010 draft are no longer with the team. Unfortunately that has been the typical outcome for Cowboy drafts. More than half of the draft picks are unproductive.

Early in the 2010 season it was clear that the Cowboys had problems, that there was a continuing deterioration of the roster (post Bill Parcells), and that this team was just not very good. They started 0-2, and were 1-3 after the first month. The offense had a tendency for drive killing penalties, turnovers, and in five of the first eight games they had less than 100 yards rushing. Dallas fell to 1-4, and then in week six, any miss-guided hope for this team evaporated in the game against the New York Giants at Cowboys Stadium. With twelve minutes remaining in the second quarter, Tony Romo was buried by the Giants blitzing linebacker Michael

Boley, and his left collar-bone was broken, ending his season.

The Cowboys would go on to lose the next three games to fall to 1-7. That would be as far as Jerry Jones would be willing to go with Wade Phillips. On November 8, 2010, and for the first time in franchise history, the Dallas Cowboys head coach was fired in mid-season. Jerry Jones named offensive coordinator Jason Garrett as the interim head coach.

The Cowboys won the first two games under Jason Garrett. Dallas would finish the season 5-3 under Garrett, for an overall 2010 record of 6-10. After the season Jerry Jones interviewed two other coaches, primarily to satisfy the "Rooney rule", and on February 1, 2011, the Dallas Cowboys announced that Jason Garrett was the eighth head coach in team history (the fifth in thirteen seasons), with a four year contract term.

In 2011 the Cowboys were forced by salary cap limitations to cut several high priced veteran players. That is the by-product of poor drafting. Before the 2011 training camp Dallas released running back Marion Barber III (2005 fourth round draft choice), wide receiver Roy Williams (2008 trade from Detroit; twenty million dollars of guaranteed money from the Cowboys), offensive lineman Leonard Davis (2007 free agent signing; eighteen million guaranteed money from the Cowboys), and offensive lineman Marc Columbo.

The Roy Williams release was confirmation that the trade in 2008 was a mistake. That trade was devastating to the salary cap, and to the draft choice inventory, and had long term ramifications on the team's depth (the lack thereof). The Leonard Davis release proved that the Cowboys had over-paid for a player who was too old for the contract that he was given. The poor drafting by the Cowboys over the years made the Roy Williams trade and the Leonard Davis free agent signing seem to make sense at the time, but both mistakes, and had harmful ripple effects on the team's roster.

The beginning of a Dallas Cowboy season is almost always heralded with high expectation and hope. That is the nature of this organization and the loyal fan base. The 2011 season was no different. This was the third year in the new Cowboys Stadium, and it was the first full year under their new head coach Jason Garrett. Never mind that they were just a few months removed from a disastrous 2010 season, with virtually the same personnel, except for the loss of some over-paid players who were not producing.

One peculiarity of the 2011 season is the fact that Jason Garrett did not have an offensive coordinator. Garrett had been the OC for Wade Phillips. Jerry Jones was expecting Jason Garrett to be a first year head coach, as well as the offensive coordinator. For reference, every single NFL team that has either played in, or won any of the last ten Super Bowls, all have a head coach and an offensive coordinator. This is an example of Jerry doing things his way, in spite of the success widely enjoyed by his NFL peers.

2011 draft:

Round	Pick	Position	Player name	University
1	9	OT	**Tyron Smith**	USC
2	40	LB	**Bruce Carter**	N. Carolina
3	71	RB	**DeMarco Murray**	Oklahoma
4	110	OL	David Arkin	C. Missouri
5	143	DB	Josh Thomas	Buffalo
6	176	WR	**Dwayne Harris**	E. Carolina
7	220	RB	Shaun Chappas	Georgia
7	252	C	Bill Nagy	Wisconsin

By Jerry's historical draft standards, the 2011 draft was an improvement over prior years. Tyron Smith is a monster NFL left tackle. Bruce Carter had some issues with pass coverage, however he developed into a relatively solid NFL linebacker. Demarco Murray improved incrementally in each of his four years with the Cowboys. He became an All-Pro in 2014, and eventually signed a free agent contract with the Philadelphia Eagles. I suspect DeMarco is going to miss the Cowboys offensive line, and I have not hidden my rancor for the Eagles organization. Dwayne Harris was a rare late round Cowboy success, and he provided good production as a kick and punt returner. The other four draft picks have been released or signed off the practice squad.

The Cowboys 2011 season was the first full season under head coach Jason Garrett. This Cowboys team would win only one game against a team with a record better than .500. Seven of their eight wins came against teams with a combined 2011 record of 35-77. The Cowboys lost two games in which they had a second half lead, but committed critical turnovers that fueled comebacks for the opposition. Against the New York Jets in week one, Dallas lead 24-17 with nine minutes to play in the game, and had the ball third and goal on the Jets two yard line. Tony Romo was sacked, he fumbled and the Jets recovered. New York tied the game 24-24. Then with 0:59 remaining, Tony Romo threw an interception that was returned to the Dallas thirty four yard line, leading to the Jets winning field goal.

In week four the Cowboys were leading Detroit 27-3 in the third quarter. Tony Romo threw two "pick-six" interceptions in the third quarter, and Calvin Johnson torched the Cowboys for two touchdowns in the fourth quarter. Dallas lost at home 34-30. In the month of November, Dallas won four straight games to get above ".500", and reached 7-4 for the season. However, after Thanksgiving, Dallas lost three of the next four games. That dropped their record to 8-7, and they faced a winner take all game with the 8-7 New York Giants. The winner would take the NFC East championship. If the Cowboys could win this game, they would move on to the playoffs, and if they lose their season would be over. This same scenario had occurred in 2008, when they were crushed by Philadelphia 44-6, and missed the playoffs. It happened again in 2009. Dallas beat Philadelphia in the season finale, and again in the wild card game, before being dismissed rudely by Minnesota in the Divisional playoff round.

The NFC East deciding game between 8-7 Dallas and 8-7 New York was all Giants, start to finish. Mid-way through the first quarter Victor Cruz took a short pass from Eli Manning, eluded the tackle attempt of Terrence Newman and outran two other pursuing Cowboy defenders for a seventy four yard touchdown. Then we got to watch the Victor Cruz salsa dance. The Giants lead 7-0 with 5:00 left in the first quarter. On the ensuing possession Dallas went three and out, and punted back to the Giants. New York took over at its thirty two yard line. Eli Manning drove the Giants by mixing deep throw attempts to soften up the Cowboys coverage, with short passes that kept the Dallas defense off balance. The Giants were aided by a Dallas defensive pass interference penalty. The Giants reached the Dallas five yard line where they faced a second and goal to go. Ahmad Bradshaw took a handoff to the right and easily scored to make it 14-0 Giants.

Two Dallas punts later the Giants got the ball at their twenty yard line with 4:33 remaining in the half. After a first down pass play for fourteen yards, Ahmad Bradshaw broke a thirty yard run to reach the Dallas thirty four yard line. You could feel that the Giants would not be denied before half time. Three short Eli Manning completions later, the Giants had a first and goal at the Dallas ten yard line. On first down Manning passed to Ahmad Bradshaw, who found the end zone for the Giants and a commanding 21-0 lead. Manning drove the Giants eighty yards in just three minutes. This reminded me of the late first half drive in the 2007 division playoff game in Texas Stadium.

In the third quarter the Cowboys went to their no-huddle offense. Tony Romo used a series of short passes to drive Dallas from their six yard line to the Giants thirty four. On first and ten, Romo hit Laurent Robinson down the right side line for a thirty four yard touchdown pass, to cut the Giants lead to 21-7 with 6:54 remaining in the third quarter.

Early in the fourth quarter, Dez Bryant returned a short Giants punt to the Giants forty one yard line, and a Giants penalty for unnecessary roughness moved the Cowboys to the twenty six. Two plays later on second and goal at the six,

Tony Romo found Laurent Robinson for his second touch-down of the day, and the Giants lead was cut to 21-14 with 10:15 remaining. However, the Giants immediately drove sixty five yards in four minutes to answer with a field goal, and go up 24-14 with 5:45 left.

Dallas went three and out on the ensuing possession. The Dallas punt went for only twenty six yards, to give the Giants possession at the Dallas forty five yard line. Eli Manning hooked up with Hakeem Nicks for thirty six yards to the Dallas four yard line. Manning then hit Nicks again on the next play for the touchdown, and New York lead 31-14 with just 3:41 remaining. After the kickoff Tony Romo completed a few short passes to reach the Cowboys forty six yard line. On the next play Romo was sacked, and he fumbled, and the Giants recovered. Game over. Cowboys season over. Dallas finished 8-8, and out of the playoffs again.

It was not ironic that the game ended with Romo being hit and sacked. He was sacked six times in this game. He had been knocked out for the season by the Giants in 2010 by a blitzing linebacker. Tony Romo spent most of 2011 running for his life due to a porous offensive line. And so ended another mediocre Dallas Cowboy season.

The Cowboys 2012 draft produced excitement when Jerry Jones traded a second round pick to St Louis to move up to

2012 draft:

Round	Pick	Position	Player name	University
1	6	CB	**Morris Claiborne**	LSU
3	81	DE	Tyrone Crawford	Boise State
4	113	OLB	**Kyle Wilber**	Wake Forest
4	135	SS	Matt Johnson	East Washington
5	152	WR	Danny Coale	Virginia Tech
6	186	TE	**James Hanna**	Oklahoma
7	222	ILB	Caleb McSurdy	Montana

the sixth pick, where the Cowboys selected cornerback Morris Claiborne. He had a relatively good rookie season, but has been less than worthy of a high first round pick in years two and three. Tyrone Crawford has shown some promise in the defensive line rotation, when he has been healthy. Kyle Wilber has shown some promise as well. These three players have the ability to develop and be successful for Dallas. The bottom half of the draft was again virtually useless.

The 2012 Dallas Cowboys were again a team that could not compete against playoff caliber NFL teams. The Cowboys have been completely absent from playoff achievement since 1996, and 2012 added to the trend. Dallas had a regular season record of 1-3 against teams that made the 2012 playoffs. The Cowboys had only two wins against teams with a record better than .500. The eight wins for Dallas in 2012 were achieved against teams with a combined record of 54-74. Dallas was consistently inconsistent, and they seemed to pick the most critical times for committing damaging penalties or turnovers. Tony Romo had a career worst nineteen interceptions, and he was sacked a career worst thirty six times. The sack total would have been much worse if not for Romo's athleticism and ability to escape in the pocket. The 2012 Cowboys running game was the worst in franchise history, averaging only seventy nine yards per game. Dallas offensive line simply could not establish an effective running game, which caused the extreme pressure from the opposition pass rush. The Dallas defense did not help matters at all. The Cowboy front seven could not stop the run when they had to, and they could not get any consistent pressure on the opposition's quarterback. The Cowboy defense was ranked number twenty four out of thirty two in the NFL, for points per game allowed.

The nearly two decades long theme of mediocrity in Dallas describes the Cowboys 2012 season. It took until week fifteen for Dallas to get its record to two games above .500. However, the NFC East was very weak in 2012, so at 8-6 the Cowboys found themselves tied with Washington and the NY Giants. Both the Giants and the Cowboys lost in week sixteen to fall to 8-7, while Washington won to go to 9-6. The Cowboys final game was at Washington. Dallas owned a tie breaker that would allow the Cowboys to win the

NFC East Division if they could beat the Redskins in the final week, and tie atop the Division with 9-7 records. There they go again! This same scenario had occurred in 2008 (Dallas lost to Philadelphia 44-6), in 2009 (Dallas beat Philadelphia 24-0), and again in 2011 (NY Giants defeated Dallas 31-14). The Cowboys were one for three in these recent, season finale playoff berth, ultimatum games. Could Dallas make it two out of four by beating Washington?

The Redskins would make the Cowboys the loser for the third time in four tries in these season finale winner take all playoff elimination games, since 2008. After falling behind Dallas 7-0 in the first quarter, the Redskins just started running the ball with Alfred Morris. Morris had 200 yards rushing and three touchdowns, and Robert Griffin III added sixty three yards and a touchdown. The Redskins controlled the ball for nearly thirty four minutes of game time. Each time the Cowboys scored to pull close in the fourth quarter, the Redskins would answer, and Washington ended the Cowboys season, 28-18. As had been the case all season for the Cowboy defense, they could not stop the run when they had to. So ended another mediocre Cowboy season (8-8). 2012 was the eleventh season in the eighteen since the 1995 Super Bowl, that the Cowboys failed to qualify for the playoffs.

After the 2012 season, Jerry Jones was quoted in an interview regarding the Cowboys mediocre results. Jerry said: "We have to do something almost unconventional to break out of this down cycle". "But how do we somehow create us an opportunity to kind of break out of this cycle? To drive across the water, if you will". "That's the challenge that I have right now". "I can tell you change is necessary at 8-8". "Change is in order when you spend the two seasons in a row down to the last two games and lose them, so we're going to have to have changes".

Jerry went on to say, "I can assure our fans this, that it's going to be very uncomfortable from my standpoint, it's going to be very uncomfortable for the next few weeks and months at Valley Ranch". Of course Jerry was making reference to the coaching staff.

As promised Jerry made changes to the coaching staff after the 2012 season. At season's end Jason Garrett spoke highly about defensive coordinator Rob Ryan: "I thought Rob did a really good job. I would say that injuries were a real challenge for the defense this year, if you think about the number of guys we lost on defense, starting, marquee players who were just simply out, and the other guys who were battling through injuries and the challenges he had bringing guys from the practice squad up, from off the street and on our team and literally playing them two days later".

That quote sounded like Jason Garrett planned on having Rob Ryan back for the final year of his contract. However, while Ryan was on vacation in the Turks and Caicos Islands, the Cowboys announced that Ryan would not be returning as the Cowboys defensive coordinator.

Ryan's reaction to the Cowboys decision was dauntless and entertaining: "I inherited a team that was 31st in the league in defense and made them better. I will be out of work for like five minutes". Rob Ryan was subsequently hired by the New Orleans Saints to be their defensive coordinator. And yes, the New Orleans defense good better in Rob Ryan's first season with them. Ryan would have an opportunity for some pay-back against the Cowboys in week ten of the 2013 season.

Jerry's changes to the coaching staff were not over. The Cowboys hired Rod Marinelli to be the new defensive line coach. They hired Monte Kiffin to be the new defensive coordinator. On the offensive side, Bill Callahan was promoted from offensive line coach to be the offensive "play-caller". That relieved Jason Garrett of in-game play calling duties.

As we have always known, Jerry Jones is in full control of all decision making regarding the coaches, draft picks, free agents, trades and any and all football operations strategy and decision making. The history of Jerry's GM performance since 1995 has not been good. However, you can mark it down right here, something changed beginning with the 2013 draft. We didn't know it then, but it would develop into something special later.

2013 draft:

Round	Pick	Position	Player name	University
1	31	C	**Travis Frederick**	Wisconsin
2	47	TE	**Gavin Escobar**	San Diego State
3	74	WR	**Terrance Williams**	Baylor
3	80	S	**JJ Wilcox**	Ga. Southern
4	114	CB	BW Webb	William & Mary
5	151	RB	Joseph Randle	Oklahoma State
6	185	LB	DeVonte Holloman	South Carolina

The 2013 season may just be one of the most bizarre in recent Cowboys history. The Cowboys found crazy, dramatic and sometimes humiliating ways to lose games in 2013. Dallas had the fifth highest scoring offense in the NFL, yet they finished only 8-8 and missed the playoffs for the fourth consecutive year, primarily because the Cowboy defense was the worst in the NFL (number thirty two in yards allowed), giving up an average of 415 yards, and twenty seven points per game.

The Dallas Cowboys won only one game in 2013 against a team with a record greater than .500. Seven of their eight wins in 2013 came against teams with a combined record of 26-54.

In week four the Cowboys were 2-1 and they were very smug after a 31-7 home win over St. Louis. In a game at San Diego, the Chargers would expose weaknesses in the Cowboy defense, and provide a model for other offensive coordinators to exploit in 2013. The Dallas defense could not cover running backs coming out on pass routes, and were also exposed in the secondary by the tight-end. Chargers tight-end Antonio Gates virtually ran free against the Cowboy defense for ten catches and 136 yards, including a fifty six yard touchdown pass to put the game away in the fourth quarter. Danny Woodhead (running back) caught five passes for fifty four yards and two touchdowns. Philip Rivers owned the Cowboy defense. Rivers was thirty five out of forty two passing for 400 yards. San Diego totaled 506 yards of offense, twenty seven first downs and thirty four minutes in time of possession. The Chargers offense was so dominant that the Dallas offense had just one possession in the third quarter, and only two in the fourth quarter. Dallas had the lead 21-13 at the half, but San Diego took the second half kickoff and drove eighty yards in 5:28 to cut the lead to 21-20. At that point the Chargers had seized the momentum, and they never let it go. The Cowboys lacked a clear leader on offense, defense, or coaching, to stop the San Diego momentum and refocus the Cowboys during the second half. San Diego won the game 31-21, after having trailed 21-6 in the second quarter. Second half collapses would be a common occurrence by the Cowboys throughout 2013.

The next week Dallas faced the league's number one offense, with the hottest quarterback (Peyton Manning); the 4-0 Denver Broncos. The game was at Cowboys Stadium. From the beginning this game was a shootout, with both offenses running up and down the field. For the second consecutive week the Cowboy defense gave up over 500 yards (517). Dallas gave up thirty four first downs and allowed nine out of thirteen third down conversions. Denver had eleven offensive possessions during the game, and they scored on all but two. The Broncos had six touchdowns and three field goals. Denver never punted. The two stops were on a lost fumble and an interception. The Dallas defense was well on the way to being ranked dead last in the NFL. The outcome of the game came down to two possessions in the last seven minutes.

With 7:19 to go in the game, Dallas was leading Denver 48-41. Peyton Manning then drove Denver seventy three yards for the tying touchdown. During the decisive touchdown drive, Manning overcame a holding penalty that saddled Denver with a second and goal at the Dallas seventeen yard line.

After the kickoff, with 1:57 left to play Dallas got the ball at their twenty yard line. On first down, Tony Romo was sacked for a six yard loss. On second down Romo's pass was intercepted at the Dallas twenty four yard line. Manning drove the Broncos inside the Cowboy ten yard line, ran the clock down to two seconds, and then Denver kicked a field goal to win 51-48 as time expired.

When Peyton Manning had to have a touchdown to tie the game in the fourth quarter, he drove his team seventy three yards in five minutes, even overcoming a holding penalty in the process. When the Cowboys needed a drive to get a game winning field goal, Tony Romo was sacked, and then on the next play he was intercepted. When Denver's defense needed a critical stop at the end, they forced a turnover. When Dallas defense needed to hold a touchdown lead in the fourth quarter, they were driven seventy three yards, and they gave up the tying touchdown. The Cowboys had no ability to make a game saving play on either side of the ball at the most critical time in the game.

Dallas won their next two games against "weak sisters" in the NFC East, Washington (1-3) and Philadelphia (3-3), to improve to 4-3 on the season. Then they went to Detroit to play the 4-3 Lions. Detroit had a dynamic offense, and a defense with several playmakers, but the Lions, like the Cowboys were a team that could find a way to lose a winnable game. For Dallas, this was a winnable game. The Cowboys were leading Detroit 27-17 with 7:30 remaining to play in the fourth quarter. Then the Cowboys began to do the things that will lose a winnable game.

Detroit drove eighty yards in 3:12 for a touchdown to cut the Cowboys lead to 27-24 with 3:30 left to play. The big play was on the first play of the drive, when Matthew Stafford saw Calvin Johnson in single coverage, and hit him for a fifty four yard gain. Dallas responded to the Detroit touchdown with a "three and out". Detroit got the ball back at their thirty three yard line with 2:25 left, and two timeouts remaining. Stafford was sacked on first down for an eight yard loss. The Lions gained six yards on second down on a short pass completion. Then there were incompletions on third and fourth down, and Detroit turned the ball over on downs to Dallas at the Lions thirty one yard line, with 1:24 remaining in the game. Detroit had two timeouts remaining, but with Dallas on the Detroit thirty one yard line, the Lions fans began leaving the stadium.

With a 27-24 lead, the Cowboys wanted to run the clock. On first down the Cowboys ran the ball straight up the middle for a three yard loss. Detroit immediately used their second timeout. On second down Dallas again ran straight up the middle for a one yard loss. Detroit then called their final timeout. There was 1:14 remaining in the game. On third and fourteen at the Detroit thirty five yard line, Phillip Tanner took the handoff (Demarco Murray was injured) straight up the middle, but when he was hit for no gain, he instinctively bounced the run out to the left side to try to gain more yards. Tanner gained nine yards to the Detroit twenty six yard line. However, there was a yellow flag on the field. When Tanner bounced outside, Tyron Smith tried to maintain a block and he was called for holding. The penalty stopped the clock, which otherwise would have continued to run because Tanner was tackled in bounds, and Detroit had no timeouts. Detroit declined the penalty because they didn't want to give Dallas another offensive play. On fourth and five from the twenty six, Dallas had the choice of running a play to run as much time off the clock as possible and try to get the first down, or to kick a field goal to force Detroit to have to score a touchdown. The Cowboys kicked the field goal to lead 30-24 with 1:05 remaining.

Detroit got the ball back on their twenty yard line, needing a touchdown to win the game, with no timeouts remaining, and just one minute to work with. On first down there was an incomplete pass. On second down Stafford completed a pass to Calvin Johnson for seventeen yards to the Detroit thirty seven. Stafford spiked the ball on first down to stop the clock. On second down, Lions receiver Kris Durham manag-ed to get behind the Cowboys Jakar Hamilton down the left sideline, and Stafford hit him for forty yards to the Dallas twenty three yard line, where he was run out of bounds. The clock stopped. On the next play Calvin Johnson went down the middle of the field. Stafford threw the pass up high and Johnson went up and got it despite double coverage. Johnson was tackled at the Dallas one yard line, with the clock still running, and approximately 0:25 remaining. Detroit's offense scrambled up to the line of scrimmage, expecting Stafford to spike the ball to stop the clock. The Cowboy defense delayed getting down the field and in to position as much as they could, in order to run the clock. However, the Cowboys front seven did not get set for a play, as they were expecting Stafford to spike the ball. Stafford was even yelling "spike" at the line before the snap. When Stafford saw how dis-organized the Cowboy front seven was at the line of scrimmage, he took the snap, jumped up over his linemen, and just stuck the ball out over the goal line for a touchdown. The replay review clearly showed that Stafford broke the plane for the touchdown. Detroit kicked the extra point to win the game 31-30. The Lions had driven eighty yards in just fifty seconds with no timeouts, against the Cowboys calamitous defense. Detroit had 623 yards of total offense on the Cowboy defense. Calvin Johnson alone had fourteen catches for 329 yards, including an eighty seven yard touchdown. It was a humiliating day for Monte Kiffin (defensive coordinator), Jason Garrett and everyone on the Dallas defense.

After the Detroit fiasco Dallas was home to face 1-6 Minnesota. The Cowboys managed to defeat the feisty Vikings 27-23 to improve their record to 5-4. Next the Cowboys would play a Sunday night nationally televised game against the New Orleans Saints, and their first year defensive coordinator, Rob Ryan. On the surface this matchup did not set up well for Dallas. The Cowboys had played three teams in 2013 (Kansas City, San Diego & Denver) who were apparent favorites to qualify for the post season, and Dallas was 0-3 against this level of competition. New Orleans was 6-2, but had lost the previous week at the NY Jets, so the Saints were sure to be motivated at home for the Cowboys.

New Orleans seized control of this game early in the second quarter. The Saints scored three unanswered touchdowns in the second quarter, and imposed their will on the Cowboys on both sides of the ball. The domination was complete and overwhelming. New Orleans offense produced forty first downs (an all-time NFL single game record), 625 total yards (a franchise record) of which 242 yards were on the ground. The Saints were nine out of twelve on third down conversions. Drew Brees completed thirty four out of forty one passes, and at one point completed nineteen consecutive. New Orleans had 39:32 in time of possession.

Then there was the Rob Ryan payback against the team that fired him the previous season. Ryan's defense shut the Cowboys down. Dallas offense produced just nine first downs, 193 total yards and were forced to punt eight times. Tony Romo was ten for twenty four for just 104 yards, and was sacked three times. The Cowboys were called for eleven penalties. The final score was New Orleans 49, Dallas 17. Dallas was now 5-5, and four of the five losses were of a devastating or humiliating nature. Clearly this team had no ability to compete with playoff contenders.

The Cowboys next game was at the New York Giants, who had started the season 0-6. The Giants had recovered to win four consecutive games and came in to this matchup at 4-6. However, the 2013 Giants were just not very good. They surrendered a defensive touchdown to Dallas on a fumble return, and the Giants defense allowed the Cowboys to drive sixty four yards for the winning field goal in the final four minutes of the game. The Cowboys got a rare road win 24-21.

On Thanksgiving Day the Cowboys beat the 4-7 Oakland Raiders 31-24, to improve their record to 7-5. That had the

Cowboys tied with Philadelphia atop the NFC East, entering the month of December.

December is the final month of the NFL regular season. It is the stretch run to the playoffs, for teams that are contending for the post season. In the years since Bill Parcells left the Cowboys (2007-2012) Dallas has a collective record in December of 10-14. In the first week of December 2013 the Cowboys went to Chicago for a Monday night game with the Bears. The national television exposure did not bring out the best in these Cowboys. The problem continued to be the league's worst defense.

The Chicago Bears played this game with their back-up quarterback Josh McCown. The Bears entered this game at 6-6, and they had lost their previous game to the 3-8-1 Minnesota Vikings. But against the Cowboys number thirty two ranked defense, Chicago scored on eight consecutive possessions in the game. The Cowboys never stopped the Bears offense. Chicago had no turnovers, and they never had to punt. Every time Chicago possessed the ball, they scored. The Bears had 490 yards of offense, 150 on the ground, and had 36:44 time of possession.

The most ridiculous drive was when the Bears got the ball with one minute to go in the first half. The Bears drove sixty yards in four plays, in thirty seconds, to go ahead 24-14 just before halftime. Jerry Jones made comments after the game: said Jones, "Basically, we will have to make some adjustments in what we are doing defensively. What that usually means is taking more risks on defense. But if you're going to have the kind of match like we had tonight or certainly in New Orleans you have to take some risks. We have to double up and I'm sure that will be part of the plan on defense; more risks."

As if the Detroit loss in week eight were not bizarre enough, the Cowboys demonstrated a new way to lose a game, that they should have won, in week fifteen against the Green Bay Packers. The Cowboys were playing at home in this game. Dallas dominated the Packers in the first half. DeMarco Murray ran through, around and over the Green Bay defense. The Cowboys had sixteen rushes for 109 yards (6.8 yard average per carry) in the first half, and they built a very comfortable 26-3 halftime lead. With that large lead and the first half rushing success, Dallas was expected to come out and run the ball in the second half, to run the clock and keep Green Bay's offense on the sideline.

Green Bay rallied for two touchdowns in the third quarter to cut Dallas lead to 29-17. So the Cowboys offensive play-calling went into panic mode. They stopped running, despite DeMarco Murray's first half dominance. In the fourth quarter Dallas ran eighteen offensive plays, and fifteen were passes.

Tony Romo was intercepted twice in the final 2:58 of the fourth quarter, allowing Green Bay to score the winning touchdown, and then to run out the clock. Green Bay defeated Dallas 37-36. It was a shocking defeat on their home field. The Dallas Cowboys offensive play calling had allowed Green Bay to have the time that it needed to rally from a 26-3 halftime deficit. Tony Romo's two interceptions gave the Packers the extra possessions that they had to have late in the fourth quarter. The Cowboys dropped to 7-7. They trailed Philadelphia (8-6) by just one game, and held the tie-breaker because they had already beaten the Eagles in the first meeting between the two teams.

Dallas next went to Washington to play the 3-11 Redskins, in a must win game. The Cowboys rallied for a late touchdown on a desperation fourth and goal to go from the ten yard line, and defeated the Redskins 24-23. The win set up another winner take-all regular season finale for the NFC East title, against the Philadelphia Eagles. This would be the fourth time in five years that Dallas would play the final game of the regular season with a playoff berth on the line. Dallas had lost three out of four of those games (2008 lost 44-6 to Philadelphia; 2009 beat Philadelphia 24-0; 2011 lost 31-14 to NY Giants; 2012 lost 28-18 to Washington).

On Monday December 23, after the Redskins game the Cowboys announced that Tony Romo had sustained a back injury during the Washington game, and that he would be unavailable for the season finale with Philadelphia, or for any playoff games thereafter in the event that the Cowboys beat the Eagles. Romo had a herniated disk that required surgery. The Cowboys would have to start their backup quarterback Kyle Orton in Romo's absence.

Fortunately for Dallas this late December matchup with the Eagles was in the friendly, climate controlled environment of AT&T Stadium in Arlington, Texas. The Cowboys outgained Philadelphia in this game 414-366, and only had one penalty for five yards. However, Dallas trailed 10-0 early in the second quarter, and could never draw even with the Eagles. As usual Dallas offensive play-calling was heavily weighted to the passing game. The Cowboys lost the turn-over battle 3-1. Dallas got the ball on their thirty two yard line with 1:49 left in the fourth quarter, and trailing 24-22. They needed about forty yards to be in reasonable field goal range for a potential game winning field goal attempt for Dan Bailey, who had already kicked three field goals in this game. But on first down Kyle Orton's pass was behind Miles Austin, and it was easily intercepted by Brandon Boykin to seal the win for the Eagles.

After the game Jerry Jones stated that "it's unthinkable to me to be sitting here three years in a row, and this game ends up putting us at .500 and this game eliminates us from going to the playoffs". But the reality for these Cowboys is that they had no business getting to the playoffs in 2013, because the team had no chance of competing against any of the strong playoff contenders. Had Dallas made the playoffs they would have faced the New Orleans Saints, whom they had played in week ten of the season, when they had been completely dominated by New Orleans 49-17.

In 2013 the Dallas Cowboys were really one of the weaker NFL teams, probably in the bottom third of the NFL. Their record at 8-8 had benefitted from winning four of their games against a very weak NFC East that included the 7-9 New York Giants and 3-13 Washington. Dallas eight wins came against teams with a combined record of 36-60. The Cowboys only win in 2013 against a team with a winning record, was against Philadelphia in week seven, the same team that would eliminate them from playoff contention when it really mattered, in the final regular season game.

Dallas Cowboys, Americas Team Is Back

Chapter Six

The Big Change,

Jerry Has "Figured It Out"

Jerry Jones has proved himself to be a bold, risk taking, brilliant and very successful business man. Jerry is also broadly recognized as being an innovator. It is the combination of his willingness to take risks, and his innovative conceptual business mind that have combined to increase the value of The Dallas Cowboys from the $140 million investment in 1989, to the current mega-franchise that is valued at approximately $3.2 billion. The Dallas Cowboys have the highest market value in the NFL. The only professional sports franchise that is valued higher is the European professional soccer club Real Madrid ($3.4 billion).

The criticisms that I have illustrated in the first five chapters of this book, which Jerry Jones has been acutely vulnerable to, pertain to his role as the club's General Manager. During the eighteen years from 1996 through 2013 the Dallas Cowboys won only two playoff games, and they never advanced beyond the divisional round of the playoffs. For a franchise with the winning history of the Cowboys, two playoff game wins in eighteen seasons is embarrassing. During this 18 year run of mediocrity and disappointment for Cowboy fans, Jerry Jones has made it clear that he is the General Manager of the Dallas Cowboys, and that he will not consider hiring someone else to be the General Manager. That is old news, and we will come back to it. First, let's look at Jerry the owner, and what he has done for Dallas, and for the league as a whole.

When Jerry bought the Cowboys in 1989, no NFL team had the right to market its franchise with commercial licensing agreements. In 1982 the NFL teams had agreed to create the "NFL Trust". This resulted in each team transferring the exclusive right to use its club emblems for commercial purposes to the NFL Trust. The NFL Trust then entered into license agreements with NFL Properties, to provide NFL Properties the exclusive right to license the Trust's property. The motivation behind creating the NFL Trust was a theory, that the critical mass of the combined NFL franchise marketing rights taken to market collectively, would be greater than if the individual teams attempted to negotiate licensing deals independently.

In 1993 the NFL Trust signed a five year contract with Coca-Cola worth a reported $250 million, to become the official soft-drink of the NFL. In 1995 the NFL Trust signed a five year contract with Visa USA worth a reported $50 million, to become the NFL's exclusive payment card sponsor. Meanwhile the enterprising Jerry Jones determined that the Dallas Cowboys were in a situation that was unique to that of most NFL teams, because he as owner of the Dallas Cowboys NFL franchise was also the owner of the stadium rights in which the Cowboys played. In September 1995 Jerry announced a seven year contract with Nike worth a reported $14 million to the Cowboys, that included a theme park at Texas Stadium, plus signage and other promotional rights. In August 1996 Jerry announced a 10 year contract making Pepsi the official sponsor of Texas Stadium, worth $20 million to the Cowboys. Pepsi received pouring rights at the stadium, some signage and other marketing privileges.

Jerry Jones felt strongly that he had not violated any of the terms of the NFL Trust, because only the NFL teams, and not the stadiums, were members of the Trust. The NFL did not agree with Jerry's assessment. Jerry Jones was served with a $300 million lawsuit at an NFL owners meeting in 1995 by NFL Properties. The lawsuit claimed breach of contract, breach of the implied covenant of good faith, unjust enrichment and tortious interference with contractual rights. Jerry responded by filing a $750 million antitrust lawsuit against the league. The Cowboys lawsuit claimed that NFL Properties centralized role violated anti-trust laws. The suit also claimed that the Texas Stadium sponsorships did not include Cowboys trademarks and were consistent with NFL Properties rules.

In addition to the legal action, Jerry Jones also informed the NFL that he intended to opt out of the trust agreement with NFL Properties when the deal expired in 1995, because Jones believed that the Cowboys could better market its brand and logo than the league could. With his counter-suit against the NFL, and his notice that the Cowboys would opt out of the NFL trust, Jerry essentially was saying, "ok, you want a war, well you've got one". And Jerry fully intended to win.

NFL Commissioner Paul Tagliabue invited Jerry Jones and several other NFL owners to the league office for a meeting about the legal dispute. According to those who were there, the commissioner was very confrontational, and as he addressed the group he chastised Jerry for having a lack of respect for the league, and as told by some in attendance, Jerry was incensed. He slammed his fist on the table and he said to Tagliabue, "I have come all the way from Dallas, Texas to meet with you. You sued me. I didn't sue you first. I don't even know if you have really read, or if any of these owners have read, what you sued me over. But let me tell you one damn thing; you're going to read it, and you're going to hear more about it!" Papers flew everywhere as Jerry Jones stormed out of the room and headed straight for the elevator. Pat Bowlen (Denver owner) and Jerry Richardson (Carolina owner) rushed out to ask Jerry not to leave.

In addition to the antitrust counter suit, the Cowboys filed a motion to dismiss the NFL Properties suit against them. This motion was granted, in part. With a portion of its suit dismissed, and facing an antitrust lawsuit, the NFL decided to settle the dispute with the Cowboys. The settlement agreement allowed Texas Stadium Corporation to maintain its contracts with Pepsi, Nike and American Express. It also allowed that every other NFL team had the opportunity to sign their own stadium sponsor agreements.

In the end Jerry was the big winner in the settlement, because the Cowboys also retained the right to enter into their own exclusive licensing agreements, in addition to the stadium rights. Yes, Jerry won. He won big.

Ultimately the actions of Jerry Jones and the Cowboys did not diminish the collective revenues of the league's other teams, as had been predicted by the NFL. The actions of the Cowboys actually opened more marketing opportunities for the individual franchises, as well as for the league. This has resulted in increased revenue for the league and for player payrolls. The financial gains for the Cowboys have been astounding. The franchise has annual revenue of over $600 million and cash flow of $250 million. This level of operating cash gives Jerry Jones an advantage in structuring long term contracts with short term salary cap benefits. What is need-ed to capitalize on this financial advantage, is better choices in the annual draft and efficient use of free agency.

Jerry Jones the General Manager had disappointing draft results from 1996 through 2010. As a result the Cowboys performance on the field was largely mediocre, and at times sub-par, with the exception of the 2007 and 2009 seasons.

Something seems to have changed beginning with the 2011 draft, that indicates that some important lessons have been learned by Jerry as the Cowboys GM. A preponderance of the evidence indicates that Jerry Jones has "figured it out". Now, not only is Jerry an innovative and financially successful NFL owner, but he also appears to be developing into a genuinely effective NFL general manager as well. This is the point at which the story changes for the Dallas Cowboy fans, and for the embattled GM Jerry Jones.

The amazing turn-around of the 2014 Dallas Cowboys, with a record of 12-4 and winning the NFC East, was fueled by key draft choices selected by Jerry in the drafts since 2011. In the 2011 draft Jerry selected left tackle Tyron Smith in the first round. Smith is the first offensive lineman that Jerry has ever taken in the first round. Tyron Smith has become a Pro Bowler and an All-Pro. He is a dominant left tackle. In the second round in 2011 Jerry selected linebacker Bruce Carter. He struggled during his first two years, but improved in 2013. In 2014 Carter had a very good year and helped stabilize what had literally been the NFL's worst defense in 2013. Carter played in 13 games and had a sack, five interceptions including one that was returned for a touchdown, and 57 tackles. Carter signed a free agent contract with Tampa Bay after the 2014 season. In the third round of the 2011 draft the Cowboys selected running back DeMarco Murray. He rushed for a solid 2,781 yards in his first three NFL seasons. In 2014 Murray became an All-Pro as he rushed for 1,845 yards, averaged 4.7 yards per rush and scored 13 touchdowns. Murray was the NFL's leading rusher in 2014. Murray signed a free agent contract with Philadelphia after the 2014 season.

In 2013 Jerry Jones took an offensive lineman in the first round for the second time in three years, when the Cowboys selected Travis Frederick from Wisconsin. He was installed as the Cowboys starting center and has started all 32 games of his career. He helped to further solidify the Cowboys offensive line, which had previously been a weakness of the team, surrendering 36 sacks in 2012. In the third round of 2013 the Cowboys drafted wide receiver Terrance Williams from Baylor. He has contributed with 81 receptions, and has averaged 16.8 yards per catch. Williams has 13 touchdowns, as the second receiver option to the primary Dez Bryant.

In the 2014 draft the change in the focus of GM Jerry Jones became undeniable, when he took an offensive lineman in the first round for the third time in four years. The Cowboys selected Zack Martin from Notre Dame. Martin was installed as the starting right guard and started all 16 games. The Cowboys offensive line was dominant in 2014. The Cowboys were second in the NFL in rushing, and fifth overall in total offense. Their ability to run the ball and control the clock was instrumental in the Cowboys resurgence in 2014. Zack Martin was named an All Pro for the 2014 season, the only rookie to be named to the 2014 All Pro Team.

#77 - Tyron Smith   #72 - Travis Frederick   #70 - Zack Martin

Jerry's draft performance of 2011-2014, and the impact that it has had on the improvement of the team in the 2014 season, is comparable to the Jimmy Johnson drafts of 1990-1993. In these four recent NFL drafts Jerry Jones has been focused and disciplined in his approach, and the key players that he has added to the Cowboys have positioned this team as a serious contender going into the 2015 season.

2014 draft:

Round	Pick	Position	Player name	University
1	16	OL	**Zack Martin**	Notre Dame
2	34	DE	**Demarcus Lawrence**	Boise St
4	119	LB	**Anthony Hitchens**	Iowa
5	146	WR	**Devin Street**	PITT
7	231	DE	**Ben Gardner**	Stanford
7	238	LB	Will Smith	TTech
7	248	SS	Ahmad Dixon	Baylor
7	251	DT	**Ken Bishop**	N Illinois
7	254	CB	Terrance Mitchell	Oregon

From the 2014 draft Zack Martin was an immediate success at offensive guard, earning All-Pro honors. Boise State defensive end DeMarcus Lawrence was drafted to help contribute to the pass rush off the edge, however he suffered a broken foot in training camp and missed most of 2014. He came back for the playoffs, and he contributed with a sack in the wild card game against Detroit, and another sack in the divisional playoff game at Green Bay. Anthony Hitchens had a good rookie season, appearing in all 16 games and he started in 11. Hitchens is expected to fill a prominent role due to the free agency losses of Bruce Carter and Justin Durant. Devin Street provides depth at wide receiver, although he didn't get many chances in 2014 due to the good health and productivity of Terrance Williams and Cole Beasley. The Cowboys got two players in the seventh round that provide depth for the defensive line rotation, with Ben Gardner and Ken Bishop. Gardner spent 2014 on the injured reserve after having surgery for a shoulder injury. Bishop spent much of 2014 on the practice squad, however he was active for the playoff game at Green Bay, and he contributed two tackles and three assists. Jerry gets a good score for the 2014 draft based on Zack Martin alone, and it appears that Lawrence and Hitchens will be solid contributors to the Cowboys defense. Adding depth to the defensive line with two players from the seventh round is an added bonus of the 2014 draft.

Jerry signed several free agents prior to the 2014 season, primarily attempting to shore up the defense, that had been so bad in 2013. The Cowboys signed defensive end Jeremy Mincey. The eight year NFL veteran would be a good signing, playing in all 16 games and producing six sacks, a defensed pass, 26 tackles and 20 assists. Mincey was signed for two years and a total of $3 million. The high profile signing was defensive tackle Henry Melton. He had made the pro bowl while playing for the Chicago Bears in 2012. Melton signed a one year incentive laden contract, as he was coming off of a serious 2013 knee surgery. Melton produced five sacks and fifteen quarterback pressures, but he missed the last six games of the year with another injury.

One of the most intriguing free agents signed by the Cowboys was linebacker Rolando McClain. He was an All-American at Alabama and was considered the best linebacker in college football. He helped Alabama win the national championship in 2010. McClain was drafted at number eight overall by Oakland in 2010. He signed with Baltimore in April 2013, but then retired having never played a game for the Ravens. The Cowboys traded a sixth round pick to Baltimore for his rights. McClain started 12 games at middle linebacker for Dallas in 2014, producing two interceptions, three defensed passes, one forced fumble, one sack, 67 tackles and 20 assists. McClain was a good emergency replacement for Sean Lee, who had injured his knee in the pre-season. McClain was also cheap, with a base salary of $750,000, plus incentives.

The remaining free agent signings included defensive tackle Terrell McClain, safety C.J. Spillman and backup quarterback Brandon Weeden. Overall Jerry's work in free agency was very productive, and also very salary cap friendly. More evidence that GM - Jerry has "figured it out".

The Cowboys went in to 2014 with relatively low expectations, given that they were coming off of three straight 8-8 seasons, and because statistically they had the worst defense in the NFL in 2013. The Cowboys had also gone four straight years missing the playoffs. The expectations were not improved by the Cowboys in their first game. Dallas hosted the San Francisco 49ers, who were coming off of a 12-4 record in 2013, that included a trip to the NFC Championship game, where they lost a close game to the eventual Super Bowl Champion Seattle Seahawks.

In game one at AT&T Stadium on September 7, 2014, the Cowboys won the toss and elected to receive. On the third offensive play of the game, DeMarco Murray was stood up on a running play while struggling for yardage, and the ball was stripped from his arm. The 49ers cornerback Chris Culliver picked up the fumble and ran 35 yards for a touchdown. One minute in to the game San Francisco lead 7-0 and the AT&T Stadium crowd was stunned. On their second offensive possession the Cowboys overcame a holding penalty and a nine yard sack of Tony Romo, to drive 69 yards to the 49ers eleven yard line, where Dan Bailey kicked a 29 yard field goal to make the score 7-3 with 7:26 left in the first quarter.

On San Francisco's next possession they drove 80 yards in four plays, taking just one minute and twenty three seconds to go ahead 14-3. The touchdown play was a 29 yard pass to a wide open Vernon Davis. On the third play of the next Cowboys possession Tony Romo's pass was intercepted by 49ers safety Eric Reid, and he returned it 48 yards to the Cowboys two yard line. On the next play Colin Kaepernick passed to Vernon Davis for the touchdown, and the 49ers lead Dallas 21-3 with 4:30 remaining in the first quarter!

The Cowboys then managed to drive to the San Francisco five yard line where they had a first and goal. Tony Romo tried to hit Jason Witten but he was covered and the pass was intercepted by Patrick Willis in the end zone. After a San Francisco punt Tony Romo tried a deep middle pass to Dez Bryant, and he was intercepted for the third time in the first half. San Francisco then drove 64 yards in two minutes and fifty seconds, using two timeouts and nine plays. Carlos Hyde scored the touchdown from four yards out and the 49ers lead the shell shocked Cowboys 28-3 at halftime.

In the second half the Cowboys defense held the 49ers to 98 total yards, and no further scoring. The Dallas offense had sustained scoring drives of 87 and 73 yards. The Cowboys committed no turnovers in the second half. The final score was 28-17, and at the time it seemed like "here we go again". The Cowboys lost to an elite team, as they typically had in the three previous 8-8 seasons.

In the second game of the regular season the Cowboys played at Tennessee. In the first week Tennessee had won at Kansas City 26-10, in a game in which the Titans held the Chiefs to 245 total yards while rushing for 160 yards and controlling the clock. Now it was the Titans home opener. This game continued the trend that the Cowboys had begun in the second half of the loss to San Francisco the week before. The Dallas defense had two sacks and two interceptions. The Cowboys offense controlled the ball with 41 minutes time of possession. Romo had no interceptions, DeMarco Murray had 167 yards rushing and a touchdown, and they converted on nine of sixteen third downs. The new offensive line with rookie Zack Martin starting at right guard was beginning to show their ability to be dominant. Dallas lead the game 16-0 at the half, and cruised to a 26-10 win, to even their record at 1-1.

Game three was at the 1-1 St Louis Rams, who started their third string quarterback, Austin Davis. The Cowboys fell behind 21-0 with six minutes remaining in the first half due to two turnovers and some weak defense. St Louis drove 80 yards in 15 plays on the game's opening possession and took a 7-0 lead. After the kickoff the Cowboys drove from their 22 yard line to the Rams 45. On a third down and four, Romo completed a short pass to DeMarco Murray for the first down, however while gaining extra yards Murray was hit and fumbled, and the Rams recovered at their 35 yard line. The Rams converted a first down and were facing a third down and thirteen to go at their 49, when Austin Davis hit Brian Quick for a 51 yard touchdown pass, to put St Louis ahead of the Cowboys 14-0 early in the second quarter.

The Cowboys and Rams traded punts, and the Cowboys got the ball at their 18 yard line with 7:35 left in the first half. On third down and eight from the Cowboys 20, Janoris Jenkins jumped a route and intercepted a Tony Romo pass that was intended for Dez Bryant, and he returned it untouched 25 yards for a Rams touchdown, to increase their lead to 21-0. On the next possession Dallas came alive. They got 39 yards rushing on three carries by DeMarco Murray, two key third down conversions, and a 26 yard pass interference call, to reach the Rams one yard line. DeMarco Murray powered in for the touchdown to cut the Rams lead to 21-7 with 2:10 remaining in the first half.

After the kickoff, St Louis drove from their 20 yard line to the Dallas 44, where they faced a third and one with just 0:42 remaining in the half. On a bizarre play, quarterback Austin Davis was in the shotgun formation, but Rams center Scott Wells snapped the ball as if Davis was "under center". The fumble was recovered by the Cowboys Henry Melton. Dallas had the ball at their own 47 with just 0:39 remaining. Tony Romo completed passes of 13 yards to Jason Witten, and 11 yards to DeMarco Murray to get the Cowboys to the Rams 11 yard line with five seconds left in the half. Dan Bailey kicked a 29 yard field goal to pull the Cowboys within 21-10 at the half.

The Cowboys got the ball to start the second half. Four plays in to the half, with a first down on their 32 yard line, Tony Romo found Dez Bryant running free behind the Rams secondary and he hit Dez for a 68 yard touchdown pass to cut the Rams lead to 21-17. The Rams responded by driving to the Cowboys 15 yard line, where they faced a fourth and one yard to go. Rather than take the easy field goal Jeff Fisher went for the first down. The Cowboys defense stuffed the run, and Dallas took over on downs at their 16 yard line. With a thirteen yard completion to Jason Witten, and a 44 yard run by DeMarco Murray, Dallas moved to the Rams 22 yard line, where Dan Bailey kicked a 40 yard field goal to cut the Rams lead to 21-20. The Rams then drove 72 yards in nine plays to get an answering field goal, and extend their lead to 24-20 with 13:31 remaining in the fourth quarter. Before the field goal, the Rams had a third and goal at the Cowboys three, when Austin Davis found his tight end Jared Cook in the end zone, but Cook dropped the pass that was right in his hands. For the Cowboys, it was a "better to be lucky than to be good" moment.

The Cowboys responded with an 84 yard drive in 12 plays to take the lead 27-24. The drive included a scramble by Tony Romo for 16 yards on a third and thirteen, a 20 yard pass to Terrance Williams on a third and fourteen, a 33 yard pass interference call on St Louis, and finally the 12 yard pass to Williams for the touchdown, with 6:21 remaining in the game. On the first play following the kickoff, Cowboys linebacker Bruce Carter intercepted Austin Davis and returned it 25 yards for a touchdown, to extend the Cowboys lead to 34-24.

St Louis would get a touchdown to cut the lead to 34-31, however the Cowboys defense forced an interception on the Rams final possession to preserve the win. The Cowboys had confirmed their newfound "commitment to the run", when they were trailing 21-0 in the second quarter. The Cowboy defense had forced three turnovers, and made stops when they had to. Dallas was 2-1, but it was not clear yet that these 2014 Cowboys were any better than the three prior 8-8 versions.

The Cowboys fourth game of 2014 was viewed as being a good measure of the Cowboys improvement, if any. The New Orleans Saints came to AT&T Stadium with a 1-2 record, however the Saints had lost two close games on the road, at Atlanta and an improving Cleveland team, then had soundly beaten Minnesota at home. In 2013 the Saints had whipped the Cowboys 49-17, and had made it to the NFC Division playoff where they lost to Seattle. So this game was considered a real test for the Cowboys. The Cowboys took the opening possession and drove 80 yards in 12 plays to take a 7-0 lead, and they never looked back. Dallas held Drew Brees to 84 yards passing in the first half, while taking a commanding 24-0 lead at the break. The Cowboys offense was physically dominant of the Saints, compiling 445 yards total offense, with no turnovers. DeMarco Murray rushed for 149 yards, and the Cowboys as a team totaled 190 yards on the ground, and 34 minutes in total time of possession. The defense sacked Drew Brees twice and forced one intercept-tion. In every phase of this game the Cowboys got pay-back for the 2013 whipping at the hands of the Saints. With the Cowboys now at 3-1 and leading the NFC East, many Cowboy doubters now had to consider that this version of the Dallas Cowboys just might be for real.

Next the Cowboys played host to the 3-1 Houston Texans. This game was "ugly". Dallas lead the Texans 3-0 at the half. The Cowboys took a 17-7 lead with 9:50 left in the fourth quarter, but then watched the Texans battle for a touchdown and a field goal to tie the game and send it to overtime. In the overtime Houston got the ball first, but was forced to punt on fourth down at midfield. Dallas then used 20 yards on four carries by Murray, and a 37 yard leaping grab by Dez Bryant from Tony Romo, to set up the game winning 49 yard field goal by Dan Bailey. Dallas improved to 4-1, having won their fourth consecutive game. They had shown that they could win against a quality NFL team even when they were not playing at their best. Next the Cowboys would travel to Seattle to play the defending Super Bowl Champion Seahawks.

Dallas went into the potentially intimidating environment of Seattle's CenturyLink Field, known for "the 12's", a reference to the extremely boisterous Seattle home crowd. Seattle got the first possession of the game. Helped by a 53 yard pass completion to Jermaine Kearse, the Seahawks got a 33 yard field goal by Steven Hauschka to take the lead 3-0, five minutes in to the game. On the Cowboys first possession, they gained a first down, but then faced a fourth and three at their 38 yard line. The Seahawks Doug Baldwin came free on the punt rush and he blocked Chris Jones punt. Mike Morgan grabbed the loose ball and returned it 25 yards for a touchdown. Eight minutes in to the game Seattle lead Dallas 10-0.

With 7:13 remaining in the first quarter, and in a hole on the road, the Dallas Cowboys offense began asserting its will on the Seattle Seahawks defense. Dallas got a 21 yard pass completion to Jason Witten and a 38 yard run by Joseph Randle, on its way to a nine play, 80 yard touchdown drive that stunned the Seattle crowd and pulled the Cowboys within 10-7. After a Seattle punt pinned the Cowboys at their own five yard line, the Cowboys offense went back to work. They mixed the running of DeMarco Murray and Joseph Randle with the passing of Tony Romo to Dez Bryant, to keep Seattle's defense on its heels. Dallas got nine rushes for 41 yards and passes to Dez Bryant of 13 and 11 yards during a 71 yard march to the Seahawks 24. When the drive stalled Dan Bailey kicked a 42 yard field goal to tie the game 10-10 with 5:20 left in the first half.

Seattle went three and out, and punted. Dallas took over at their own 20 with 3:04 remaining in the first half. Again, the Dallas Cowboys offense proceeded to impose its will on the Seattle defense. There were nifty catch and runs by Lance Dunbar of 21, and 18 yards, and a 23 yard catch by Dez Bryant, beating Richard Sherman and getting an extra 10 penalty yards on a tripping penalty on Sherman. Finally there was the three yard touchdown pass from Romo to Jason Witten. The Cowboys had driven 80 yards in 10 plays in 2:48 to take the lead on Seattle 17-10, at the half.

In the third quarter with 7:09 remaining Seattle was forced to punt. The Cowboys Dwayne Harris muffed the punt catch and fumbled, and Seattle recovered the loose ball at the Dallas 14 yard line. It took just two plays for Seattle to score and tie the game at 17-17. On third down of the ensuing Dallas drive Tony Romo was hit and fumbled, and Seattle recovered on the Dallas 20 yard line. The Cowboys defense was up to the task, and on a fourth and 13 from the Cowboy 23, Seattle kicked a 33 yard field goal to lead 20-17 with 3:25 left in the third quarter.

On the first play after the kickoff, from the Dallas 19 yard line Tony Romo hit Terrance Williams for 47 yards to the Seattle 39 yard line. Then on fourth and nine from the 38, Dan Bailey kicked a 56 yard field goal to tie the score 20-20 with 1:08 left in the third quarter. Seattle and Dallas exchanged punts to start the fourth quarter. Then Seattle had a short drive that stalled at the Cowboys 30 yard line, and the Seahawks kicked a 48 yard field goal to lead again 23-20, with 8:21 left to play in the game.

Once again the Dallas Cowboys offense reasserted its will upon the Seattle defense. During this drive the Cowboys would have to overcome a holding penalty and three plays that resulted in no gain. The Cowboys converted a 16 yard pass completion on a third and five. They also got a pass completion for 23 yards to Terrance Williams on a third and twenty. This completion to Williams was reminiscent of the Drew Pearson "toe tap" completion on December 28, 1975 that gave the Cowboys the first down, that lead to the famed "hail Mary" touchdown pass that helped Dallas defeat Minnesota. On the next play DeMarco Murray went through right tackle for 25 yards to the Seattle 21 yard line. On first and ten Murray ran for six yards. On second and four from the fifteen, Murray burst up the middle for 15 yards and the go ahead touchdown. Dallas took the lead on Seattle 27-23 with just 3:23 remaining in the game.

Seattle had four desperation plays trying to convert a first down, and they failed. Dallas took possession at the 23 yard line with 2:35 remaining. Dallas ran the ball three times and kicked a field goal to lead 30—23 with one minute remaining. On Seattle's second play after the kickoff Russell Wilson's pass was intercepted by Cowboys linebacker Rolando McClain, to end the game. Dallas had won their fifth straight game to improve to 5-1. Now everyone in the NFL world was paying attention to what was going on in Dallas. And I was starting to think, there is more going on here than just this five game winning streak. This is about the last four drafts, and our GM's new approach to his job. This is a really big story, not just wishful thinking.

Next up the Cowboys hosted the division rival NY Giants. The Giants came in to this game with a record of 3-3, but having won three of its last four games. Dallas actually fell behind the Giants for about five minutes in the second quarter (14-7), but relatively controlled the game with their ball control offense. The Cowboys had 33:49 time of possession, and rushed for 156 yards. DeMarco Murray had 128 yards on the ground, and became the first NFL running back to ever begin a season with seven straight 100 yard games. Tony Romo had three touchdown passes and Dez Bryant had 151 yards receiving. When the Giants pulled within 28-21 with 5:28 left in the fourth quarter, the Cowboys went on a clock killing drive that resulted in a game clinching field goal with less than a minute remaining. Dallas won 31-21 for their sixth straight win, to improve to 6-1. This was the second game of 2014 in which DeMarco Murray had more rushing attempts than Tony Romo had pass attempts. Amazing.

Next up was a Monday night game in AT&T Stadium against the 2-5 Redskins, who had not won an NFC East game since the final game of the 2012 season. Washington was starting their third string quarterback, Colt McCoy. On paper this looked like the Cowboys seventh win in a row, and a 7-1 start to 2014. But there is an old saying in the NFL, "on any given day"...and this was one of those. Tony Romo was sacked five times, and in the third quarter Tony was knocked out of the game. Romo took a brutal direct hit to his lower back from Keenan Robinson. Tony reached for his back after the hit and stayed flat on the ground, as the crowd was in shock. He lay motionless on the field for several minutes before getting up and walking off under his own power. There was 7:59 remaining in the third quarter and the Cowboys trailed Washington 10-7. The Cowboys would get a 51 yard run by DeMarco Murray to set up a short field goal and tie the game at 10-10. Colt McCoy then drove the Redskins 80 yards, with the help of a 45 yard completion to DeSean Jackson, and McCoy capped the drive with a seven yard quarterback draw to give Washington a 17-10 lead with 13:44 left in the fourth quarter. Brandon Weeden then took the Cowboys on an 80 yard drive in eight plays, that took just over four minutes, to tie the game at 17-17. Each team had one possession in the final nine minutes, however the regulation time ended in a tie.

In overtime Washington got the first possession. Colt McCoy took the Redskins on a 58 yard drive that included a 23 yard completion to Pierre Garcon, and a nifty scramble in the pocket that allowed McCoy to complete a 16 yard sideline route to Jordan Reed. Washington stalled at the Cowboys 22 yard line. Kai Forbath kicked a 40 yard field goal to give Washington the lead 23-20. The Cowboys were unable to convert a first down on their possession, and the Redskins prevailed 23-20, to drop Dallas record to 6-2.

Next was another home game, this time hosting the 6-1 Arizona Cardinals. The Cowboys would have to play without the injured Tony Romo, so Brandon Weeden got the start. The Cowboys got a good break in the first quarter when rookie Tyler Patmon stepped in front of a Carson Palmer pass and returned it 58 yards for a touchdown. It was all downhill from there for the Cowboys though, as Brandon Weeden was just bad. Weeden was 18 of 33 for 183 yards, and threw two interceptions. With Romo out the Cardinals defense keyed on DeMarco Murray, and held him to 92 yards rushing. Unable to run the ball consistently, and with Weeden out of sync, the Cardinals took control of the game late in the second quarter. The Cowboys never threatened. Arizona won 28-17. The post-game conversation was not about Brandon Weeden needing to improve, it was about the time line for Tony Romo's return. The 6-3 Cowboys had one more game to play before their bye week, so speculation was to rest Romo one more week, and with the bye week following he would effectively have four weeks of recovery before taking contact again.

The next game was in London against the 1-8 Jacksonville Jaguars. The talk early in the game week was that Tony Romo would make the trip to London with the team. So much for resting Tony's injured back. Romo did make the trip to London, and he prepared for the game. Romo was very sharp and the Cowboys offense was clicking as a result. This was an easy win for Dallas from start to finish. The Cowboys lead Jacksonville 24-7 at the half, 31-7 after three quarters, and 31-9 in the fourth quarter before the Jaguars got a late touchdown to make the score closer. DeMarco Murray had 100 yards rushing and another 31 yards receiving. Dez Bryant had 158 yards receiving on six catches including two for touchdowns. Romo was a nifty 20 for 27 for 246 yards and three touchdowns. The Cowboys won in London to improve to 7-3, and would now have a bye week to rest and to heal the bumps and bruises.

After the bye week break the Cowboys traveled to New York to face the 3-7 NY Giants in a Sunday night nationally televised game. On this "big stage" Giants wide receiver

Odell Beckham Jr made what has been widely called one of the greatest catches in NFL history. But Beckham's heroics would be upstaged by a late Cowboy come back. This was a classic NFC East matchup. The Giants started strong by driving 80 yards for a touchdown on the game's first possession. The Cowboys got a Dan Bailey 38 yard field goal to pull within 7-3 with 2:50 left in the first quarter. Then Beckham amazed everyone with his one handed catch of Eli Manning's 43 yard rainbow pass, while being interfered with by the Cowboys Brandon Carr, and falling backward into the end zone to put New York ahead 14-3 on the first play of the second quarter.

Tony Romo and the Cowboys offense responded with a 77 yard drive that was capped by a shovel pass to Jason Witten for a four yard touchdown to cut the Giants lead to 14-10. On the Giants next possession Beckham went to work again on the Cowboys secondary. Beckham made three catches for 32 yards to help the Giants on another 80 yard march, that culminated in a three yard touchdown run by Andre Williams. The Giants lead Dallas 21-10 at the half.

The Cowboys did not have much going offensively until Tony Romo completed a short pass to Cole Beasley, who then turned it into a 45 yard catch and run touchdown to pull Dallas within 21-17 with 6:48 left in the third quarter. Eli Manning then drove New York to the Dallas 18 yard line,

271

where they had a first and ten. On the next play Manning overthrew his receiver and Barry Church intercepted the errant pass and returned it 45 yards to the Cowboys 48 yard line. Four plays later Tony Romo hit Dez Bryant who fought his way to the end zone to put Dallas ahead 24-21 with 1:19 left in the third quarter.

The fourth quarter would be a fight to the finish. The Giants got the ball on their seven yard line with 9:12 left in the game. Manning drove the Giants 93 yards in 14 plays, using 6:12, with the touchdown coming on a one yard pass to Adrien Robinson to put the Giants ahead 28-24 with 3:06 left in the game. This is when the three first round draft choices of the last four years on the Cowboys offensive line took over the game. Tony Romo had a clean pocket with which to work as he methodically drove the Cowboys 80 yards in seven plays in 1:59. The touchdown came on a 13 yard pass to Dez Bryant, to put Dallas ahead for good 31-28. The Giants could not get a first down, and the Cowboys ran out the clock. Dallas improved to 8-3 and they were 5-0 on the road in 2014.

After playing a Sunday night game in New York, the Cowboys had to quickly turn around and play on Thursday for the Thanksgiving Day game. They hosted the 8-3 Philadelphia Eagles, with first place in the NFC East on the line. From the opening kickoff the Eagles dominated the

Cowboys on both sides of the ball. Philadelphia scored touchdowns on their first two drives to take a 14-0 lead in the first quarter. With the help of a 38 yard pass from Romo to Dez Bryant the Cowboys cut the lead to 14-7 early in the second quarter. The Cowboys had to put up three defensive stands to hold the Eagles to field goals in the second quarter, and Philadelphia lead 23-7 at the half.

The Cowboys got a field goal early in the third quarter after recovering an Eagles fumble, to make it 23-10, but that was as close as they would ever get. Philadelphia pulled away to win 33-10 and take over first place in the NFC East. Tony Romo looked out of sync and inaccurate. The Cowboy offensive line lacked the dominance they showed in New York four days earlier. Philadelphia dominated every phase of this game. The Cowboys had 93 yards rushing, and only 267 total yards. They committed three turnovers and were called for six penalties. They were just four of twelve on third down conversions. Dallas fell to 8-4. It was a game to forget, as they would have just seven days to prepare for their next game, on a Thursday night at Chicago.

The NFL schedule makers did the Dallas Cowboys no favors at the end of November 2014. First they scheduled them on a Sunday night in New York, three days before the Thanksgiving Day game. Then they scheduled the Cowboys for a Thursday night game on the road right after playing on

Thanksgiving Day! The trip to Chicago was a return to the scene of a massacre one year earlier on December 9, 2013, when Chicago hosted the Cowboys, and the Bears scored on eight consecutive possessions to embarrass Dallas on national television, 45-28. This trip to Chicago was made by an entirely different Cowboy team than the one that was there in 2013.

In the first half DeMarco Murray had 65 yards rushing and 40 yards receiving, as he gave Tony Romo a check down pass option to beat the Bears rush. Romo completed 17 of 21 first half passes for 123 yards, including a 13 yard touchdown to Cole Beasley just 0:13 before the half ended, to take a 14-7 lead over the Bears. Early in the second half the Cowboys Anthony Spencer stripped Matt Forte of a screen pass and the Cowboys recovered at midfield. Tony Romo then hit a leaping Cole Beasley for a 24 yard touchdown pass to go up 21-7. On their next possession, after Tony Romo hit Dez Bryant for a 43 yard gain, Romo hooked up with tight end Gavin Escobar in the back of the end zone to stretch the lead to 28-7. After a Chicago punt, DeMarco Murray broke a 27 yard run to move the Cowboys inside the Chicago 20 yard line. Two plays later Joseph Randle broke off a 17 yard touchdown run for a commanding 35-7 lead with 2:18 left in the third quarter. The Cowboys finished the Bears off 41-28, to improve to 9-4, and 6-0 on the road in 2014. Now the

Cowboys would get ten days to prepare for a rematch with the Philadelphia Eagles.

The Cowboys went to Philadelphia to face the 9-4 Eagles. Two weeks earlier the Eagles had come to Dallas on Thanksgiving Day and dominated the Cowboys 33-10. To start the game the Cowboys special teams alertly recovered the kickoff when the kick was short, and it landed between the Eagles deep returner and their short man, at about the Eagles 15. The Cowboys CJ Spillman covered the loose ball at the Philadelphia 18 yard line. Four plays later, and just two minutes in to the game DeMarco Murray scored from the one yard line to put Dallas up 7-0.

After the Eagles were forced to punt, Dallas started at their twelve yard line, and drove 88 yards in 16 plays, with the touchdown coming on a four yard pass to Dez Bryant. With 3:08 left in the first quarter Dallas lead 14-0. The Eagles had a three and out and punted. Dallas started at their own 44 yard line, and they faced a second down and eleven, when Tony Romo found Dez Bryant down the right sideline for 26 yards and a touchdown, to go ahead 21-0 with 12:01 to go in the second quarter.

Philadelphia finally found some life offensively, and starting from their 16 the Eagles drove 84 yards in 11 plays, taking just 3:24 to cut the lead to 21-7. After the Cowboys were forced to punt, the Eagles took over at their own 28. They drove to the Cowboys 29 yard line where they faced a fourth and thirteen, so they settled for a 47 yard field goal to make the score Dallas 21 Philadelphia 10, at the half.

The Cowboys were forced to punt on their first possession of the third quarter. The Eagles responded by quickly covering 86 yards in seven plays in just 2:46, to cut the Cowboys lead to 21-17. On the fifth play of the Cowboys next possession, Tony Romo was sacked and he fumbled, and the Eagles recovered at the Dallas 14 yard line. It took just three plays to score and Philadelphia had come back to take the lead 24-21 after having trailed the Cowboys 21-0 early in the second quarter.

The Cowboys quickly regrouped, and they drove 78 yards in eight plays, with Murray scoring from the two, to put Dallas back ahead 28-24. Three plays in to the Eagles next possession the Cowboys J.J. Wilcox intercepted Mark Sanchez and returned to the Eagles 42. Four plays later Tony Romo hooked up with Dez Bryant for 25 yards, and the Cowboys lead the Eagles 35-24 with 12:55 left to play. The two teams would trade field goals, and the Cowboys defense held the Eagles in check, as the Cowboys won 38-27 to improve to 10-4, and avenge the Thanksgiving Day loss, and take over first place in the NFC East. The Cowboys also stretched their 2014 road record to 7-0.

The Cowboys next hosted 10-4 Andrew Luck and the Indianapolis Colts. Dallas came in to this home game on a three game home losing streak. The Cowboys started the game with an opening drive 80 yard touchdown march to lead 7-0. Dallas defense forced a fourth and eleven, and then the Colts had Dallas beaten on a fake punt, but the punter's perfect pass was dropped when it hit the receiver in the hands. This gave Dallas possession on the Colts 19 yard line. On the next play Tony Romo hit Dez Bryant with a 19 yard touchdown pass to put the Cowboys ahead 14-0. The Cowboys pushed the lead to 28-0 by halftime.

The Cowboys went ahead 35-0 in the third quarter when Tony Romo hit Jason Witten for a 25 yard touchdown pass. On the play Tony Romo broke Troy Aikman's franchise record for total yards passing. The Colts finally scored with 5:29 remaining in the game. The Cowboys won 42-7 to up their record to 11-4, and they clinched the NFC East as Philadelphia lost at Washington.

The final game of the season was at the 4-11 Washington Redskins. The Cowboys had the NFC East and their playoff spot clinched, but they had one piece of business to resolve. They needed to avenge the overtime loss to the Redskins from week eight. The Cowboys also had the chance to finish the season 8-0 on the road. Dallas scored on their first five possessions to take a 27-7 lead in the second quarter, including touchdown passes of 65 and 23 yards to Dez Bryant, and a DeMarco Murray touchdown run of nine yards.

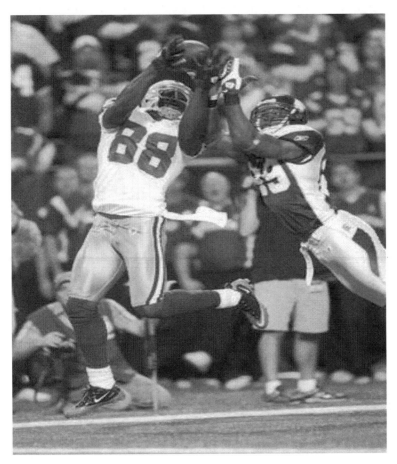

2014 All-Pro Dez Bryant

The Cowboys stretched the lead to 37-17 in the fourth quarter when defensive tackle Terrell McClain sacked Robert Griffin III and forced a fumble, which was picked up by Anthony Spencer and run into the end zone for a defensive touchdown. The Cowboys scored again with 1:49 left in the fourth quarter when Joseph Randle broke a 65 yard run on an off tackle running play, making the final score Dallas 44 Washington 17. Payback delivered. The Cowboys finished the year 12-4, with an 8-0 road record. Champions of the NFC East. In this game DeMarco Murray passed Emmitt Smith's single season rushing record of 1,773 yards, as Murray totaled 1,845. Dez Bryant topped Terrell Owens single season touchdown catch record (15) with his sixteenth touchdown pass of 2014.

At 12-4 the Cowboys tied with Seattle and Green Bay for the best record in the NFC. However, the tie breaker was win percentage in the conference. Dallas lost that tie breaker with Seattle and Green Bay, so the Cowboys hosted the Detroit Lions in a wild card playoff game. The Lions had gone 11-5 in 2014, and they had the second best defense in the league, based on average yards allowed per game. The leaders were Ndamukong Suh (8.5 sacks), DE - Ezekiel Ansah (7.5 sacks) and DE – George Johnson (6 sacks). Detroit also had play makers on offense with Matthew Stafford, Calvin Johnson ("Megatron"), and first year free agent Golden Tate had made the pro-bowl as well. Detroit was a very worthy wild card opponent for the Cowboys.

The Cowboys got the first possession of the game, and the Lions stout defense held them to three yards in three plays, forcing a punt. The Lions then went 62 yards in four plays in just 2:04 to go ahead 7-0 just over three minutes in to the game. The big play was a 51 yard pass to Golden Tate for the touchdown.

The Cowboys gained one first down and were forced to punt again. The punt pinned the Lions on their one yard line. The Lions did not get a first down and were going to punt from their six yard line, but the Cowboys were called for running in to the kicker, so Detroit got a new set of downs at their 11 yard line. Detroit went on to drive 99 yards in 7:10 to take a 14-0 lead on Dallas with 2:06 left in the first quarter. The Lions and Cowboys then exchanged four punts through the second quarter, until the Cowboys took possession at their own 26 yard line with 2:15 left in the first half. On a third and two the Cowboys were called for offensive pass interference, and then faced third and twelve at their 24 with 1:50 left in the first half, still trailing 14-0. It didn't look good, but on the next play Terrance Williams took a short pass over the middle from Romo, and he turned it into a 76 yard touch-down catch and run to pull the Cowboys within 14-7. But Detroit was not through. Matthew Stafford drove the Lions 59 yards in ten plays, using two timeouts, and they managed a 39 yard field goal to lead the Cowboys 17-7 at the half.

The second half seemed to start well for the Cowboys, when on the first play Matthew Stafford was intercepted by the Cowboys Kyle Wilber at the Detroit 19 yard line. On third and one at the Detroit ten, Tony Romo was sacked for a thirteen yard loss, and the Cowboys were forced to kick a field goal. However, Dan Bailey missed from 41 yards. The Lions then drove to the Dallas 19 yard line, where on fourth and three they kicked a field goal to go ahead 20-7 with 8:44 left in the third quarter.

The Cowboys then started their next drive at their own 20 yard line. DeMarco Murray got a seven yard pass, followed by two runs totaling 23 yards to reach mid-field. Then, on a third and ten, Tony Romo hit Dez Bryant for 43 yards to the Lions seven yard line. After a holding penalty backed the Cowboys up, Romo hit Cole Beasley for fifteen yards to the Detroit two yard line. DeMarco got the touchdown run to bring the Cowboys within 20-14 with 2:55 left in the third quarter.

Detroit had a three and out and punted. Dallas took over at their 31 yard line. Tony Romo hit Cole Beasley for 19 yards, and then 12 yards, and on the second catch Detroit was called for unnecessary roughness (15 yards) moving the ball to the Detroit 18 yard line. Then Ndamukong Suh sacked Tony Romo two consecutive plays, to give Dallas a fourth and 25 at the Detroit 33 yard line. Dan Bailey kicked a 51 yard field goal to pull Dallas to within 20-17 with 12:21 left in the fourth quarter.

Dallas pinned Detroit on their five yard line on the kickoff coverage. Detroit managed to drive to the Dallas 46 yard line where they faced a third and one. This is where significant controversy ensued. Rather than run for the one yard, the Lions tried a pass to tight end Brandon Pettigrew. Matthew Stafford's pass was underthrown, and it actually hit Cowboys linebacker Anthony Hitchens on his shoulder and fell incomplete. The back judge flagged the Cowboy's Hitchens for pass interference. The referee announced the penalty, and marked it off giving Detroit the first down. Then, after a huddle of the officials the head linesman overruled the call and waved off the penalty. Points of fact are, the pass was underthrown, there was no significant contact by Hitchens, and there is no longer a penalty for "face guarding" in the NFL. Detroit then faced a fourth and one at the Cowboys 46 yard line. The Detroit offense lined up to go for it on fourth down, but just tried to draw the Cowboys defense off side. When that didn't happen, they took a five yard delay of game penalty and lined up to punt. The Detroit punt, however was very poor and only netted ten yards.

Dallas got the ball at their 41 yard line trailing 20-17 with 8:10 left in the game. Dallas got a 13 yard run by DeMarco, but then faced a fourth down and six yards to go at the Detroit 42 yard line. The Cowboys called timeout to talk it over. There was 6:00 remaining in the game. Jason Garrett decided to go for it. Tony Romo found Jason Witten for a short pass to get the first down, and Witten turned it into a 21 yard gain to the Detroit 21 yard line. Two defensive holding calls on Detroit got Dallas to the eight yard line. The Cowboys faced third and goal from the eight when Tony Romo hit a streaking Terrance Williams for the touchdown to put Dallas ahead for the first time in the game 24-20 with 2:39 left to play.

After the kickoff Detroit started at their 20 yard line with plenty of time (2:32) to get the potential winning touchdown. On second and four at their 26, Matthew Stafford was sacked by the Cowboys Anthony Spencer, and Stafford fumbled. The fumble was picked up by the Cowboys DeMarcus Lawrence, but he was hit and fumbled back to the Lions with 2:10 remaining. Detroit drove to the Dallas 42 yard line where they faced a fourth and three with 1:00 left to play. Stafford dropped back to pass and he was hit by DeMarcus Lawrence, and he fumbled again, and this time Lawrence secured the fumble recovery. Tony Romo kneeled down and the game was over. Dallas defeated Detroit in the wild card game 24-20.

The Cowboys advanced to the NFC divisional playoff round for the first time since 2009, and only the second time since 1996. This was the first time the Cowboys would play a playoff game at Lambeau Field since the famed 1967 Ice

Bowl. The Green Bay Packers were 12-4 in 2014 and champions of the NFC North Division. Dallas got the first possession of the game, and they went three and out. On Green Bay's first possession they went 60 yards in 10 plays to take a 7-0 lead. Eddie Lacy rushed for 45 of the 60 yards. The touchdown was a four yard pass from Aaron Rodgers to Andrew Quarless in the back of the end zone. The Cowboys answered with a 62 yard drive in 12 plays in 7:25, to tie the score 7-7. The touchdown was a "1 yard" pass from Romo to fullback Tyler Clutts, who was wide open and made a nice catch for the score with 1:09 left in the first quarter.

On the following possession Aaron Rodgers had driven the Packers to the Dallas 27 yard line where they faced a third down and seven. Rodgers was in the shotgun in his snap count, and was clapping his hands when rookie center Corey Linsley snapped the ball. Rodgers dropped it, but then picked it up. The Cowboys defensive end Jeremy Mincey rushed in and hit Rodgers causing him to fumble. Mincey recovered the fumble for Dallas at their 36 yard line. Dallas got three carries for fifteen yards from DeMarco Murray, and an 11 yard completion from Romo to Cole Beasley to reach the Packers 38 yard line. On second and seven Romo hit Terrance Williams with a quick slant, and Williams broke Tramon Williams tackle and turned up the field and raced 38 yards for the touchdown to put Dallas ahead 14-7 with 8:29 remaining in the half.

Green Bay managed to convert one first down on their next possession, but then were forced to punt. Dallas took over at their 19 yard line. They got one first down and then faced a third and seven on their 35 yard line, when Romo hit Jason Witten for 18 yards to the Packers 47. A five yard run by Murray and two completions to Witten got Dallas to the Green Bay 27 where they faced a fourth and one with 0:34 left in the half. Dallas lined up for a field goal attempt of 45 yards, but they were called for a false start. The field goal attempt from 50 yards was blocked by Datone Jones, and the Packers got the ball on the 40 with 0:29 left. The Packers did not kneel down to end the half. First Rodgers hit Randle Cobb for 12 yards to the Cowboys 48, where they called a timeout. On the next play DeMarcus Lawrence sacked Aaron Rodgers back to the Packers 42. Green Bay called timeout with 0:16 left in the half. On second and 20 Randle Cobb found a hole in the Cowboys zone and Rodgers hit him for 31 yards to the Dallas 27. Another completion to Davante Adams got them to the Dallas 22, where Mason Crosby kicked a 40 yard field to end the half.

Rather than Dallas extending their lead to 17-7, Green Bay had narrowed the gap to 14-10 at the half. This was a critical six point swing.

Early in the third quarter there was another critical game changing play for Green Bay. On the play Dallas had a first down on their 41. Romo handed off to DeMarco Murray, who had a huge hole on the right side and it appeared that he would have a long gain. However, Julius Peppers who was not in position to make the tackle, was able to poke the ball from Murray's grasp, and Green Bay recovered the fumble at the Dallas 44. The Packers were able to turn this possession into a field goal to cut the Dallas lead to 14-13 with 7:49 left in the third quarter.

Dallas responded with an 80 yard drive in six plays in just 3:30, to go up 21-13 with 4:16 left in the third quarter. The drive included a 20 yard completion to Dez Bryant, 15 yards to Jason Witten and a 26 yard run by DeMarco Murray. The Packers came right back. Aaron Rodgers got completions of 16 yards to Davante Adams, and 26 yards to Randall Cobb to reach the Dallas 46 yard line. Then Aaron Rodgers hit Davante Adams for what appeared would be another Packer first down, but Adams shook off a tackle, and beat three Cowboy defenders for a 46 yard touchdown to cut the Cowboys lead to 21-20 at the end of the third quarter.

After the Green Bay touchdown Tony Romo was sacked two consecutive plays to put Dallas in a third and 23 hole. The Cowboys were forced to punt. Green Bay took over at their 20 with 13:29 left in the game. Aaron Rodgers had seven straight completions to drive the Packers 80 yards in eight plays to give Green Bay the lead 26-21 with 9:10 left to play. The Packers tried a two point conversion but it failed.

What followed was the bizarre of the NFL and its rule makers, as well as a great NFL team forcing its will to win upon its opponent. Dallas started at its 18 yard line. On first down DeMarco Murray went for 30 yards to the Dallas 48. Romo completed to Bryant for a first down to the Green Bay 40 yard line. After another critical sack of Romo, Dallas faced third and 11. Romo hit Cole Beasley but he was stopped two yards short of the first down. Dallas had a fourth and two at the Packers 32 yard line, with 4:42 remaining in the game. Jason Garrett decided to go for it. The Cowboys lined up in the shotgun, with no backs in the backfield, and with four wide receivers. On the snap Romo made his decision quickly, and he threw deep down the left sideline to Dez Bryant who was covered by Sam Shields. Romo's pass was slightly underthrown, so while Shield's coverage was good the underthrow gave Bryant a chance to make a play on the ball. Bryant leaped high in the air and caught the ball with both hands. Dez pulled the ball in against his shoulder as he began to come back down to the ground. Then as both feet touched the ground and his momentum carried him forward, he switched the ball to his left hand, and his right arm made contact with the field at about the one yard line.

Dez extended his left hand with the ball cradled in it against his arm, toward the goal line. As his body made full contact with the ground his left arm and hand bounced on the ground, and the ball popped up slightly, and he regained his grip on the ball without dropping it. On viewing the play in live action it appeared to be a good catch, giving the Cowboys a first and goal at the Packers one yard line. Packers coach Mike McCarthy threw the challenge flag, and upon further review the NFL review officials overruled the catch, turning over the ball on downs to Green Bay at their 32 yard line with 4:06 remaining.

Green Bay proceeded to convert two first downs. The Cowboys defense could not stop Aaron Rodgers, Davante Adams and Randall Cobb. The Packers ran out the clock with Tony Romo and his offense watching helplessly on their sideline, and Green Bay won the NFC Division playoff game over Dallas 26-21.

This game was not decided by the controversial catch over-rule in the fourth quarter. This game was decided by the blocked field goal late in the second quarter that caused the six point swing in 34 seconds, by the Cowboys inability to slow down Davante Jones and Randall Cobb, by Julius Pepper's forcing the fumble on the potentially big run in the third quarter, by the poor tackling of the Cowboys secondary, and by the excellent play of the hobbled Aaron Rodgers.

The Dallas Cowboys 2014 season was a great success, and was not foreseen by any NFL preseason projections. The 2014 Cowboys came together with a blend of talent, effort and some good fortune. There is a lot to build upon from the 2014 season. For the first time in 20 years the Dallas Cowboys are genuinely good, and a serious contender in the NFC. Their weaknesses are primarily on defense, but they did improve in 2014 to the 19th ranked defense, as compared to number 32 in 2013.

Looking forward to 2015 The Dallas Cowboys should be stronger than the 2014 team. They will return a top five NFL offense that features a young and dominant offensive line, a receiving core with All-Pro Dez Bryant, Terrance Williams, All-Pro Jason Witten and slot receiver Cole Beasley, as well as the four-time Pro Bowl quarterback Tony Romo. There is a question at running back with the free agency loss of DeMarco Murray. However it is widely known that Murray's emergence with the Cowboys paralleled that of Jerry's building of this offensive line with three first round choices in four years between 2011 and 2014. The Cowboys currently have Joseph Randle, Lance Dunbar, Ryan Williams and newly added free agent Darren McFadden. With the threat of the Cowboys vertical passing game and Romo's accuracy, as well as the solid offensive line, there will be continued production from the Cowboys running game. Look for the

Cowboys to be active in the free agent running back market in the 2015 summer.

Four-time Pro Bowl quarterback Tony Romo

The Dallas Cowboys will be a favorite in the NFC, along with Seattle and Green Bay, to compete for a spot in Super Bowl 50. The Cowboys chances for success will hinge on the improvement of their defense, as well as the health of Tony Romo. The defense should be better with the return of Sean Lee, and the additions of first round pick Byron Jones (cornerback), second rounder Randy Gregory (linebacker), free agent Greg Hardy (although suspended part of 2015) as well as the re-signing of linebacker Rolando McClain.

It is great to be a Cowboy fan, and 2015 could be our year to get back on top. Go Cowboys!

AT&T Stadium, home of the five time world champion Dallas Cowboys

"Mr. Cowboy" -- Bob Lilly

Dallas Cowboys, Americas Team Is Back

Chapter Seven

The 70's Cowboys
The Glory Years

I have spent all of my time in this book to this point, covering the events of the Jerry Jones ownership since 1989. Now I will spend some time recounting some of the glorious and fun memories of the Cowboys colorful history. The 1970's are just full of great performances and historical events. I hope that reading this chapter will bring you as much enjoyment as it brought to me in recounting it.

I am not old enough to actually remember first-hand the Dallas Cowboys of the 1960's. As with most expansion teams the Cowboys were pitiful in their early years. It took the Cowboys seven years to have their first winning record. But once they got good, they stayed good for a long time. The Cowboys first draft pick in franchise history was Bob Lilly. He has been appropriately dubbed "Mr. Cowboy". What a way to start a franchise! A defensive lineman from the Southwest Conference. Bob Lilly was elected to the NFL Hall of Fame in 1980.

The Cowboys had some legendary names on the roster in the late 60's: Larry Cole, Walt Garrison, Cornell Green, Bob Hayes, Chuck Howley, Lee Roy Jordan, Bob Lilly, Don Meredith, Ralph Neely, John Niland, Don Perkins, Jethro Pugh, Dan Reeves, Mel Renfro, Lance Rentzel, Rayfield Wright, Mike Ditka, and Calvin Hill to name a few.

The Cowboys made it to the 1966 NFL Championship Game, where they were defeated by the Green Bay Packers 34-27. Green Bay went on to win Super Bowl I over Kansas City (AFL) 35-10.

In 1967 the Cowboys again advanced to the NFL Championship Game, again playing the Green Bay Packers. This was the famed "Ice Bowl game", played at Lambeau Field. The game time temperature was reported to have been minus 15 degrees. It is said to be the coldest playoff game ever played. It is also considered to be one of the most famous NFL playoff games ever played. The Packers won the game 21-17 on a Bart Starr quarterback sneak with just sixteen seconds left. Green Bay went on to win Super Bowl II 33-14 over the Oakland Raiders (AFL).

The Dallas Cowboys went into the 1970's being called "next year's champions", with the reputation of not being able to "win the big one". In 1970 the Cowboys won the NFC with a regular season record of 10-4, and had playoff game wins over Detroit and San Francisco. They played the Baltimore Colts in Super Bowl V, in Miami at the Orange Bowl. The Colts won the game 16-13 on a field goal with sixteen seconds left in the game. This is the only Super Bowl game in which the MVP award was given to a member of the losing team (Chuck Howley).

In 1971 the Cowboys got off to a slow start in the first half of the season with a record of just 4-3. The Cowboys also inaugurated their new home, Texas Stadium, in Irving Texas. Tom Landry was splitting time at quarterback between Craig Morton and Roger Staubach. After a bad loss to the Chicago Bears, Tom Landry made the decision to give Roger Staubach the starting job at quarterback. The Cowboys then went on to win the final seven games of the regular season.

Dallas won the Division playoff game over Minnesota, and the Conference championship over San Francisco, to reach Super Bowl VI against the Miami Dolphins. The game was played in Tulane Stadium, in New Orleans. The Cowboys dominated Super Bowl VI, beating the Dolphins 24-3. Dallas set Super Bowl records for the most rushing yards (252), the most first downs (twenty three), and the least points allowed (three). Dallas remains the only team ever to prevent their opponent from scoring a touchdown in the Super Bowl. This was the first Super Bowl win for the Dallas Cowboys, and the beginning of a legend. Roger Staubach was named the Super Bowl MVP.

Roger Staubach, Hall of Fame Quarterback (1969 – 1979)

In 1972 the Cowboys lost Roger Staubach in the preseason to a separated shoulder. Roger would have surgery and miss most of the season. So Craig Morton was back in as the starting quarterback. The Cowboys also traded disgruntled running back Duane Thomas to San Diego. The Cowboys finished the regular season 10-4, and made the playoffs as a wildcard team. In the Divisional playoff game the Cowboys went to San Francisco. The 49ers had beaten Dallas a month earlier in the regular season 31-10. The 49ers had a 28-13 lead on the Cowboys late in the third quarter, when Tom Landry benched Craig Morton and put Roger Staubach in at quarterback. After struggling through most of the fourth quarter, Roger hit Billy Parks with a twenty yard touchdown pass with a minute left to play to cut the lead to 28-23. The Cowboys went for the on-side kick and they recovered it. Staubach scrambled and passed the Cowboys to the San Francisco ten yard line, where from there he hit Ron Sellers for the touchdown to shock the 49ers 30-28. This is the game that produced the famous footage of Larry Cole rolling around on the field in celebration of the Cowboys comeback win. This was the first of many late game comeback miracles that Roger Staubach became famous for, earning him the nickname "Captain Comeback". Unfortunately the Cowboys were ambushed in the Conference Championship game by the Washington Redskins 26-3. Washington went on to lose in Super Bowl VII to the undefeated Miami Dolphins.

In 1973 the Cowboys added a couple of great players in the draft. In the first round they selected Billy Joe Dupree, and in the third round they got Harvey Martin. The Cowboys got off to a good start at 3-0, but then lost three out of the next four to drop to 4-3 at mid-season. The Cowboys would then win six of their last seven games to close strong and finish atop the NFC East at 10-4. The Cowboys hosted the Los Angeles Rams in the Divisional Playoff round, and they defeated the Rams 27-16. In the Conference Championship game the Minnesota Vikings hammered Dallas 27-10. Roger Staubach was intercepted four times, and one was returned for a touchdown. Golden Richards scored the Cowboys only touchdown on a punt return. In Super Bowl VIII Minnesota lost to Miami 24-7.

In 1974 Dallas added two memorable players from the draft. In the first round they selected Ed Too Tall Jones, and in the third round they added Danny White. The Cowboys opened the season going 1-4. The Cowboys then won seven out of nine games to improve to 8-6. One of the highlights of 1974 was the Thanksgiving Day game against the Washington Redskins. Roger Staubach was knocked out of the game early in the third quarter, with Dallas trailing 16-3. Rookie quarterback Clint Longley engineered two third quarter touchdown drives to give Dallas a 17-16 lead. The Redskins then got a 19 yard touchdown run (by Duane Thomas) to go ahead 23-17. Dallas got the ball back with 1:45 remaining in the game. Longley had to convert a fourth and six at the Dallas forty four yard line, which he did, to get the ball to midfield with time running out. With just thirty five seconds remaining, Longley dropped back, and moved in the pocket to avoid the rush, then heaved a bomb to the end zone. Drew Pearson ran by two defenders and caught the pass for the thrilling winning touchdown, and the Cowboys won a memorable Redskins matchup 24-23. But the Cowboys missed the playoffs for the first time in nine years. Minnesota would lose their third Super Bowl in as many appearances at the end of the 1974 season. Pittsburgh won Super Bowl IX, 16-6.

1975 was a very memorable season for Dallas for several reasons. The Cowboys had 12 rookies make the team from the draft. These rookies became known as "the dirty dozen", and included: Randy White, Thomas "Hollywood" Henderson, Bob Breunig, Pat Donovan, Herb Scott, Randy Hughes, Scott Laidlaw, Burton Lawless, Kyle Davis, Roland Woolsey, Percy Howard and Mitch Hoopes. The Cowboys finished the regular season 10-4, but made the playoffs as the wildcard, as St Louis won the NFC East at 11-3. The Cowboys had to win all of their playoff games on the road, in order to get to Super Bowl X.

Dallas played one of its most memorable playoff games ever at Minnesota in 1975 (the "Hail Mary" pass). The Cowboys trailed Minnesota 14-10 with 1:50 remaining in the fourth quarter, and Dallas got the ball at their own fifteen yard line. Most people think only of the Hail Mary pass, and don't remember that the Cowboys faced a fourth down and seventeen yards to go from their thirty three yard line, before getting in to position for the miracle play. Roger Staubach hit Drew Pearson on an out pattern at the sideline with just enough to get the first down, with less than a minute to play. There was an incompletion on first down, and then with thirty two seconds remaining, Staubach again lined up in the shotgun, took the snap, pump-faked left, and then unloaded a desperation bomb to Drew Pearson. Minnesota cornerback Nate Wright was covering Pearson. As the pass arrived Nate Wright over ran the ball (and Pearson), and Wright stumbled while trying to adjust to the trajectory of the throw, allowing Pearson to make the catch by trapping the ball against his right hip at the 5-yard line, with his back momentarily to the end zone. Pearson then turned and scored standing up with twenty four seconds left in the game. Pearson then heaved the football in to the stands, in celebration. The Vikings claimed that Pearson pushed off, however Pearson used a "swim move" to maneuver to the ball without shoving Wright, as Wright ran by him and then stumbled. Pearson nearly dropped the pass, but was able to hold it up against his hip, and trot in to the end zone. The Cowboys won 17-14, and Vikings fans have never forgotten it. Dallas then went to Los Angeles and destroyed the Rams 37-7, in the NFC Championship game.

After rolling the Rams for the NFC Championship, the Cowboys played in Super Bowl X against the Pittsburgh Steelers. Dallas was the first ever wild card team to reach the Super Bowl. Pittsburgh was making their second consecutive Super Bowl appearance. The Cowboys got great field position in the first quarter when they recovered a fumbled punt snap at the Pittsburgh twenty nine yard line. Dallas scored on a twenty nine yard touchdown pass from Roger Staubach to Drew Pearson on the next play to lead early 7-0. The Steelers immediately responded with a drive that included a leaping catch by Lynn Swann down the sideline for 32 yards. The Steelers scored on a seven yard touchdown pass from Terry Bradshaw to Randy Grossman, to tie the game 7-7. Dallas responded by driving fifty one yards, and scoring on a thirty six yard field goal by Toni Fritsch, to take a 10-7 lead early in the second quarter.

In the third quarter Lynn Swann would make a much heralded acrobatic reception for fifty three yards, where Swann leaped and then had to tip the ball to himself while still in the air, after it was first tipped by Dallas cornerback Mark Washington. This drive would stall with no points for Pittsburgh, but the catch by Swann lives in Super Bowl lore.

The Cowboys lead the Steelers 10-7 after three quarters. Early in the fourth quarter the Steelers blocked a Cowboys punt through the end zone, and the safety cut the lead to 10-

9. After the free kick, Pittsburgh drove and got a field goal to take the lead 12-10. On the ensuing Dallas drive the Steelers intercepted Roger Staubach, and a short drive resulted in another Pittsburgh field goal to lead Dallas 15-10.

Late in the fourth quarter, on a third and two, Terry Bradshaw beat the blitz and hit Lynn Swann for a sixty four yard touchdown pass, to take a commanding 21-10 lead over Dallas. Roger Staubach responded with an eighty yard drive in five plays, capped by a thirty four yard touchdown pass to Percy Howard, to cut the lead to 21-17.

Dallas attempted an on-side kick, but Pittsburgh recovered. However, on fourth and two at the Dallas forty yard line, Chuck Noll elected to go for it rather than punting, and the Cowboys stopped them short, to get the ball back with just over one minute remaining. The Cowboys drove to the Pittsburgh thirty eight yard line, where there was just enough time for two desperation heaves to the end zone. The first pass was incomplete, and the second was intercepted, and Pittsburgh won Super Bowl X, 21-17. It was the Steelers second consecutive Super Bowl win. The Steelers sacked Roger Staubach seven times in this game. Pittsburgh kicker Roy Gerela missed two relatively short field goals, which kept the game close.

In the 1976 draft the Cowboys added three significant players. In the first round they drafted Aaron Kyle, in the third round they selected Butch Johnson, and in the fourth round they added Tom Rafferty. In the 1976 regular season Dallas went 11-3 and they won the NFC East Division. The Cowboys hosted a Divisional round playoff game against the LA Rams. Los Angeles upset the Cowboys 14-12. The Oakland Raiders would defeat the Minnesota Vikings in Super Bowl XI, to give Minnesota their fourth Super Bowl loss in four tries. Minnesota has not been back to the Super Bowl since 1976.

In 1977 the Cowboys engineered a trade with the expansion Seattle Seahawks for their number one pick in the draft, the second pick overall. The Cowboys coveted Tony Dorsett, and Dorsett had stated before the draft that he did not want to play for Seattle. In return for their first pick, Seattle received the Cowboys number fourteen first round pick, and three second round selections. The Cowboys selected Tony Dorsett, and he would have a hall of fame career with Dallas. Other notable players from the 1977 draft include Tony Hill (third round), Guy Brown (fourth round), Andy Frederick (fifth round) and Steve DeBerg (tenth round). The Cowboys were 12-2 in the regular season, with their only losses to the St Louis Cardinals, and the Steelers. Dallas started the season

8-0, lost two in a row, and then finished with four straight wins.

In the playoffs the Cowboys rolled the Chicago Bears 37-7, and then dismissed Minnesota 23-6, to earn a trip to Super Bowl XII, against the Denver Broncos, whom the Cowboys had defeated in the final regular season game, 14-6. Super Bowl XII was the first to be played in a domed Stadium (Louisiana Super Dome) and the first Super Bowl to be played in prime time. Denver had been 12-2 in the regular season, was quarterbacked by former Cowboy Craig Morton, and had to defeat Pittsburgh and Oakland to win the AFC Championship. Denver had the "orange crush" defense.

Dallas took a 10-0 lead in the first quarter by capitalizing on two interceptions. Dallas lead 13-0 at the half. The Cowboys stretched the lead to 20-3 in the third quarter on a diving touchdown catch by Butch Johnson, that is repeatedly shown in all-time Super Bowl highlights. Denver cut the Cowboys lead to 20-10 late in the third quarter. In the fourth quarter Dallas got a tricky twenty nine yard half-back option pass by Robert Newhouse for a touchdown to Golden Richards, to put the game out of reach 27-10. It was the Cowboys second Super Bowl win in four appearances.

The Cowboys defense dominated Super Bowl XII by forcing eight turnovers, and allowing only sixty one yards passing on eight completions. The Super Bowl MVP was shared by Randy White and Harvey Martin, the first time that a defensive lineman had won the Super Bowl MVP.

Tony Dorsett became the first football player in history to win an NCAA National Championship one year (University of Pittsburgh) and a Super Bowl the next season. Remarkably, Dorsett won both championships in the Super Dome, as Pitt won the 1976 national championship by defeating the Georgia Bulldogs in the Sugar Bowl on January 1, 1977.

In 1978 the Cowboys got off to good start in the regular season at 6-2, but then lost two consecutive games to fall to 6-4. Dallas then went on a six game winning streak to close the season at 12-4. By the end of the season Dallas had the league's number two ranked offense and defense (yards). In the playoffs the Cowboys defeated Atlanta in the Divisional round 27-20, after trailing 20-13 at halftime. The Cowboys won the NFC Championship on the road in Los Angeles, by beating the Rams 28-0 in the Coliseum.

Then came Super Bowl XIII, and a rematch (of Super Bowl X) with the Pittsburgh Steelers. On the game's opening possession the Cowboys drove to the Pittsburgh thirty eight yard line. The Cowboys then tried a reverse that was designed for Drew Pearson to pass to Billy Joe DuPree. DuPree was open down field, but Pearson fumbled the handoff, and Pittsburgh recovered at the forty seven yard line. The Steelers then drove to the Dallas twenty eight yard line, and Terry Bradshaw hit John Stallworth for a touchdown to put Pittsburgh ahead 7-0. With about one minute to play in the first quarter, Bradshaw was sacked by Harvey Martin, and he fumbled. It was recovered by "Too Tall" Jones. Three plays later, Staubach beat an all-out blitz and hit Tony Hill for a thirty nine yard touchdown to tie the game 7-7 at the end of the first quarter.

Opening the second quarter the Steelers drove to the forty eight yard line. Bradshaw and Franco Harris had a mix up and ran into each other in the backfield, and Bradshaw dropped the ball. Bradshaw picked up the loose ball and attempted to roll out. Dallas linebackers Mike Hegman and Hollywood Henderson blitzed, and Henderson caught Bradshaw. Before he was tackled the ball came loose and Hegman pulled it away from Bradshaw, and raced thirty seven yards for a touchdown to put Dallas ahead 14-7. On the third play of the ensuing possession, Bradshaw completed a ten yard pass to John Stallworth. Stallworth broke the tackle attempt by Aaron Kyle and outraced the defense to a seventy five yard touchdown on what should have been just a first down. Dallas 14 – Pittsburgh 14.

After a Dallas punt, the Steelers got the ball at their forty four yard line with under two minutes to play in the half.

Bradshaw completed passes of twenty and twenty one yards to Lynn Swann to reach the Cowboys sixteen yard line. Two plays later Bradshaw completed a seven yard pass to Rocky Bleier for the touchdown, to give Pittsburgh a 21-14 half time lead.

The defenses "ruled the day" for most of the third quarter. However Dallas started a possession at their forty two yard line late in the quarter, and they drove to the Pittsburgh ten yard line. Then came one of the most famous blunders in Super Bowl history, and the most heartbreaking for Cowboy fans. On third down Roger Staubach saw Jackie Smith open in the end zone. Staubach's pass was low and slightly behind a wide open Smith as he ran across the end zone. As Smith was trying to stop and adjust to the ball, he slipped and fell straight down in a sitting position as the ball arrived. The ball clanked off of his hands, and the Cowboys had to settle for a field goal. Pittsburgh 21 – Dallas 17 at the end of the third quarter. Jackie Smith played sixteen years in the NFL, and is in the Hall of Fame. But that drop haunts him from the archives of NFL Films.

In the fourth quarter the Steelers had the ball at their forty four yard line, when Bradshaw attempted a deep pass to Lynn Swann. The pass was incomplete, but the officials called a questionable pass interference on Dallas, moving the ball to the Cowboys twenty three yard line. On third and nine from the twenty two, Franco Harris took a handoff and burst up the field untouched for the touchdown. Dallas safety Charlie Waters had an angle to get to Harris before the end zone, however an official pursuing the play got in the way and screened Waters, allowing Harris to score untouched. The Steelers lead 28-17 early in the fourth quarter.

After the touchdown and the extra point, the kickoff was inadvertently squibbed down the field. The ball rolled to Randy White, who picked it up and attempted to return. White, who was wearing a cast on his broken left hand, fumbled and Pittsburgh recovered at the Dallas eighteen. On the next play Bradshaw hit Lynn Swann for the touchdown to put Pittsburgh ahead 35-17 with under seven minutes to play.

Some of the Steelers were starting to celebrate on the sideline, sensing the win was near. The Cowboys did not quit. On the next possession, Dallas drove eighty nine yards in eight plays, including an eighteen yard scramble by Roger Staubach on a third and eleven, and a twenty nine yard run by Dorsett. The Cowboys scored on Staubach's seven yard touchdown pass to Billy Joe Dupree, to cut the lead to 35-24 with 2:20 remaining.

Dennis Thurman recovered an onside kick for Dallas with just over two minutes remaining. Drew Pearson caught two passes for twenty two and twenty five yards. The second catch was on a fourth down and eighteen. The Cowboys drove fifty two yards in nine plays, and scored on Staubach's four yard touchdown pass to Butch Johnson. With the extra point, the Steelers lead was cut to 35–31 with just 0:22 left in the game.

The Cowboys attempted another on-side kick, however the Steelers recovered this one, and Pittsburgh ran out the clock. The Steelers won 35-31 to become the first team to win three Super Bowls. Terry Bradshaw was named the Super Bowl MVP.

After the 1978 season NFL Films made a "year in review" video for each of the NFL teams. During the Cowboys video, the dialogue recognized the fact that at many of the road games that the Cowboys play in, there is a significant percentage of the fans in the stadium wearing the Cowboys colors, and clearly cheering for the Cowboys. Because of this, NFL Films called the Dallas Cowboys "Americas Team". The term stuck and has been a reference to the Cowboys since, even throughout their mediocre years from 1996 through 2013, when Dallas has only won two playoff games in eighteen years.

The Cowboys defense lost several prominent defensive players in 1979. Defensive tackle Jethro Pugh and safety

Mark Washington retired. Safety Charlie Waters missed the season due to a knee injury. Ed "Too Tall" Jones left the team to pursue a professional boxing career, although Jones would return in 1980. Thomas "Hollywood" Henderson was cut in November for erratic play and bad behavior. The season began 7–1, and then the Cowboys lost three straight games to Philadelphia, Washington and the Houston Oilers, to drop to 8-5. After Houston defeated Dallas 30–24, Oilers coach Bum Phillips declared the Oilers to be "Texas Team". Uh, no Bum, I don't think so – that just sounds like Cowboys envy. Dallas recovered to win their final three games to finish at 11–5 and gain the number one seed in the NFC.

The most important and colorful game of the season was the final game against the malodorous rival Washington Redskins. Both teams entered this game at 10-5. However because of tie breakers, the Redskins had to win the game to make the playoffs. The Cowboys could enter the playoffs as a wildcard had they lost, but if they won Dallas would have the home field advantage throughout the playoffs. The Redskins had whipped the Cowboys in their first regular season meeting a month earlier in D.C., 34-20. The Redskins had won their last two games in a row, in convincing fashion, so they were feeling confident to face the Cowboys.

Washington got off to a fast start, thanks in part to some sloppy play and turnovers by Dallas, and the Redskins lead 17-0 in the second quarter. Dallas battled back with a touchdown to pull within 17-7. Then later at the end of the half, Staubach faced a third and twenty at the Washington twenty six yard line. Roger found Preston Pearson for the twenty six yard touchdown pass that cut the Redskins lead to 17-14 at halftime. The touchdown finished an eighty five yard drive, with less than ten seconds remaining in the half. Clutch!

Dallas scored the only touchdown of the third quarter to take the lead 21-17 going to the fourth quarter. But Washington took control of the game in the fourth quarter. First, Mark Moseley kicked a twenty four yard field goal to make it 21-20 Dallas. Later the Redskins drove, and then John Riggins bulled his way in to the end zone from a yard out to put Washington up 27-21. A little later Riggins broke a shocking sixty six yard run for a touchdown. With just under seven minutes left to play, the Redskins held a seemingly insurmountable 34-21 lead, considering that the Cowboys offense had bogged down in the fourth quarter.

After the Cowboys forced a Washington punt, they got the ball back with 1:46 remaining, and two timeouts, trailing 34-28. Roger Staubach threw a twenty yard pass to Tony Hill, and then connected twice with Preston Pearson for twenty two and twenty five yards to reach the Washington eight yard line with just 0:45 remaining in the game. Staubach, facing an all-out blitz by the Redskins, tossed a high, arching pass that Tony Hill caught in the back corner of the end zone for the touchdown. Captain Comeback had done it again, and the Cowboys won the game 35-34, to win the NFC East.

The Cowboys faced the Los Angeles Rams in the Divisional round playoff game in Texas Stadium. The Cowboys were favored to win this game, as they had pounded the Rams in the NFC Championship game the year before 28-0, and had again soundly beaten the Rams in October of the 1979 regular season, 30-6. There would be a very different outcome on December 30, 1979. Big plays were the difference, as the Rams got them and the Cowboys did not. Vince Ferragamo threw first half touchdown passes of thirty two yards to Wendell Tyler, and forty three yards to Ron Smith, as the Rams held a 14-5 lead at halftime. Dallas scored touch-downs in the third and fourth quarters to take a 19-14 lead. However, Faragamo hit Billy Waddy with a fifty yard catch and run touchdown pass with two minutes remaining in the game to regain the lead 21-19. The Rams defense held off a last minute rally attempt by Staubach. The Rams would go on to win the NFC championship. They would lose to the Pittsburgh Steelers in Super Bowl XIV.

Roger Staubach retired from football after the 1979 season. His remarkable career included: six pro bowls; five NFL passing championships; five NFC titles; two Super Bowl championships; the Super Bowl MVP (Super Bowl VI). "Captain Comeback" engineered twenty three fourth quarter come-backs, including fourteen in the final two minutes, during his eleven year career. He was inducted in to the Cowboys Ring of Honor in 1983, and the Pro Football Hall of Fame in 1985.

After Roger's retirement, Danny White got an opportunity to be the Cowboys starting quarterback. In 1980 Danny lead the Cowboys to a regular season record of 12-4. The Cowboys tied the Eagles at 12-4 overall, at 6-2 in the division and at 9-3 in the conference. However, Philadelphia won the NFC East on the tie breaker of largest point differential (overall margin of victory). So the Cowboys went in to the playoffs as the wild card team.

In the wildcard game Dallas faced the Los Angeles Rams, who had knocked the Cowboys out of the playoffs in 1979 and advanced to the Super Bowl (losing to Pittsburgh), and had beaten Dallas 38-14 in week 15, just two weeks earlier. The first half was a back and forth struggle and the score was tied at the half 13-13. Dallas took control in the third quarter, scoring two touchdowns to open a 27-13 lead. They added another score in the fourth quarter while shutting down the Rams offense, to win 34-13. The Cowboys eliminated Los Angeles from the playoffs for the second time in the last three years (1978, 1980).

In the Divisional playoff round Dallas traveled to Atlanta to play the Falcons (12-4 regular season). Atlanta lead the Cowboys 17-10 at halftime, and 27-17 with 6:37 left to play in the fourth quarter. Danny White drove the Cowboys sixty two yards for a touchdown to cut the Atlanta lead to 27-24. The Cowboy defense forced Atlanta to punt, and Dallas got the ball back down three, at their thirty yard line with 1:48 remaining to play. From the Atlanta twenty three yard line, Danny White scrambled in the pocket and found Drew Pearson for the touchdown to put Dallas ahead 30-27 with under a minute to play. The extra point was missed, giving Atlanta a chance to tie with a field goal. The Cowboys defense kept Atlanta from reaching mid-field, and time ran out on the Falcons. Dallas won 30-27.

So Danny White took Dallas to the NFC championship game in his first year as the starter. The Cowboys would face the Eagles in Philadelphia. Dallas lost at Philadelphia in week seven, 17-10, and defeated the Eagles 35-27 in the final regular season game, in which Dallas had lead 35-10 at one point. January 11, 1981 was a very cold day in Philadelphia (twelve degrees at game time) and it was very windy. The Eagles defense was stifling, holding the Cowboys to 206 total yards and forcing four Cowboy turnovers. Philadelphia ended the Cowboys season, 20-7. The Eagles lost in the Super Bowl to the Oakland Raiders. The Eagles have never won the Super Bowl.

In 1981 the Cowboys won their first four regular season games. Then they lost two straight games. The second loss was to San Francisco, and it would come back to haunt the Cowboys in the playoffs. The Cowboys then won four straight games to improve to 8-3. Then on November 15 the Cowboys played at the 4-6 Detroit Lions. They lost to Detroit 27-24, a bad loss for the playoff bound Cowboys that would further hurt their chances of gaining home field advantage in the playoffs. The Cowboys won four straight games again, to improve to 12-3. They lost the final game to the 8-7 NY Giants to finish the regular season 12-4. The Cowboys won the NFC East, however they were second in the conference, so San Francisco held the home field advantage throughout the playoffs.

In the 1981 playoffs the Cowboys faced Tampa Bay in the Divisional playoff round. The Buccaneers had won the NFC Central with a record of 9-7. Tampa Bay was no match for the Cowboys. Dallas lead 10-0 at the half, then scored three answered touchdowns in the third quarter, and went on to win 38-0. This advanced Dallas to the NFC championship game against the San Francisco 49ers. San Francisco advanced by beating the NY Giants 38-24.

For San Francisco 49ers fans, the 1981NFC Championship meeting with the Dallas Cowboys was a daunting endeavor. San Francisco had not enjoyed a lot of playoff success, as Dallas had during the 1970's. When San Francisco did advance to the NFC championship game after the 1970 and 1971 seasons, it was the Dallas Cowboys that had ended their season both times. In the 1981 regular season San Francisco had beaten the Cowboys soundly in week six at Candlestick Park, 45-14. These were the new 49ers, with Joe Montana at quarterback, Ronnie Lott at corner and the innovative coach Bill Walsh.

This was an epic conference championship game. It was a close, back and forth game throughout. It was not a cleanly played game as there were a lot of turnovers (nine), penalties (twelve) and sacks (seven). The Cowboys lead San Francisco 10-7 after one quarter, and 17-14 at halftime. San Francisco took the lead after three quarters 21-17. Early in the fourth quarter the Cowboys got a field goal to cut the 49ers lead to 21-20. Then mid-way through the fourth quarter the 49ers fumbled and Dallas recovered at the fifty yard line. Four plays later Danny White hit tight-end Doug Cosbie for a twenty one yard touchdown pass to give Dallas a 27-21 lead with less than seven minutes left in the game.

With 4:54 remaining in the game, San Francisco got the ball at their own eleven yard line. Using some short passes and runs by running back Lenvil Elliott, the 49ers drove methodically down the field. After the two-minute warning, the 49ers ran a reverse with Freddie Solomon, and he gained fourteen yards to the Dallas thirty five yard line. Avoiding a heavy Dallas pass rush, Joe Montana completed passes of ten yards to Dwight Clark and twelve yards to Solomon. Lenvil Elliott gained seven-yards around right end. The 49ers then had a third-and-three yards to go at the Dallas six yard line with fifty eight seconds remaining in the game. Montana took the snap and rolled out to his right. Dallas defenders Larry Bethea and Ed Too Tall Jones were in close pursuit of Montana, and as he reached the sideline, and his primary receiver (Solomon) was covered, Montana appeared to be throwing the ball out of the end zone to come back and try again on fourth down. However, Dwight Clark was coming across the back of the end zone. The 6'4" receiver went high and caught the pass for a touchdown ("The Catch"). The extra point put San Francisco ahead 28-27. It is a legendary play.

The Cowboys got the ball back with fifty one seconds remaining in the game. It seemed as if the Cowboys might pull off a miracle comeback of their own. Danny White completed a pass to Drew Pearson for thirty one yards to the

San Francisco forty four. Pearson nearly got away for the touchdown, but he was caught with a horse-collar tackle by cornerback Eric Wright, the only 49ers defender who could reach Pearson. On the next play 49ers tackle Lawrence Pillers sacked Danny White and caused a fumble, and Jim Stuckey recovered for the 49ers. Game over. San Francisco went on to win the Super Bowl over the Cincinnati Bengals.

The 1982 season was shortened by the NFL players strike. The Cowboys went 6-3 and earned a wild card playoff berth. Dallas defeated Tampa Bay and Green Bay to advance to the NFC championship game for the third straight year, this time at Washington. The Redskins had gone 8-1 in the regular season and had won the NFC East. Washington whipped the Cowboys 31-17 to advance to the Super Bowl. 1982 was the third consecutive year that Danny White and the Cowboys had made it to the NFC championship game, unfortunately losing all three.

The Cowboys would go 12-4 in 1983 but would lose in the wild card game. The rest of the decade of the 80's saw the Cowboys decline to what became the team that Jerry Jones acquired in 1989.

I cannot end this discussion about the Dallas Cowboys early history without a discussion of the team's only General Manager prior to Jerry Jones, Tex Schramm. Tex Schramm is credited with building the Dallas Cowboys from scratch, starting in 1960, into an NFL power house by 1967, that went on to have twenty consecutive winning seasons. It was Tex Schramm who selected and hired Tom Landry as the Dallas Cowboys first head coach.

Tex Schramm, Dallas Cowboys GM 1960 - 1989

Tex gets the credit for creating "America's Team". In 1966 Schramm negotiated the deal with the NFL, insuring that Dallas would host a Thanksgiving Day game every year. This exclusive national television broadcast every Thanksgiving holiday, combined with the Dallas Cowboys on field success, built the popularity of the team across the nation, in the early years of the NFL.

Tex Schramm was an innovator for the Dallas Cowboys and for the NFL as well. As chairman of the NFL's competition committee, Schramm lead the NFL owners to merge with the AFL. His counterpart in the AFL was Lamar Hunt, owner of the Kansas City Chiefs. Together they persuaded the leagues' other owners to agree to the merger. Eventually, the leagues merged at the start of the 1970 season after having agreed to play a championship game the three previous years, the game that became known as the Super Bowl.

A list of Tex Schramm's innovations, that we take for granted today, includes: moving the goalposts from the front of the end zone to the back; putting the official time on the scoreboard; overtime in the regular season; using computer technology in scouting; extra-wide sideline borders; wind-direction strips on the goal post uprights; instant replay; multi-color striping of the twenty and fifty yard lines; the thirty second clock between plays; the referee's microphone; and of course, the all-important Dallas Cowboy Cheerleaders. Yes, Tex did that too!

Tex Schramm laid the foundation, and built the Cowboys through the 1960s, and maintained the excellence in the organization through the 1970s and into the 1980s. Tex remained the Cowboys GM through the acquisition of the club by Jerry Jones. Tex was with Jerry when he fired Tom Landry.

Tom Landry was the only head coach of the Dallas Cowboys from 1960 through 1988. Landry is a legendary head coach with an extraordinary record. Landry presided over five NFC championships and two Super Bowl championships. His regular season record was 250-162, and 20-16 in the playoffs. Under Landry the Cowboys made the playoffs in eighteen of twenty years (1966-85) and had a winning record for twenty straight years.

Tom Landry, Dallas Cowboys head coach 1960 – 1988 (29 seasons)

The final piece to this look into the Dallas Cowboys remarkable history is to rank the top ten Dallas Cowboy players in the history of the franchise. The Cowboys did a lot of winning and enjoyed a lot of success through the 1970's, in the early 1980's, and of course in the 1992 – 1995 Super Bowl championship run. Because of all of that success, the list of great players that have played in Dallas is very lengthy. In addition to the players who were great on the field, there were a lot of players that were great characters, and as a result who became fan favorites, even beyond their on the field accomplishments. As a result, this is a difficult list to reduce to just ten names. I am sure that this list will be subject to disagreement and debate. I tried to limit my emotional attachment to the players, and make my evaluation on the basis of their on the field contributions to the team's success.

The top ten Dallas Cowboys of all time, in my opinion, are:

#10   Don Meredith

9   Darren Woodson

8   Tony Dorsett

7   Randy White   (The "Manster")

6   Drew Pearson (The original "88")

5   Emmitt Smith (NFL all-time leader - rushing yards)

4   Michael Irvin   (The "Play Maker")

3   Troy Aikman

2   Bob Lilly ("Mr. Cowboy")

1   Roger Staubach ("Captain Comeback")

Honorable mentions: Chuck Howley, Mel Renfro, Ed "Too Tall" Jones, Harvey Martin, Billy Joe Dupree, Charlie Waters, Cliff Harris, Mark Tuinei, Daryl Johnston, Eric Williams and Jay Novacek

*** The End ***

Dallas Cowboys History by Season

Year	Record	Coach	Season accomplishment
2014	12-4	Garrett	Wildcard beat DET 24-20
'			lost divisional at Green Bay 26-21
2013	8-8	Garrett	missed playoffs lost * 24-22 to PHIL
2012	8-8	Garrett	missed playoffs lost * 28-18 at WASH
2011	8-8	Garrett	missed playoffs lost * 31-14 at NYG
2010	6-10	Phillips	missed playoffs (Garrett replaced
'			Phillips week 10)
2009	11-5	Phillips	defeated PHIL in wildcard 34-14
			lost divisional at MINN 34-3
2008	9-7	Phillips	missed playoffs lost * 44-6 at PHIL
2007	13-3	Phillips	lost Division (NYGiants 21-17)
2006	9-7	Parcells	lost Wildcard (Seattle 21-20)
2005	9-7	Parcells	missed playoffs
2004	6-10	Parcells	missed playoffs
2003	10-6	Parcells	lost Wildcard (Carolina 29-10)
2002	5-11	Campo	missed playoffs
2001	5-11	Campo	missed playoffs
2000	5-11	Campo	missed playoffs

'* Dallas would have made playoffs if they won season finale.

Dallas Cowboys History by Season

Year	Record	Coach	Season accomplishment
1999	8-8	Gailey	lost Wildcard (MINN 27-10)
1998	10-6	Gailey	lost Wildcard (Arizona 20-7)
1997	6-10	Switzer	missed playoffs
1996	10-6	Switzer	Wildcard beat MINN 40-15
'			lost Division (CAR 26-17)
1995	12-4	Switzer	**won Super Bowl XXX 27-17 (PITT)**
'			NFC champ beat Green Bay 38-27
'			Division beat PHIL 30-11
1994	12-4	Switzer	lost NFC championship @ SF 38-28
'			Division beat Green Bay 35-9
1993	12-4	Johnson	**won Super Bowl XXVIII 30-13 (BUFF)**
'			NFC champ beat San Francisco 38-21
'			Division beat Green Bay 27-17
1992	13-3	Johnson	**won Super Bowl XXVII 52-17 (BUFF)**
'			NFC champ beat San Francisco 30-20
'			Division beat Philadelphia 34-10
1991	11-5	Johnson	Wildcard beat Chicago 17-13
'			lost Division @ DET 38-6
1990	7-9	Johnson	missed playoffs
1989	1-15	Johnson	missed playoffs

Jerry Jones ownership of Cowboys commenced 1989.

Dallas Cowboys History by Season

Year	Record	Coach	Season accomplishment
1988	3-13	Landry	missed playoffs
1987	7-8	Landry	missed playoffs *
1986	7-9	Landry	missed playoffs
1985	10-6	Landry	lost Division game to LA Rams 20-0
1984	9-7	Landry	missed playoffs
1983	12-4	Landry	lost Wildcard to LA Rams 24-17
1982	6-3	Landry	lost NFC championship to WASH 31-17
'			Division beat Green Bay 37-26
'			Wildcard beat Tampa Bay 30-17

(1982 season was shortened by players strike)

Year	Record	Coach	Season accomplishment
1981	12-4	Landry	lost NFC championship to SF 28-27 **
'			Division beat Tampa Bay 38-0
1980	12-4	Landry	lost NFC championship to PHIL 20-7
'			Division beat Atlanta 30-27
'			Wildcard beat LA Rams 34-13

'* 1987 lockout shortened season to 15 games

'** "The catch" (Montana to Clark)

Dallas Cowboys History by Season

Year	Record	Coach	Season accomplishment
1979	11-5	Landry	lost Division game to LA Rams 21-19
1978	12-4	Landry	lost Super Bowl XIII to Pittsburgh 35-31
'			NFC championship beat LA Rams 28-0
'			Division beat Atlanta 27-20
1977	12-2	Landry	**won Super Bowl XII Denver 27-10**
'			NFC championship beat Minnesota 23-6
'			Division beat Chicago 37-7
1976	11-3	Landry	lost Division game to LA Rams 14-12
1975	10-4	Landry	lost Super Bowl X to Pittsburgh 21-17
'			NFC championship beat LA Rams 37-7
'			Division beat Minnesota 17-14 *
1974	8-6	Landry	missed playoffs
1973	10-4	Landry	lost NFC championship to MINN 27-10
'			Division beat LA Rams 27-16
1972	10-4	Landry	lost NFC championship to WASH 26-3
'			Division beat San Francisco 30-28
1971	11-3	Landry	**won Super Bowl VI vs. Miami 24-3**
'			NFC champ beat San Francisco 14-3
'			Division beat Minnesota 20-12
1970	10-4	Landry	lost Super Bowl V to Baltimore 16-13
'			NFC champ beat San Francisco 17-10
'			Division beat Detroit 5-0

* 1975 the "Hail Mary" pass from Roger Staubach to Drew Pearson

Dallas Cowboys History by Season

Year	Record	Coach	Season accomplishment
1969	11-2-1	Landry	lost Division vs. Cleveland 38-14
1968	12-2	Landry	lost Division vs. Cleveland 31-20
1967	9-5	Landry	**lost Conf. champ to G.Bay 21-17 ***
1966	10-3-1	Landry	lost Conf. championship to G.Bay 34-27
1965	7-7	Landry	missed playoffs
1964	5-8-1	Landry	missed playoffs
1963	4-10	Landry	missed playoffs
1962	5-8-1	Landry	missed playoffs
1961	4-9-1	Landry	missed playoffs
1960	0-11-1	Landry	missed playoffs

* this was the famed "Ice Bowl" game at Lambeau Field

Bibliography:

The opinions in this book are my own, based on my experiences as I have followed the Dallas Cowboys as a die-hard fan for nearly 50 years. I sourced factual information from numerous public venues, including:

pro-football-reference.com

knowyourdallascowboys.com

espn.com

sportsillustrated.cnn.com

cbssports.com

Some of the photographs are used with publication rights and permission granted by the owner, St. Angelo Photography LLC.

Others are from my private collection of Cowboys memorabilia.

The "Triplets"

Michael Irvin, Emmitt Smith and Troy Aikman

Three Hall of Famers, and three time Super Bowl Champions

Troy Aikman

The number 1 overall draft pick in 1989 by Dallas

1992 Super Bowl MVP

Three time Super Bowl Champion (1992, 93, 95)

Six time Pro-Bowler

NFL Hall of Famer

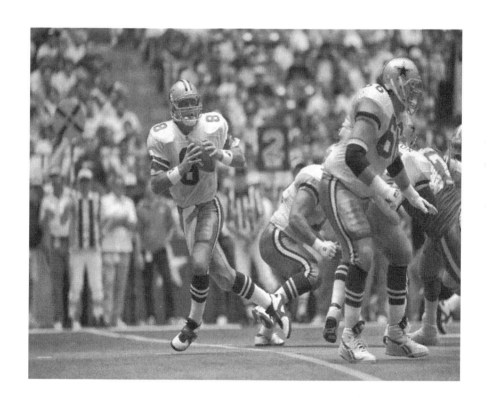

Michael Irvin

The number 11 overall draft pick in 1988 by Dallas

Three time Super Bowl Champion (1992, 93, 95)

Five time Pro-Bowler

NFL Hall of Famer

Emmitt Smith

The number 17 overall draft pick in 1990 by Dallas

1993 Super Bowl MVP

Three time Super Bowl Champion (1992, 93, 95)

Eight time Pro-Bowler

NFL Hall of Famer

All-time NFL leading rusher with 18,355 yards

The only NFL running back to accomplish in a single season:
(1) Super Bowl Champion, (2) NFL MVP, (3) NFL rushing
leader, and (4) The Super Bowl MVP (1993)

Jimmy Johnson

Dallas Cowboys head coach 1989 - 1993

Two time Super Bowl Champion (1992-93)

44-36 overall regular season record with Dallas Cowboys

25-7 regular season record in Super Bowl years (92-93)

7-1 playoff record with Dallas Cowboys

Jay Novacek

Tight end – Dallas Cowboys 1990 – 1995

Averaged 10.5 yards per catch in Cowboys career

Three time Super Bowl Champion (1992, 93, 95)

Five time Pro Bowler; Five time All-Pro

Darryl Johnston ("Moose")

Full Back, Dallas Cowboys 1989 – 1999

Averaged 7.6 yards per reception for career

Lead blocker for NFL career rushing leader Emmitt Smith

Drafted second round in 1989 by Dallas

Three time Super Bowl Champion (1992, 93, 95)

Two time Pro Bowler

Roger Staubach

Drafted 10th round 1964 by Dallas (served four years U.S. Navy)

Dallas Cowboys quarterback 1969 - 1979

1971 Super Bowl MVP

Two time Super Bowl Champion (1971, 1977)

Six time Pro-Bowler

NFL Hall of Famer

Tom Landry

Dallas Cowboys head coach 1960 – 1988

Five NFC Championships

Two Super Bowl Championships (1971, 1977)

20 consecutive winning seasons (1966 – 1985)

Third most wins in NFL history (250)

Texas E. Schramm ("Tex")

Dallas Cowboys General Manager 1960 – 1988

Instrumental in the merger of the AFL – NFL (1970)

Brought the traditional Thanksgiving Day game to Dallas

Formed the Dallas Cowboys Cheerleaders

Chaired the NFL Competition Committee

Responsible for multiple NFL game innovations (page 321)

From "Worst to First", 1989 – 1992

Dallas Cowboys, Americas Team Is Back

Jeff Stevenson, Author

Copyright 2015 Paul J. Stevenson – Publisher

19766041R00190

Printed in Great Britain
by Amazon